THE RACING ENGINE BUILDER'S HANDBOOK

How to Build Winning Drag, Circle Track, Marine, and Road Racing Engines

Tom Monroe

HPBOOKS

HPBooks

Published by the Penguin Group
Penguin Group (USA) Inc.
375 Hudson Street, New York, New York 10014, USA
Penguin Group (Canada), 90 Eglinton Avenue East, Suite 700, Toronto, Ontario M4P 2Y3, Canada
(a division of Pearson Penguin Canada Inc.)
Penguin Books Ltd., 80 Strand, London WC2R 0RL, England
Penguin Group Ireland, 25 St. Stephen's Green, Dublin 2, Ireland (a division of Penguin Books Ltd.)
Penguin Group (Australia), 250 Camberwell Road, Camberwell, Victoria 3124, Australia
(a division of Pearson Australia Group Pty. Ltd.)
Penguin Books India Pvt. Ltd., 11 Community Centre, Panchsheel Park, New Delhi—110 017, India
Penguin Group (NZ), Cnr. Airborne and Rosedale Roads, Albany, Auckland 1310, New Zealand
(a division of Pearson New Zealand Ltd.)
Penguin Books (South Africa) (Pty.) Ltd., 24 Sturdee Avenue, Rosebank, Johannesburg 2196, South Africa

Penguin Books Ltd., Registered Offices: 80 Strand, London WC2R 0RL, England

While the author has made every effort to provide accurate telephone numbers and Internet addresses at the time of publication, neither the publisher nor the author assumes any responsibility for errors, or for changes that occur after publication. Further, publisher does not have any control over and does not assume any responsibility for author or third-party websites or their content.

THE RACING ENGINE BUILDER'S HANDBOOK

Copyright © 2006 by Tom Monroe
Text design and production by Michael Lutfy
Cover design by Tresa Rowe/Bird Studios
Cover photos *Stock Car* magazine, Tom Monroe and Harold Hinson

First edition: September 2006

ISBN: 1-55788-492-7

PRINTED IN THE UNITED STATES OF AMERICA

10 9 8 7 6 5 4 3 2 1

NOTICE: The information in this book is true and complete to the best of our knowledge. All recommendations on parts and procedures are made without any guarantees on the part of the author or the publisher. Tampering with, altering, modifying, or removing any emissions-control device is a violation of federal law. Author and publisher disclaim all liability incurred in connection with the use of this information.

CONTENTS

ACKNOWLEDGMENTS

I started collecting engine-building information when I built my first engine, a "3/4 race" flathead Ford. The local dirt trackers were replacing their flathead Fords and Jimmys with the newer pushrod V8s, so there were a lot of surplus performance parts available for my engine. Wanting more power, I managed to scavenge many 8BA flat-head parts. But more importantly, I learned about full-race cams, clearances, boring, honing, valve/seat grinding, stiff valve springs, high compression and porting, polishing and relieving. Although I farmed out boring and honing, I managed to pull off a successful engine build by using these parts and good information I gathered in the form of tips from local racers, specifications from *Motor's Auto Repair Manual* and a series of *Hotrod Magazine* articles on how to modify the flathead Ford by Roger Huntington. I learned early on the value of good basic information.

I continued to learn from many top engine builders during my years of involvement in racing. Engines ranged from a 110-hp Formula Ford four banger to a 900-hp 3.2L turbo Buick Indy Car engine. In between there were numerous big- and small-block Chevrolet, Ford and Mopar engines for stock car, TransAm, CanAm, IMSA, drag, off-road, pro stock and Bonneville Salt Flats racing.

I put this book together with considerable help from a few key people. First was Kevin Hartley of Hartley Equipment Sales in Boone, North Carolina. An engine machinist in his own right, Kevin brought me up to speed on the availability and operation of the latest engine-building equipment. He also introduced me to key individuals in shops that build engines for the racing community. Most of the photos in this book were taken over several months at Powell Motorsports in Hickory, North Carolina. Allan Powell and Bob Curl allowed me to shoot pictures and answered many questions about building and dyno testing everything from late-model stock-car engines to NASCAR Cup and road-racing engines.

Mike Williams of Action Automotive in Mooresville, North Carolina, took time to show me the fine art of crankshaft balancing. Bill Wheatly and John Stilley of CVProducts showed me through their immense race-parts facility and supplied me with many photos and illustrations. Tom Malaska gave me a tour of Xceldyne Technologies' titanium-valve production facility. Jeff Joyner of Bill Davis Racing allowed me to look over his shoulder while he set up a five-axis CNC machining center for block machining. Others who helped with their engine-building expertise were Mark Smith of TriStar Racing Engines, Joey Robinson of Robinson Racing Engines, Charlie Buck of Buck Racing Engines, Bruce Jacobson of Glendale Machine & Balance, Freddie Turza of Labonte Racing, Frank Leisson of Victory Racing Engines and the guys at Penske Racing South's engine shop.

Racing parts and equipment suppliers who helped with information or product photos include Jerry Elhart of Calico Coatings, Lee Morse and Brad Green of Mahle Motorsport. Also helping were Michael Zeranski of Canton Racing Products, Harold Bettes of SuperFlow, Bob Misata and Brian Clarke of BHJ Products, William Dailey of Dailey Engineering and John Swartz of Aviaid Oil Systems.

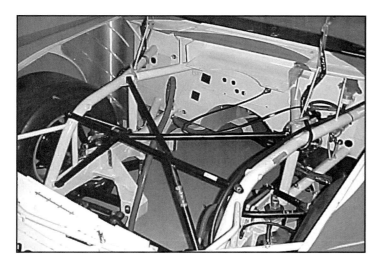

Your job as an engine builder is to build an engine to fill a space like this to make a winning combination.

It's no secret the four-stroke engine hasn't died as was predicted in the '90s, nor is the end in sight! This is particularly true for pushrod racing engines as evidenced by the many high-performance equipment suppliers and racing classes that require them. Further support comes from automotive manufacturers that supply new parts for pushrod engines. And the life of the pushrod engine has been extended even further by the introduction of new OEM high-performance pushrod engines. Who would have thought Toyota would build a pushrod V8 in order to gain entry into NASCAR racing? Apparently the only thing that can bring an end to the spark-ignition pushrod racing engine would be the lack of fuel to power them.

I wrote this book with the assumption that you have the basic skills and equipment needed to build an engine. With these skills and equipment coupled with the information in this book should allow you to build a competitive, efficient and reliable pushrod engine. When I say "build," I mean choose, inspect, machine and assemble the parts. Do this with care to ensure your engine will perform reliably and at maximum potential. Start by taking nothing for granted, never quit checking and stay with the basics. Treat tricks as just that, but always be open to the latest ideas and new technology. Be patient, pay attention to details and don't compromise. Various types and makes of engines are illustrated. This shows that the basics of building a pushrod racing engine apply regardless of make or application.

I emphasize inspection, machining and cleanliness throughout the book. This is because most engine failures involve errors made in one of these areas. Bottom line: Your engine will do the job providing the correct parts are sound, fit correctly and you keep them clean. Keep in mind that taking extra care will make your engine a cut above the others rather than it being just another engine. Go beyond what is considered to be blueprinting, or building an engine within factory tolerances. A racing engine must be built to tighter tolerances for it to be a consistent winner.

Finally, it was once common practice to pour in as much fuel to match the highest volume of air an engine could draw or pump in without much consideration to efficiency. The game has changed, particularly in endurance racing where efficiency is used to both maximize power and minimize fuel consumption. So pay attention at every step in a build to think about how you can improve the quality of the air/fuel mixture that enters the cylinders will be burned efficiently. Also think about how you can reduce parasitic friction and pumping losses so power that is produced ends up at the flywheel flange. Use the information in this book and all you can collect from manufacturers and competitors to make yourself more than a parts assembler, but a race-engine builder.

—*Tom Monroe*

Taking a break while enjoying my favorite toy, an ERA Cobra powered by old technology, a 427 Ford side oiler with tunnel-port heads.

LET'S GET TECHNICAL

Technical, that's what engine building is about. Loosely translated from Webster, technical is the skill employed in a specific science, art, profession or craft. This means you'll have to apply science and art with skill when building your engine. So get accustomed to using numbers along with your mechanical skills during all aspects of your engine-building project. Understand what must go on in an engine for it to produce power and every step through to final assembly. Then there are the basics you must understand and master.

Measuring is a major portion of engine building, so you should have the basic tools and skills to use them—feeler gauges, micrometers, dial gauges and the sort. I cover the use of each as the tool is used. Then there's the aspect of converting units such as from metric to English, and vice versa. You must be consistent with units. For example, if you want displacement in cubic inches, you must use bore and stroke expressed in inches. On the other hand, to find displacement in cubic centimeters, use centimeters for bore and stroke. You should also be able to convert back and forth between English and metric. I give some examples, but refer to page 199 for conversion units.

Dyno testing reveals torque and power of engine. Air- and fuel-flow data are also used to determine efficiency in the form of brake specific fuel consumption (BSFC). The rate of fuel consumed in terms of pounds per horsepower hour, or how much fuel an engine uses every hour for every horsepower produced, BSFC should be 0.50—0.55 lb/hp-hour for gasoline and double that for alcohol engines.

HORSEPOWER

James Watt came up with the term *horsepower* in 1780 by basing it on the most common method of how things were moved at the time—with the horse. He determined one horse could lift 32,500 pounds one foot in one minute. Rounding it off, lifting the 33,000 pounds makes 33,000 ft-pound of *work*. Moving it in one minute makes it *power*, or one *horsepower*. So torque—force times distance in the case of an engine—applied to rotate a crankshaft once is work. Doing it in a given amount of time, or revolutions per minute (rpm), produced power. Rounding off the number as Watt did, one horsepower equals 33,000 ft-lb/min., which equates to the familiar 550 ft-lb/sec per horsepower.

So much for the history lesson. To put this in a usable form, torque and rpm are used to represent force, distance and time, respectively. Once an engine is loaded to obtain these values, such as on a dyno, we can then calculate

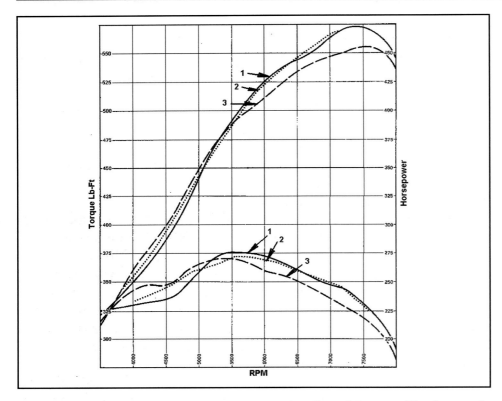

These typical horsepower/torque curves compare the effect of three modifications made to a 5.0-liter engine. All torque and horsepower curves cross at 5,252 rpm as torque begins to fall off and horsepower increases.

horsepower by plugging them into the formula:

Power = (T x S) ÷ 5,252 where T is torque and S is rpm.

An engine that has a torque of 425 lb-ft @ 6,500 rpm will produce:

Power = (425 lb-ft x 6,500 rpm) ÷ 5,252 = 526 hp.

When looking at torque and horsepower curves, notice that as torque falls off as horsepower rises, the two curves cross as they should at 5,252 rpm. This is due to the constant 5,252 being cancelled out by 5,252 rpm, making horsepower and torque numbers the same at 5,252 rpm.

In Metric Terms

With the move toward metrics, you may see engine power output expressed in kiloWatts (kW), or 1,000 Watts (W). This is what the SAE uses in its publications, so you should be familiar with making this power conversion. To do so, convert kW to hp by multiplying kW by 1.341 hp/kW, or HP = kW x 1.341. For example, a 400 kW engine equates to 400 x 1.341 hp/ kW = 536 hp.

Similarly, torque in metrics is expressed in Newton-meters (N-m) as opposed to ft-lb. To convert from N-m to lb-ft, use 0.7385 lb-ft/N-m. A 450 N-m engine is equivalent to 0.7385 lb-ft/N-m x 450 N-m = 332 lb-ft. Fortunately, time is universal...no conversion is required for rpm.

DISPLACEMENT

There are three variables to work with when determining engine displacement: Bore, stroke and number of cylinders. Assuming you've chosen the number of cylinders, you're down to two variables; bore and stroke. To determine displacement in cubic inches or cubic centimeters use the formula:

Displacement (CID) = $\pi D^2 \div 4 \times L \times N$

π is the constant 3.141593 regardless of units used for bore and stroke.
D = bore in inches or centimeters
L = stroke in inches or centimeters
N = number of cylinders
Displacement is in cubic inches (in.^{3}) or cubic centimeters (cc), respectively.

Example: Beginning with a V8 and a common bore and stroke; D = 4.0010 inches; L = 3.2500 inches; N = 8. Plugging in the numbers:

CID = π (4.0010 in.)^2 ÷ 4 x 3.2500 in. x 8
= 40.8611 in.^{3} x 8
= 326.8890 in.^{3}

The displacement of one cylinder is 40.8611 in., which is also the swept volume (SV) of that cylinder. SV is the volume displaced as the piston moves between top dead center (TDC) and bottom dead center (BDC). Keep swept volume in mind. It will be used for calculating compression ratio later in the cylinder head chapter.

Metric Conversions

Suppose you need to work in

centimeters and the dimensions are in inches? You'll need to convert to metric units. Since there are 2.54 centimeters (cm) in one inch, multiply dimensions in inches by 2.54 cm/in., or:

D = 4.0010 in. x 2.54cm/in.
= 10.1625cm
L = 2.54 cm/in. x 3.2500 in.
= 8.2550cm

Displacement in cubic centimeters (cc) is then found using the same formula, or:

CID = π(10.1625cm)^2 ÷ 4 x 8.2550cm
x 8 = 669.5886cc x 8 = 5,356.7091cc,
or 5.3567 liters (L)

That's a lot of work to arrive at the displacement in metrics providing dimensions are given in inches. So if you prefer making life easier and would rather work in English units, not to mention it is more accurate to read measuring instruments calibrated in English units, find displacement in cubic inches first, then convert to metrics. That's simple enough since there are 61.02 in.^{3} for each liter, or 61.02 in.^{3}/L. To go the other way, there are 0.01639 L/in.^{3}, which is the inverse of 61.02. Make the conversion as follows:

Displacement in liters = 326.8890 in.^{3}
÷ 61.02 in.^{3} per L = 5.3570L.

The difference in the last figure occurs from rounding off numbers between English and metrics units.

You've probably recognized that we're dealing with a common displacement, or 327 in.^{3} in English units and 5.4L in metrics.

Auto manufacturers like nice even numbers for emblems and literature, so they round off displacement to an even number because it looks neater.

At some stage during an engine build, you will need displacement in cubic centimeters (cc) and not liters. Fortunately, working with metrics is easy. The conversion from one metric unit to another is usually a matter of simply moving the decimal point. For instance, when converting between cubic centimeters and liters, move the decimal point one way or the other three places. Or because there are 1,000cc per liter, simply multiply displacement in liters by 1,000, or 5.3570L x 1,000cc/L = 5,3570cc. Keep in mind that converting to metrics is particularly handy when determining compression ratios. Combustion chamber volumes are typically given in cc's, as are burette graduations, so you'll need SV—displacement of one cylinder—in cubic centimeters.

Effects of Boring and Stroking on Displacement

Consider you have a particular engine and want to increase displacement by some amount—a small increase or a large one. The question is what is best done to increase displacement in the increment you want? If it's a small increase, one method is best; another if it's a large increase. Let's take a look at the effect of one versus the other.

Overboring—Using the example above, let's suppose you overbore the engine 0.030 in.—0.015 in. removed—which increases bore diameter to 4.0310 in. Stroke

remains the same at 3.2500 in. Plugging in the numbers, displacement then becomes:

$CID_{0.030 \text{ overbore}}$ = (4.0310 in.)^2 ÷ 4 x
3.2500 in. x 8
= 41.4762 in.^{3} x 8
= 331.8100 in.^{3}, or an increase of
4.9210 in^3.

This is just over 1.6 cubic inches per 0.0100-inch bore increase for a four-inch bore. Not much, but boring is useful if you are trying not to exceed, but want to maximize displacement that's legislated by the rules of a sanctioning organization.

Stroking—To increase stroke with the same engine, let's see what the effect is on displacement. Assuming there is room in the bottom end to swing the bigger crankshaft and other mechanicals work, an increased stroke of 0.25 in. will result in a new stroke of 3.5000 inches. Displacement is then:

$CID_{3.50 \text{ stroke}}$ = (4.0010 in.)^2 ÷ 4 x
3.5000 in. x 8 = 44.0043 in.^{3} x 8 =
352.0343 in.^{3}, or an increase of
25.1453 in.^{3}.

This is a significant displacement increase, but the gain is about even compared to the gain from the bore size change in terms of actual dimensional increases, or 0.030-in. bore increase versus a 0.250-in. stroke increase. The reason for this is bore size is squared in the formula and stroke is not. To make significant bore-size changes would require a different block due to cylinder-wall thickness limitation. Therefore, the point here is to bore when making incremental displacement increases, but increase stroke to make major displacement changes. Ideally, though, work with both bore and stroke to make displacement changes.

COMPRESSION RATIO

Within limitations, increasing compression is the single most effective easy way to increase the power output of a naturally aspirated engine. But compression ratio is usually limited by racing rules. No wiggle room here. For instance, if compression is limited to 9.5:1, that's it. Compression ratio must not exceed 9.5:1 or you're out. But if compression is not limited by rules, your next limitation is the octane rating of available fuel. For instance, if you'll be using pump gas, figure on not much more than 10:1. However, if you can run unlimited racing gas, then compression can push 15:1. You can go even higher with alcohol, or up to 16:1. Camshaft grind/timing, airflow, combustion-chamber efficiency, port flow and a combination of factors have a major influence on compression and the ultimate limitation—*detonation*.

Detonation

Detonation is a condition that causes some or all of the fuel charge to explode rather than burn. Very bad. Allowed to occur under high-speed engine load, damage from detonation can range from bearing distortion to catastrophic engine failure. Instead, fuel should burn, although rapidly. Fuel burns at a speed of 70 to 170 feet/second. The higher the octane, the slower the burn rate. To put into

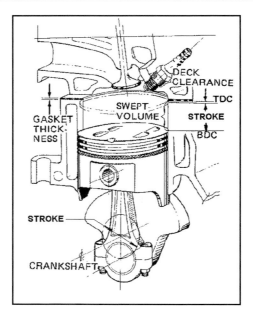

Static compression ratio is the ratio between swept volume (SV) and clearance volume (CV). CV is cylinder displacement. SV is volume above piston at TDC.

perspective, once ignition takes place complete burning of the air/fuel mixture is about 3/1,000 second.

Static and Dynamic Compression

Static, or mechanical, compression ratio is determined though calculations. *Dynamic* compression is the true compression the engines builds while running. It's varies with engine load and rpm. More or less air/fuel mixture is getting crammed into and is retained in the combustion chamber to support combustion. So cam grind, flow and combustion-chamber effici-ency have a considerable effect on compression ratio, thus the term *dynamic compression ratio*. But we have to start with static compression, or compression determined through calculations. Do this by determining the ratio of the volume above the piston that will be squeezed—compressed—into a

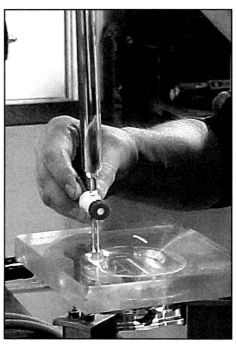

Determining piston-dish volume using burette and plate.

smaller volume as the piston moves from BDC to TDC.

Typically expressed in cubic centimeters, the two volumes to work with are swept volume (SV) and clearance volume (CV). Previously discussed, SV is the displacement of one cylinder. As for CV, it is the volume above the piston at TDC created by a combination of volumes made up by the cylinder-head combustion chamber, head-gasket compressed thickness, piston-to-deck clearance, top compression ring to top of piston and shape of the piston top.

Let's take a look at how static compression ratio is determined using SV and CV. For how to measure the amount each component makes up clearance volume for your engine, refer to the cylinder-head chapter. For now let's use a real-world example using the following:

First, using an engine with a bore and stroke of 4.23 in. and 3.784

in., respectively, swept volume is:

$$SV = \pi(4.23 \text{ in.})^2 \div 4 \times 3.784 \text{ in.} = 53.1767 \text{ in}^3, \text{ or } 871.46cc.$$

If you have SV in cubic inches, convert to cubic centimeters by dividing 53.1767 in.^{3} by 61.02 in.^{3}/cc and multiplying the result by 1,000cc/L, which yields the same 871.46cc.

Second, CV consists of five volumes: cylinder head combustion chamber (CV_1), gasket (CV_2), deck clearance (CV_3), ring position on piston (CV_4) and top of piston (CV_5). Clearance volume created by CV_1 is nearly always positive. CV_2 and CV_4 are always positive, but CV_3 is sometimes negative. CV_5 can be positive or negative. For this example the volumes in cubic centimeters are:

CV_1 = 89cc
CV_2 = 10.4cc
$CV3$ = 2.7cc
$CV4$ = 1.3cc
$CV5$ = −10cc (Negative indicates the piston has a popup or dome, thus reducing CV by 10cc.)
CV_{tot} = 93.4cc

$$CR = (SV + CV) \div CV$$

SV plus CV, or 871.46 + 93.4cc = 964.86cc is the volume in the cylinder above the cylinder at BDC. CV, or 93.4cc is the volume above the piston at TDC. With that in mind, the 964.86cc is compressed into the 93.4cc combustion chamber. Plugging the numbers into the equation shown above:

$$CR = (871.46cc + 93.4cc) \div 93.4cc$$
$$= 10.33{:}1$$

or making it simpler,
$$CR = SV \div CV + 1$$
$$= 871.46cc \div 93.4cc + 1$$
$$= 9.33 + 1 = 10.33{:}1$$

As can be seen from this example, anything done to increase CV will reduce compression. This includes removing metal from the combustion chamber, installing a thicker head gasket or using a piston with more dish, or reverse dome. Conversely, milling the head, installing a thinner gasket or increasing piston popup size will reduce CV, thus increase compression. Similarly, a change in SV will change compression, albeit slightly. For instance, overboring a cylinder increases SV, thus increases compression. So always recheck CR after boring.

VOLUMETRIC EFFICIENCY

Power depends on trapping as much air/fuel charge in the cylinder as possible. Technically speaking, how much air trapped in a cylinder is known as *volumetric efficiency,* or VE. This is simply the ratio of air molecules retained in a cylinder compared to the molecules in the same volume at ambient—surrounding—pressure and temperature. A better term would be *density ratio,* or the ratio of air density in the cylinder compared to the density of the outside air just before it is drawn into the intake track of the engine. Mike Urich, coauthor of HPBooks' *Holley Carburetors, Manifolds and Fuel Injection,* also says VE should be called density ratio.

But whatever you call it, increase the VE of an engine and you increase its power output. A VE of 100% or better should be your primary objective as a racing engine builder.

Prior to government emissions regulations, mileage standards coupled with the resulting use of fuel injection, high-energy ignition systems and multiple valves, typical grocery-getter engines had VEs around 75%. Performance models of the same era offered engines with VEs of 85% at peak efficiency. As for the best race engines, VE went up to 90% at maximum rpm and 95% at maximum torque. However, this could be increased to 100% or slightly more by tuning the intake and exhaust systems for a certain engine speed. With the testing equipment coupled with the available knowledge we have today, VE of the internal combustion engine can be pushed higher through with highly efficient intake and exhaust systems.

Airflow, Power, and Engine Speed

Just how VE and total airflow relates to horsepower at a particular engine speed can be illustrated by the formula:

$$CFM = (CID \times rpm) \div 3{,}456 \text{ where } CID \text{ is engine displacement in cubic inches.}$$

A 370-in.^{3} engine is turning at 9,000 rpm flows:

$$CFM = (370 \text{ in.}^3 \times 9{,}000 \text{ rpm}) \div 3{,}456$$
$$= 964 \text{ in.}^3 \div \text{min. total flow, providing VE is 100\%}$$

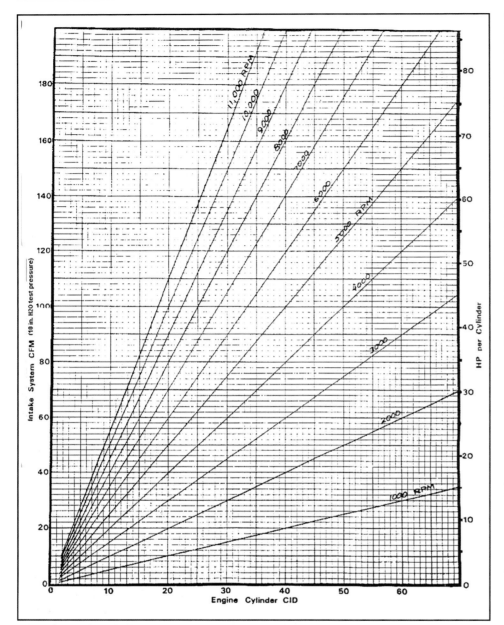

Use chart to relate airflow in CFM at test pressure of 10 inches of water to displacement, rpm and horsepower. <u>Convert airflow using the relationship</u> $CFM_1/CFM_2 =$ $\sqrt{(\text{Test Pressure}_1)} \div \sqrt{(\text{Test Pressure}_2)}$. Chart courtesy SuperFlow Technologies Group

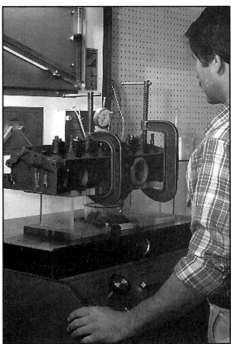

The author flowing head on SF600 flow bench. Head flow relates directly engine power output.

However, if VE is reduced to 95%: $CFM = 964$ in.$^3 \div$ min. x 0.95 = 915 in.$^3 \div$ min., drop of nearly 50 in.^{3} min.

Airflow Chart—Total engine airflow is more easily obtained using the accompanying chart that graphs airflow versus engine rpm. The chart is based on 100% VE, so multiply the assumed VE of your engine by the airflow obtained from the chart to arrive at actual airflow. While keeping in mind you know what assume means, lean toward the conservative side when estimating engine efficiency. Being over optimistic concerning the capability of an engine is typically a bad thing to do.

Fuel Flow Chart—In addition to the airflow chart there is a fuel flow chart. Refer to it to obtain fuel flow in pounds per hour (lb/hr). Because you don't deal with fuel weight, convert to gallons per hour by dividing fuel flow in lb/hr by 6.016 lb/gal. for gasoline. Fuel flow will be about double for straight alcohol. The chart reflects a 12.5 A/F (air/fuel) ratio; typical of the A/F mixture of a race engine on gasoline at full power. An engine with high burn efficiency could go leaner, but 12.5:1 is a safe assumption. As with the airflow chart you need to factor in the VE ratio to obtain fuel flow at full power.

For example: From the Fuel Flow vs. Rpm chart on the next page, the example engine should flow about 340 lb/hr of fuel at 100% VE, or 323 lb/hr at 95% VE. Dividing 323 lb/hr by 6.016 lb/gal., fuel flow is nearly 54 gal./hr. So at wide-open throttle continuous, fuel consumption for

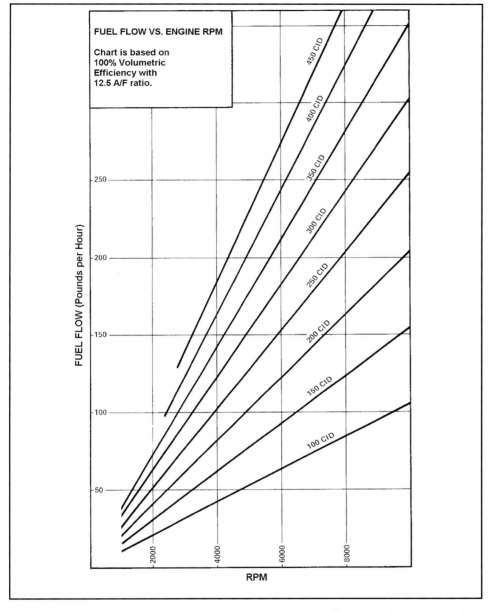

FUEL FLOW VS. ENGINE RPM

Chart is based on 100% Volumetric Efficiency with 12.5 A/F ratio.

Determine fuel consumption by going up from rpm on horizontal axis to appropriate displacement line, then across to vertical line and read fuel flow in pounds per hour. Convert to gallons per hour by dividing pounds per hour by 6.016 lb/gallon.

each hour will be approximately 54 gallons.

AIRFLOW, POWER & RPM

Airflow trapped in the combustion chambers is required to get power, but fuel burned at the correct air/fuel mixture is what ultimately produces power. The problem is, it's always more difficult and expensive to improve airflow than it is fuel flow. Consequently, we must first deal with increasing airflow. Once that is accomplished, you can add more fuel by carburetor rejetting or changing injector nozzle or pill size. Also, fuel pressure can be changed, depending on the system used.

The relationship to power output of one cylinder and maximum airflow through one intake port is expressed by the formula provided by SuperFlow Corporation:

Power expressed in horsepower = 0.43 x CFM @ 10 in.H_2O

Once you find horsepower of one cylinder using this formula, multiply it by the number of cylinders to get total power output.

The airflow used in the formula is that obtained at a test pressure of 10 in.H_2O. If you use a flow figure found at any other test pressure, you must convert it to what the flow would be at 10 in.H_2O pressure. Also note that engine displacement is not used in this formula, illustrating that the amount of airflow into an engine can be more important than displacement, all things considered. What this implies is a lower-displacement engine with high a VE can produce more power than a larger engine with a low VE. The condition is the smaller engine must be operated at a higher rpm to obtain this power.

But first, making this flow conversion based on test pressure is important because airflow of a cylinder head or whatever is almost never given at a pressure of 10 in.H_2O. A more typical cylinder-head test pressure is 28 in.H_2O, but some are given at 25 in.H_2O. Also, if you're comparing the flow of one cylinder head to another that was flowed at a different test pressure, you must make this conversion to make a direct comparison. Let's take a look at airflow first, beginning with converting airflow at one pressure to airflow at another pressure.

FLOW TEST PRESSURE CONVERSION

From Test Pressure in.-H$_2$O	To Test Pressure: in.-H$_2$O							
	10	**12**	**15**	**18**	**20**	**22**	**25**	**28**
10	1.00	1.09	1.22	1.34	1.41	1.48	1.58	1.67
12	.913	1.00	1.12	1.22	1.29	1.35	1.44	1.53
15	.816	.894	1.00	1.09	1.15	1.21	1.29	1.37
18	.745	.816	.912	1.00	1.05	1.11	1.18	1.25
20	.707	.744	.866	.949	1.00	1.05	1.12	1.18
22	.674	.739	.826	.905	.935	1.00	1.07	1.13
25	.632	.693	.775	.849	.894	.938	1.00	1.06
28	.598	.694	.732	.802	.845	.886	.945	1.00

Use chart to convert flow from one test pressure to flow at another test pressure.

Airflow vs. Pressure Conversion— It makes sense that a head flowed at a higher test pressure will flow more air and vice versa. However, because air is compressible it does funny things, such as not providing a flow change that's directly proportional to pressure change—the relationship is not linear.

To convert from one flow to another at different pressures, use the relationship:

$$CFM_1 + CFM_2 = \sqrt{P_1} \div \sqrt{P_2}$$

In usable form:

$$CFM_2 = CFM_1 \times \sqrt{P_2} \div \sqrt{P_1}$$

As an example, suppose the heads for a V8 flow 295 cfm @ 28 in.H$_2$O on the intake side. The first step is to determine flow at 10 in.H$_2$O, or CFM$_2$. Using the accompanying chart or formula above:

$$CFM_2 = 295 \text{ cfm} \times (\sqrt{28 \text{ in.H}_2\text{O}} \div \sqrt{10 \text{ in.H}_2\text{O}}) = 295 \text{ cfm} \times (3.1623 \div 5.292)$$
$$CFM_2 = 295 \text{ cfm} \times 0.598 = 176.3 \text{ cfm}$$

Now for power, providing there are no flow losses in the intake track:

Power per cylinder = 0.43 x 176.3 cfm = 75.8 hp
Total power = 8 x 75.8 hp = 606.5 hp.

To make use of the maximum airflow required to produce this power, use the following formula from SuperFlow or the accompanying graph to determine the rpm the engine must be turned.

RPM = 2,000 ÷ displacement in in.^{3} x flow @ 10 in.H$_2$O

For a 350 in.^{3} engine, displacement for each cylinder is 43.75 in.^{3}

RPM = 2,000 ÷ 43.75 in.^{3} x 176.3 cfm = 45.71 x 176.3 cfm = 8,059 rpm

STANDARD TEMPERATURE & PRESSURE

Temperature and pressure affect power output because they directly influence the number of air molecules that will enter the cylinders. As pressure goes down, power drops in direct proportion. And since pressure drops with an increase in altitude, power drops as altitude increases. Why? Air at lower pressure is less dense, which means fewer air molecules occupy the same volume. A similar phenomenon occurs with temperature. As temperature goes up, air density goes down. Consequently, there are fewer air molecules at higher temperatures to support combustion. So high altitude and high temperature have a detrimental effect on power.

Engine testers eliminate atmospheric pressure and temperature as a variable by correcting airflow and power readings. They do this by converting power readings to what they would be at standard sea level pressure and temperature, or 14.7 pounds per square inch (psi) and 59° Fahrenheit, respectively.

Rather than using psi, pressure is typically expressed in inches of Mercury (in.Hg), where one psi is approximately 2 in.Hg. Therefore, standard pressure is 29.92 in.Hg, which is equivalent to 14.7 psi. And for every 1,000 ft increase in elevation, there's an approximate pressure drop of about 1 in.Hg, or 0.5 psi. Aircraft altimeters, which are nothing but barometers, read out in altitude instead of pressure. **Note**: Humidity has some effect on air density, although much less than temperature and pressure. As humidity increases, water molecules displace air molecules, which has an inverse effect on air density. That is, as humidity increases, air becomes less dense and vice versa.

Keep in mind that airflow in CFM is stated in inches of water (in.H_2O) rather than inches of Mercury (in.Hg). This is because reading the scale from a taller water-filled manometer is much more accurate than a short one filled with mercury. Cost, handling and environmental considerations are other reasons for using water.

Air Weight——Air density is really a gauge of how much a unit of air weighs. As pressure goes down with higher elevations and lower temperatures, density decreases as does weight. For example, the weight of a Standard Cubic Foot of air weighs about 0.0764 lb/ft³. This is arrived using the formula:

D = 1.325 (Pb/T) where D = weight of one cubic foot of air; Pb = Barometric pressure in inches of Mercury; T = ambient temperature in degrees F + 460.

Harold Bettes of SuperFlow offered this extreme example: In Denver on a typical race day, temperature is about 85°F and the barometer reads 24.9 in.Hg. Plugging in the numbers:

D = 1.325 (24.9 in.Hg/545) = 0.0605 lb/ft³.

The following chart illustrates standard air pressure and temperature change with elevation. Note that one psi is 2.036 in.Hg. Every 1000-ft increase in elevation decreases local barometric pressure by approximately 1 in.Hg up to about 20,000 feet.

Elevation (feet)	Approximate Pressure	in.Hg PSI*	Temperature (deg.F)
0	29.92 in.Hg	14.7	59°F
1000	28.86 in.Hg	14.17	55.4°F
2000	27.82 in.Hg	13.66	51.9°F
3000	26.82 in.Hg	13.17	48.3°F
4000	25.84 in.Hg	12.69	44.7°F
5000	24.89 in.Hg	12.23	41.2°F
6000	23.98 in.Hg	11.78	37.6°F
7000	23.09 in.Hg	11.34	34°F
8000	22.22 in.Hg	10.91	30.5°F
9000 **Pikes Peak Hillclimb start**	21.38 in.Hg	10.5	26.9°F
14110 **Pikes Peak Hillclimb Finish**	17.57 in.Hg	8.63	9.1°F

*numbers rounded off

Chart courtesy Harold Bettes

2 THE CYLINDER BLOCK

Performance block work typically consisted of cleaning, then visually checking for cracks, cylinder-bore condition, deck-surface condition and main bearing-bore alignment. The block was next declared acceptable or unacceptable. If irregularities were found they were either corrected or the block was replaced. Things have changed. For instance, tolerances are tighter, components are more precisely manufactured using higher quality materials and finishes are critical. So you need to be very attentive when inspecting and preparing a block. The block is the foundation of an engine, much like the foundation of a house. If the foundation of a house collapses, the house goes with it. The same applies to an engine. The block supports all major engine components in close proximity to one another; seals pressurized liquids at the heads, crankshaft, pistons and passages. At the same time these components must operate under very high stress. So skimp on any steps outlined in this chapter and you'll compromise the power and durability of your engine.

CLEANING

Begin your block work by cleaning it. Skimp on this critical phase and you risk early failure of your engine. A friend who built Rolls Royce aircraft engines for

Block work begins with a thorough cleaning. After tanking, scrub block and clean lifter bores with a gun-bore brush.

unlimited Reno air racers said that most failures of these incredibly rare and expensive engines was caused by the d-one-r-t additive, commonly known as dirt. So don't short-cut cleaning. Not only may deposits result in damage left in place, they may hide imperfections. They can lead to clogged oil passages, scored bearing journals and bound up oil pumps, so consider dirt deadly in terms of engine life.

Dirt ranges from mud, oil and grease on the outside to sludge, abrasive grit, metal particles and varnish on the inside. Don't

overlook cleaning even a new block. It will have debris in the oil galleries, on machined surfaces and in the water jacket. The debris can take the form of machining lubricant, abrasives and metal cuttings. So don't assume a block is clean just because it's new.

Cleaning is not a one-shot process. You're not done after cleaning a block once. Cleaning is an ongoing process. Start by cleaning the exterior with a pressure washer or steam cleaner if it's really dirty. As for cleaning the block, start with an initial cleaning followed up by additional cleanings as you go.

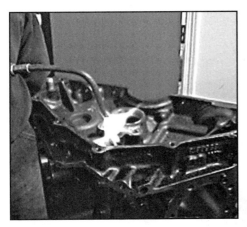

Remove stubborn oil gallery plugs by first heating in the center with a torch until cherry red.

Hold paraffin against plug to cool and shrink it.

Restrictors for Chevrolet limit oil to lifters and rocker arms.

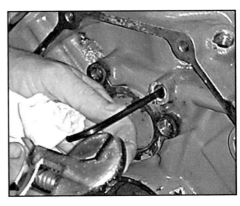

Removing threaded oil restrictors installed behind plugs in Ford block. Gallery at right is also fitted with restrictor.

What you use to clean the block with depends on its material. If it's cast iron, your options are wide open. Although not used for engine blocks, the same goes for steel, brass and copper. As for aluminum, you can't use a hot tank. That's unfortunate because a hot tank with caustic soda is an excellent cleaning solution. But the caustic solution attacks soft metals such as aluminum, zinc and lead. Also, there are environmental implications. Caustic solution is not EPA friendly. All is not lost, though. Jet sprayers with hot high-pressure water-based solutions work well. But whatever you use, the cleaning solution must be heated to near boiling to ensure maximum cleaning.

Strip Block

The cleaning solution must have access to all hidden areas in the block such as oil passages, water jackets and blind bolt holes. So remove all brackets, bearings, plugs, bolts, studs, screws, old gasket material, seals—everything.

Removing oil gallery plugs is particularly important. This will allow deposits in the galleries to be flushed out by the cleaning solution now so they won't be loosened later when the engine is back in operation. If this happens they will be circulated with the oil to the pump and bearings. Even worse, large chunks can block oil passages, causing oil starvation to main bearings and rod bearings. Not a pretty picture.

Oil Plugs—Blocks typically have three oil galleries drilled the length of the block. Sometimes there are as many as five. Additionally, there is a connection of oil passages drilled 90° to these passages.

The ends of the oil galleries are sealed with plugs; cup type at the front and pipe plugs at the rear or pipe plugs at both ends. Pipe plugs are usually in very tight, so tight that you can't remove them without the use of heat. You'll need an acetylene torch and a paraffin wax stick for this job. You can find wax sticks, the kind for lubricating drawer slides or sealing toilets, at your local hardware store. Fit the torch with a large welding tip such as Victor's #5.

With torch lit and adjusted to a small white inner cone, apply heat in a circular pattern to center of plug, heating it evenly until it is cherry red, no hotter. Once it reaches this color, remove the heat and immediately hold wax, or paraffin, against the plug to cool it rapidly. With or without using wax, the plug will shrink and loosen so you can remove it. Remove plug with a 3/8-in. to 1/4-in. socket adapter, Allen wrench or eight-point socket. Tighten plug slightly, then remove it. Shrink and remove all oil gallery plugs in the same manner. After removing plugs, check for oil restrictors. At the end of two galleries at the rear, some are an integral part of the plugs and some install behind the conventional oil gallery plugs.

O-ringed plugs seal oil galleries on this Mopar NASCAR Cup engine. After removing TruArc retaining ring, pull out plug with bolt threaded in hole at center of plug.

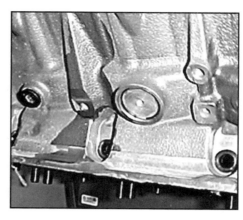

O-ringed core plugs similar to oil gallery plugs in Mopar NASCAR Cup block.

Drain plugs and epoxied core plugs in Chevy and Ford blocks. Don't remove either if water jackets look clean.

Make a note of which holes these install in.

If cup-type plugs are installed in the front end of oil the galleries, drive them out by sliding steel rod in from back of block after rear plugs are out. Use a four-foot long, 1/4-in. diameter steel rod and hammer to knock out the plugs.

You're not finished. Check for plugs in galleries running 90° to the main oil galleries. Don't overlook these. They should be removed so the cleaning solution will flow into the darkest remote corners of the oil galleries. You'll find such plugs at the top or side of the block,

either front or rear. If cup plugs are used, use your ingenuity to remove them. What works for me is to drill a 1/8-in. hole in the center of the plug and thread in a large sheet-metal screw until it is tight. This provides something to grasp. Clamp onto the head of the screw head with ViseGrip pliers then pry under the head of the pliers to pull out the plug.

Core Plugs—Sometimes called freeze plugs, soft plugs, cup plugs or whatever, these are used to seal core holes in the water jacket, thus the term *core plugs*. You'll find these at the sides of the block and

sometimes at the front and rear. Cup-type plugs are usually used, but large-diameter pipe plugs have been used in some Ford and Mopar cast-iron blocks. If the block is aluminum, chances are it's fitted with O-ringed thread-in plugs.

On some race-prepped blocks such as the Mopar block pictured, the core holes are counterbored to provide a ledge at the bottom of the bore and a groove for a retaining ring. A plug fitted with an O-ring for sealing is installed in each core-plug hole and retained with a retaining ring. A blind hole is drilled and tapped in the center of each plug for removal purposes. To remove this type of plug, remove the retaining ring and thread a bolt into the center of the plug. Using a slide hammer, grasp the bolt head and knock out plug.

You usually don't have to remove the core plugs from a race block, but if the interior of the water jacket appears to be dirty or the plugs rusted, remove them. The best way to remove a cup plug is drive one side of it in using a 1/2-inch diameter punch and hammer. Check first to see if the plugs are pinned. Typically, there will be three pins per plug spaced evenly around the plug. If so, remove each one by carefully driving a small cape chisel under the pin head just enough to raise it. This will allow you to get under the head of the pin with the jaws of a small pair of diagonal wire cutters and lever it out. Once all pins are removed, drive out the plug. As for plugs retained with epoxy, remove them as you would any plug and remove the remaining epoxy.

Be careful when removing a cup-

Remove studs by double-nutting as shown or with stud remover.

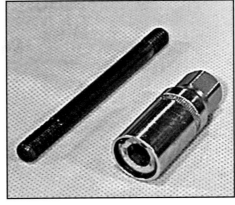

Stud extractor shown beside stud. Make sure when using extractor that it grasps unthreaded section of stud.

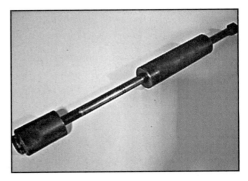

Slide hammer with interchangeable collet for removing dowels.

Slide hammer and collet positioned to knock out solid dowel.

Thick-wall hollow is threaded, making removal easier.

type core plug that's near a cylinder. When driving in a cup-type core plug, offset punch to the side of the plug that's farthest from a cylinder. The object is to rotate the plug in its hole and not knock it in. Take care not to drive the plug in against a cylinder. If it butts against the cylinder, stop. Cylinder walls have been cracked by overenthusiastic engine builders. After rotating the plug, clamp on its flange with water pump pliers and lever it out. Remove all core plugs at the side, front and back. If

a plug falls into the water jacket, fish it up to the hole with a magnet, then clamp on the flange with your pliers and pry it out.

Finally, there will be a drain plug at the bottom of the water jacket, one on each bank of a V-type block. Remove them. These shouldn't be in as tight as oil gallery plugs, but if they are use the heat-and-wax method to loosen them.

Studs—Your block may be fitted with studs in the deck, main bearing webs and pan rails. To ease the jobs of checking, machining and handling your block, remove studs from the deck and pan rails. Leave the main cap studs in place. Use the

double-nut method or use a stud extractor, particularly for removing the head studs.

Dowels—Dowels are used to position heads to deck or bellhousing to rear face of the block. Some, but not all engines, use dowels to position the front cover. For now remove dowels from the deck. How to do this depends on the dowel type. These may be small-diameter solid, thin-wall hollow, thick-wall hollow or split hollow dowels.

First, try removing each dowel with your fingers. If a dowel is missing, check to see if it came out with the head. You'll need more pulling force if they are tight. The best way to remove solid or thick-wall dowels is with a slide hammer and collet. With the right size collet clamped on the dowel, slide the hammer to bang it out. If you don't have a slide hammer, try ViseGrip pliers, but be careful not to collapse a hollow dowel. Clamp on the dowel with the smooth part of the jaws, then pull while rocking the pliers back and forth. Check to see if the dowel moves. Remove all dowels.

Cam Bearings—Cam bearings should come out, particularly if you'll be hot tanking the block. Not only will it ruin the

Drive out cam bearings using an adjustable or snug-fitting solid mandrel.

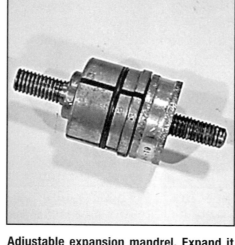

Adjustable expansion mandrel. Expand it so it's snug, then drive out the bearings.

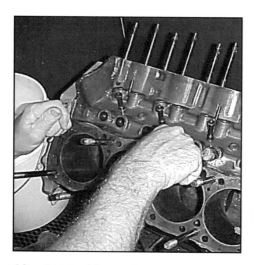

After hot tanking or jet-spray cleaning, scrub the block inside and out with soapy water.

A jet spray cleaner is large enough to handle a block.

bearings—you should replace them anyway—it will contaminate the caustic cleaning solution.

You will need a hammer, drive bar and a set of mandrels, either solid or the collet-type expansion type. A solid mandrel should fit snugly in the cam bearing, but not tight. As for an expansion mandrel, expand it to fit the ID of the bearing. For engines using different diameter bearings, you will need a series of solid mandrels. One expansion mandrel adjusted to fit should work.

Start by knocking out the rear cam plug. These are usually a low-profile cup plug, but *expansion plugs* are sometimes used. Expansion plugs have no flange, but a slight hemispherical shape prior to installation. Regardless of the type plug used, remove them in the same manner. Slide the bar through the cam bore, butt it against the plug, then strike the bar to knock it out.

Next to remove are the cam bearings. Choose the mandrel that fits snugly into the bearing, but not

tight, or fit the expansion mandrel into the bearing and expand it to fit. Check that the mandrel flange is against the side of the bearing, and then center the drive bar through the cam tunnel into the mandrel. Here's where a big hammer is appropriate. While holding the drive bar hard against the mandrel, drive out the bearing. Continue removing the bearings until they are all out. Be aware that you may have to use different solid mandrels or readjust the expansion mandrel. Cam bearing may not be sized the same front to back.

Clean Block—After stripping block, set it in the hot tank or jet sprayer. Save your back. Use a hoist or cherry picker to lift the block, particularly when using a hot tank. Drop the block and you will get splashed with caustic soda—not a nice experience. Remember: Don't use a hot tank if the block is aluminum or cam bearings are in block.

For efficient cleaning, the jet-spray or hot-tank temperature should be at maximum and soap at full strength. Caustic soda must be washed off with water and machined surfaces rust proofed. Using compressed air, immediately blow off all water and coat machined surfaces with WD-40 or an equivalent water-displacing lubricant. Pay particular attention to the cylinder bores and lifter bores. To complete the cleaning, run a gun-bore brush through the oil galleries to dislodge stubborn deposits. Also, if you have a steam cleaner or pressure washer, fire it up and direct the high-pressure spray into each oil gallery to force out remaining deposits. Blow out the oil galleries with compressed air and protect machined surfaces with WD-40.

STRESS RELIEVING

When a casting is made, internal stresses, or forces pushing and pulling against each other, are built up in the part. This is due to factors such as differing cross sections and uneven cooling that occurs during the casting process. If not relieved, these stresses can result in cracks and instability, or movement, neither of which can be tolerated in a racing engine block. The good news is these stresses can be removed from a *green* block by aging, or seasoning, over long time. Better news is stresses are relieved if the block has been used.

If you don't have the time to season a green block, stresses can be relieved artificially. So if you are not working with an existing engine or the block has been sitting out in a field for years, there's is no other option than to stress-relieve the block artificially. Fortunately, most manufacturers that supply parts in the high-performance and racing industry do this for us. Check to make sure. The following are methods used for stress relieving.

Heat Treating

This is the traditional way of stress-relieving a metal part, whether it is cast iron, aluminum or steel. One process used for an aluminum block involves heating it in an oven to about 500°F, then quenching it, cooling rapidly, in 80°F water. The block is then aged by bringing it up to just over 200°F and holding it there for two hours. For stress-relieving a cast-iron block, it is uniformly heated

COMPACTED GRAPHITE CAST IRON

CGI, or compacted-graphite cast iron, was developed in the 1970s in an effort to find a higher strength cast iron as a replacement for gray cast iron. As is usually the case, there were problems. CGI had casting and machining problems that needed to be addressed, but the need to find lighter, stronger materials in the auto industry forced manufacturers' hands. Consequently, these problems have been largely overcome. This result is CGI is now used to manufacture lighter diesel engines and to make cast iron competitive with aluminum. As a result, CGI has found its way into the racing industry and is now used in many high-performance engine blocks. The advantage of CGI is it's 35% stiffer than gray cast iron, has a 75% higher tensile strength and is more resistant to cracking at higher temperatures, all without the need to do a lot of alloying. The bottom line is, CGI blocks are stronger and lighter.

As mentioned above, there were machining problems with CGI that had to be overcome. Because of the metallurgical properties of CGI, more power and higher machining speeds on the order of 10–30% are needed. In addition, CGI has a lower manganese sulfide content than gray cast iron, which provides lubrication. This reduces tool life to about half of that for milling and to one-tenth for boring compared to that for gray cast iron. Also, CGI is more sensitive to notching, or stress risers, which makes it even more important to smooth the surface of a block and provide large radii in all corners if the block is cast with compressed graphite. So if you are working with a CGI block, expect to replace or sharpen cutting tools more often.

in an oven to about 1,050°F and held there for approximately two hours. The block is then cooled at a controlled rate, or no more than 200°F per hour.

Taking the "heat treating" procedure further, *cryogenics*—super cooling—provides additional stress relieving for all metals. Cryogenics requires that the traditional stress-relieving process is done first, then the part is cooled in nitrogen to near absolute zero, or –300°F. This process not only stress relieves the block, but improves its wear properties.

Vibratory Treating

An alternative to stress relieving by using thermal methods is inducing controlled vibrations into metal parts. This is accomplished by clamping the block to a table or an inducer to the part and inducing sub-harmonic vibrations into it for a short time as shown. Harmonic vibrations are those at which a part or assembly would naturally "dance," typically called natural frequency, much like an unbalanced tire would do when it vibrates at a certain speed, or frequency, say 55 or 60 mph. It follows that sub-harmonic vibrations are a lower frequency.

Once the natural frequency is found, a sub-harmonic frequency is induced into the part for 20 minutes. Natural frequency is again checked. If it has shifted, or changed, stress relief has occurred.

INSPECTION

Regardless of whether your block is aged or green, it should be inspected, both visually and with inspection equipment. Your best scenario is working with a block that's part of a previously run engine that didn't have problems. That doesn't mean the block shouldn't receive any less attention, though. Keep in mind as you work that the earliest you discover a problem the sooner you can make a decision as to how to correct it. Also, you won't have to invest any more time or money if the block can't be used.

Although inspecting is something you do throughout the entire engine-building process, you need to inspect the block for serious problems now. Specific problems to look for include cracks, inclusions, surface irregularities, oversizes and undersizes. Although some of these can be corrected, others render a block useless. Inspection can be done using one or a combination of methods.

Crack Inspection

The first thing you need to look for is cracks. How you do this depends on your equipment or access to specific equipment. Crack detection can be done by using magnetic-particle inspection and dye testing, both of which are non-destructive testing methods.

MPI Testing—The most

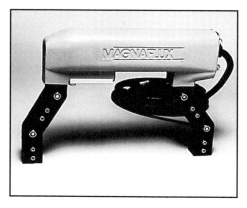

Portable AC crack detector has adjustable yokes for magnetizing large or small areas. Rotate in different positions to align magnetic field for detecting cracks running in different directions. Goodson photo.

Powdered iron particles are sprayed or sprinkled on magnetized area to align with and expose cracks.

commonly used method of checking for cracks is by magnetic-particle inspection, or MPI, commonly know as *Magnafluxing*. A limitation of MPI is it can't be used to check non-magnetic materials such as an aluminum, copper and some stainless steels, but it works great for inspecting cast-iron blocks, connecting rods (unless they are aluminum), and crankshafts. I cover methods for inspecting non-magnetic materials later in this chapter.

MPI uses black or colored iron oxide particles, either dry or wet, to inspect for surface cracks using an AC unit. A more expensive DC unit can detect cracks accurately from the surface to 0.100-inch below the surface. These particles are applied dry by sprinkling from a saltshaker-like container, squeeze bulb or atomizer bulb. The dry method is better for detecting sub-surface cracks. With the wet method, called Magnaglo by Magnaflux, a division of Illinois Tool Works, magnetic particles are flowed over the area being checked in solvent or water treated with wetting and anti-corrosion agents.

To improve detection, the iron oxide particles used in the wet MPI method are available with fluorescent material. This makes cracks highly visible when viewed under a UV lamp (black light). Do this in a darkened room or booth.

Using MPI, magnetize the part to be checked. For checking a large area such as a block deck, magnetize it in sections. Use the portable yoke to magnetize small areas. Magnaflux recommends you use Model Y-7 AC-DC yoke for this operation. Once magnetized, use a magnetic field meter, a specialized compass, to check for sufficient magnetism, then sprinkle or flow magnetic particles over the area. If a crack exists, the magnetic field will attract the particles, aligning them with the crack to highlight it. Move across the deck, checking it as you go until you've checked every square inch. Use the same process to check the lifter area, main webs and front and rear faces of the block.

Check the bores, too. Fold the yokes of the Magnaflux unit so you can reach down in each bore to magnetize its length in sections. Apply iron particles to the magnetized area, check it and continue working around the bore. Check all bores in the same manner.

Caution: A magnetic field aligns between the North and South poles of the magnet yokes. This means that cracks running in the same direction as the magnetic field may not be sufficiently strong to attract enough particles that will be visible. So, to make sure all cracks will be fully magnetized, turn the magnet 90° in each location you're checking and recheck. Unfortunately, you can't turn the magnet 90° when checking a bore, so you'll have to look very closely. With this in mind, double check the bores using a dye test.

Demagnetization—Once a part has been checked using the MPI method, it must be degaussed, or demagnetized. If it's not, the part—block in this case—will attract and retain metal particles where they can cause damage. Demagnetization can be done by heat treating, but a more convenient method is to use the portable AC unit and reverse the magnetic unit. Use your field meter to check for residual magnetism. It should read zero. After you've finished with demagnetizing, remove the iron particles by either washing or wiping them off.

Dye Penetrant Testing—The major advantage of dye-penetrant testing is it can be use on magnetic and non-magnetic materials. This includes even plastic, although it's doubtful you'll ever see a plastic engine block. But it's your only option with an aluminum block.

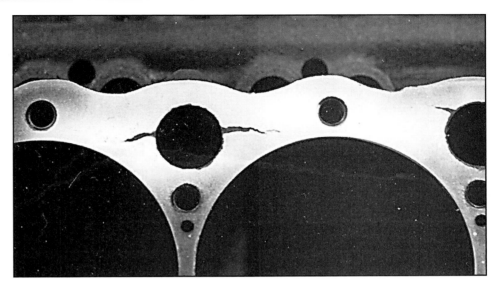
Dye testing. After cleaning block and applying penetrant, clean area again, then spray with white developer to reveal surface cracks.

And like the MPI process used with an AC magnet, it will only detect surface cracks. Although it's not as sophisticated as the Magnaflux/Magnaglo process, dye-penetrant testing is a valid crack-detection method. It is used in the aerospace industry for inspecting non-magnetic materials.

With that said, two types of dye-penetrant inspection systems are available. One uses a dry developer to highlight cracks. The other depends on a black light much like the Magnaglo process. Generally, both involve applying a penetrant to the area being checked. To be effective, it's critical that the part is free of grease, rust, oil, paint, water, scale and plating. Be aware that even though an area may appear to be clean, contaminates can "clog" surface defects and block the penetrant.

The simplest and easiest to use method of crack detection involves using what I call the three-can or red-dye system. Magnaflux markets this as Spotcheck. The first aerosol can is a cleaner, the second a penetrant and the third a developer. To use this system, spray the area to be checked with the cleaner. Allow it to dissolve dirt and film, then wipe the area dry with a clean cloth. Let it dry thoroughly and apply the penetrant to the area. Allow time for it to penetrate fine cracks. After no more than 30 minutes has elapsed, wipe off the penetrant with a clean cloth. Developer that penetrated a crack will still be there. Shake up can of developer just as you would a paint can. Spray the area treated with penetrant so it's wetted thinly, no more. Correctly applied, the developer will dry to an even white layer. Cracks show up as red lines that become brighter as the developer dries.

A more sophisticated and more accurate penetrant crack-detection system uses a fluorescent penetrant and black light. Magnaflux's Zyglo process is used in a manner similar to Spotcheck, but differs in important respects. The most obvious is how the developer is viewed—with a black light. Other differences include four optional methods used to remove or clean penetrant from the surface, six rather than three steps are used to perform a total inspection and the use of a dry or wet developer. Lots of choices here that are too complex to describe in detail.

Dealing with Cracks—What do you do if you've found a crack? As for me, I don't like cracks anywhere, but it depends on where you find it. If you find a crack in one of the main bearing webs, junk the block. Weakness in this highly stressed area can't be tolerated. One in the deck may or may not be terminal. For instance, a crack extending into a bore is bad. However, a short crack from one of the water passages can be stop-drilled. One that's 1/2-in. long can be tapped and threaded for a small pipe plug. If a crack or porosity is found in a cylinder bore, it can be sleeved.

Main Caps and Bolts—Because the main caps and bolts are steel, you can use MPI for checking them. And rather than using a portable magnet, use a full-circle magnet as shown on page 77 for inspecting connecting rods and crankshafts. Whichever method you use, check them closely.

Bore Inspection

Although you've checked the bores for cracks and have dealt with any problems, there are other issues you must address. Specifically, these are bore size and wall thickness. For instance, if a bore is too large for some reason such as wear that can't be cleaned up by boring or honing without going oversize, a decision must be made.

Jeff Joyner at Bill Davis Racing checks bore sizes.

If it's one bore you're dealing with, sleeving is an option. If it's all the bores, you'll have to address the practicality of sleeving them all. Then there's bore-wall thickness. A bore must be sufficiently thick, particularly on the thrust side, to have sufficient strength.

Bore Diameter—At this point in your engine build, you should have a finished bore size in mind. Using this figure, a notebook and dial bore gauge, make some quick measurements and record the results.

Set your dial bore gauge in a setting fixture to the desired bore size. Although super accuracy is not critical at this point, you should have a setting fixture to ensure your dial bore gauge will provide accurate readings for later boring and honing operations. Record measurements as you go. Check bore diameter in at least six locations: position of top ring at TDC, piston travel halfway down bore and at the bottom of the bore.

Turn the bore gauge 90°, repeat and record the measurements. Your readings should indicate any undersize condition, how true each bore is and the amount it needs to be enlarged to clean it up or obtain the desired size. Retain these figures for later reference. If the bores are too big, find another block.

Ultrasonic Testing—Even though a bore may be perfectly round, its walls could be too thin due to core shift or bore shift. Although not as prevalent with blocks of today because of more precise casting techniques, core shift results from the water jacket core moving out of position when the block is cast. Even though a bore center may be correct, the bore ID and OD they are not concentric, or on the same centers. Consequently, the bore is thick on one side and thin on the other side. The same condition results if a cylinder is bored off center in a good casting.

Ideally, cylinder wall thickness should be the same all around and from top to bottom. For a naturally aspirated engine, finished bore wall thickness should be 0.250-in. minimum on the thrust side and 0.200-in. minimum at all other locations for gray cast-iron blocks, but can go as low as 0.150 in. for CGI nodular or alloy cast iron. The thrust side is on the right side of the bores of a normal rotating—counterclockwise— engine as viewed from the rear of the block. These numbers can be slightly less if the cylinders are siamesed, have reinforcing ribs or filled, such as with HardBloked. With that said, wall-thickness minimums depend on cylinder pressure, so as pressure goes up, so should wall thickness. Therefore, minimums for supercharged, turbocharged, and nitrous-injected engines should be higher.

To check bore wall thickness you'll need your notebook and an ultrasonic tester. Add to this list a Sharpie marker and a sheet specifically for recording wall thickness. Record wall thickness of each bore in eight locations; four quadrants about 2 in. down the bore and directly below each of these in four locations halfway down the bore. Using the marker, record each thickness on the block deck above where you made the measurement. Record as you go.

The first step is to calibrate the ultrasonic tester. Manufacturer instructions will give you details on how to use it, but here are the basics: Calibrate the tester using a known piece of material and thickness. Several standards are usually part of a tester kit. If not,

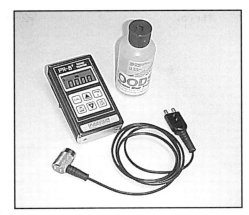
Ultrasonic tester with gel.

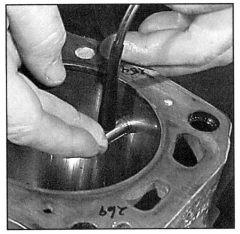
After applying gel to sensor, hold it firmly against bore wall to get accurate reading. Note thickness recorded on deck in position checked.

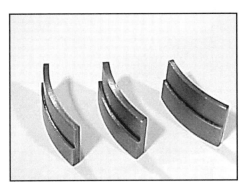
Use a standard of known thickness and material to calibrate ultrasonic tester. Standards are curved to simulate bore wall shape.

Readout indicates 0.305-in. thickness at section being checked. Check in eight places, 2-in. down bore and another 2-in. down 90° from each other.

make your own standard using a known piece of material and thickness measured with a micrometer. Coat the sensor probe with coupling gel, then hold it firmly against the standard. Calibrate the readout to the thickness of the standard.

Using your calibrated ultrasonic tester, start by measuring the first bore. Remember to apply coupling gel to sensor first. Also, offset measure when checking the front and rear walls of siamesed bores. Also note unusually high readings. Some bores have vertical reinforcing ribs cast into the bores.

You can detect these by moving the probe to the side and noting big jumps in thickness as you would when measuring a siamesed section. Record bore wall thickness on the deck as shown, then make your next measurement. Record measurements you take down in the bore under those taken at the top to differentiate them. Using the same procedure, measure all bores, then copy the figures from the deck to your notebook or form supplied with the tester.

Review your numbers, checking them against the minimum bore

Ultimate deburring and lightening tool is CNC programmed to machine smooth entire surface of block, interior and exterior. Note partially machined side of block.

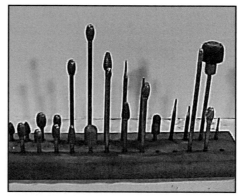

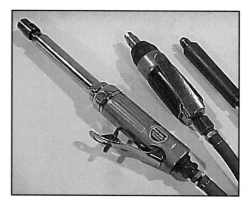

Assortment of die grinders, burrs, and stones for deburring and smoothing block.

wall thickness for your block. If you find an area that is substandard, recheck to verify that it is too thin. If it is, you may be able to salvage the block by sleeving that bore. However, if you find the bores on one bank are thin at the front or rear sides, a core or bore shift is the likely cause. Such a problem can be corrected by boring the block so the bore centers on that bank are offset—shifted—away from the thin sections toward the thicker section. To do this, consider how much you'll be increasing bore size. Whatever your figure is, don't thin the walls too much. Consider that at least 0.004-in. should be left for honing stock on the thin side, so at least that much will have to be removed from the thin side. As an example, if you intend to increase bore size by 0.030 in., and one side is 0.020-in. thicker than the other, and you couldn't shift the bore any more than half this figure minus 0.002 in., that leaves 0.0004 in. for honing. That means you can shift the bore a maximum of (0.020 in.÷2) −0.002 in., or 0.008 in.,

providing his amount doesn't thin the bores excessively.

I didn't mention shifting bores toward or away from the thrust sides. The reason is the bores must be on center with the crankshaft main bearing bore. Shifting, or offsetting, the bores in this manner would offset them with the crank centerline, which is unacceptable.

SMOOTH & DEBURR

Reasons used for doing the tedious work of smoothing the interior of a block includes allowing oil to flow more easily, which is debatable, and to remove residual casting sand and flashing that may otherwise break off and end up in the lubrication system. It was once common practice to paint the interiors of blocks to accomplish the same thing, but this is not recommended. True, paint will smooth and seal a block, but it is something else that can chip or break off to contaminate the oil. So I recommend that you smooth the block to accomplish the same thing. Don't just work the lifter area because it's easier to do and more visible, but smooth the crankcase area, including the main webs and the front face of the block in the timing chain area. If

you are really fanatical, smooth the entire cast surface of the block, both inside and out. This will reduce weight and minimize stress risers, which is particularly important with a CGI block.

Deburring Tools & Technique

Deburring and chamfering requires a wide range of hand tools. Chamfering tools and files are helpful, but a die grinder with an assortment of burrs, stones and paper rolls are best for doing most deburring and smoothing work. Starting with the die grinder and burr or stone, knock off the roughest areas, especially in corners and edges. Take care not to damage machined surfaces. Keep in mind that your objective should be to smooth the rough casting surface and not to produce a mirror finish. Such a finish would actually impede oil flow. Once you've smoothed off the rough stuff with the burrs, switch to paper rolls for the fine work. You'll go through a bunch of these.

Clean Threads—Cleaning threads was typically done by chasing them with a thread tap. This method is fine for rebuilding a "grocery gettter," but not so for cleaning critical threads of a racing engine.

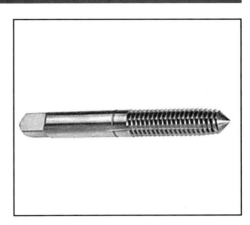

Use long-reach die grinder fitted with flame-shape carbide burr to deburr and smooth block interior. Finish with paper rolls.

Instead of chasing threads, clean first with a gun-bore brush, then run a thread-roller tap to bottom of threads.

Thread-roller tap.

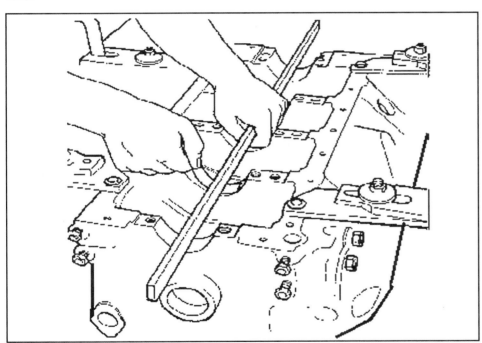

Using a precision straightedge and feeler gauge is a quick way to check main bearing bore alignment.

Material removed will weaken threads, albeit slightly. But slightly is too much, particularly if the engine is refreshed several times. Add up a bunch of "slightlys" and you have way too much. Instead, dirt and debris is removed from threaded holes by an initial cleaning. And if you deburred the block, many of the holes were loaded up with metal and abrasive particles. Remove most of

this debris by blowing out the holes with compressed air and pressure washing. To finish, run a tight-fitting copper bristle brush in the threaded holes and blow them out again.

Make sure the main cap and head-bolt-hole threads are straight by using a thread-rolling tap of the correct size and pitch. Such a tap looks similar to a thread tap, but

doesn't have sharp cutting edges. Rather, it moves the threads back into alignment instead of removing material, thus restoring the threads to their original cross section. Use a thread-rolling tap the same as you would a cutting tap.

Modifications for Improved Oiling—Considerable work can be done to the internals of a block to improve oiling and limit power losses. For making such modifications refer to Chapter 7.

BLOCK MACHINING

Blueprint the block, or measure and machine it so all dimensions are correct and within close tolerances. Start by inspecting the main bearing bore axis because all other block dimensions are referenced to it. The main bearing bore axis must be straight, and then the cam bearing bore must be straight and parallel to it. The same goes for the deck surfaces; they must be parallel to the main bearing bore axis as well as flat. Then there are the lifter bore centers, which must be square to and intersect the cam bearing bore axis. But first comes the main bearing bores.

Run a large mill file lightly across each cap to remove burrs that could force the cap out of alignment.

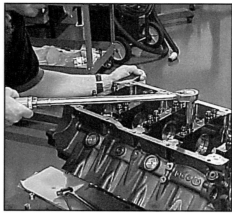

Install and torque main caps to specification prior to checking. Install all bolts, including cross bolts, as with this Mopar block.

Allan uses a dial bore gauge to check mains for out-of-round and size.

Main Bearing Bore

Align Boring & Align Honing—
Also called *line boring* and *line honing*, respectively, your block may have to be align bored or honed for more than one reason. The obvious reason is it is not straight. Another is because one or more of the bearing bore diameters is out of spec, or not round, too small or too large. This may be due to a warped block, distorted main bearing caps or you've installed new caps. Misalignment of the main bearing bore can show up as wiped bearings that get progressively worse toward the center bearing. Such a condition could also be caused by a bent crankshaft, however if the crank is straight, suspect the block.

If you're using new caps or a bearing has spun, the block must be align bored or honed. As for original caps, check to see if there's any problem. Even some engine builders line hone just to make sure the bearing housings are right, but I prefer checking first. If all checks out okay, line honing should not be necessary, certainly

not line boring. If you're going through an existing engine and the crank turned without binding and bearing wear was even from top to bottom and front to back, it's reasonable to assume the mains are straight. In this case use the rule, "If it ain't broke, don't fix it."

Checking Procedure—To check the main bearing bore, install the caps and torque them to specification. Before doing this, set each cap on a large flat file and run it lightly across the file. This will ensure there are no burrs or projections that would prevent the cap from being pulled down in the register and sit square against block. Likewise, file the parting faces in the block. Lay the file on the registers and run it lightly across them. Break any sharp corners on the caps and block parting faces with a stone or fine flat file. Wipe off the block and cap parting faces, then install the caps in their positions and in the right direction. With the bolt threads and underside of the head clean and lubricated, thread in main cap bolts and torque them to spec. Check that the caps are numbered.

If not, stamp them and indicate forward with an arrow or so the numbers read when you're looking at them standing in front of the block.

Don't check the main bearing bore alignment with the block hanging from an engine stand. Instead, the block should be supported flat on a bench. As you would when checking and honing cylinders, install deck plates, main caps and other components that may cause block or cap distortion. An example of this is the oil pump on a small-block Chevrolet. With the block upside down, carefully slide a precision straightedge into the main bearing bore. Try to slide a feeler gauge under the straightedge. If nothing thicker than a 0.001-in. feeler gauge fits between the straightedge and bore, consider the bore straight. However, if a 0.003-in. or thicker feeler gauge will fit, you need to align-bore and -hone the mains. Hone only if the gap is between 0.001 in. and 0.003 in.

Although a very old method, another way to check the main bearing bores is with a precision round checking bar that's ground

0.001-in. under the specified bearing bore diameter. If you happen to have such a rare piece, lay the bar in the block on clean bearing housings, then install the caps. If the bar turns, consider the bore to be straight. If the bar won't turn, the housings are either out-of-round or not straight. It's unlikely they are too small. However, the bore could be too big, which you will check later.

A more practical check is to use a straight crankshaft. This requires that you install the crankshaft on the bearings. Begin by coating the main bearing journals with machinist's blue. Install the bearings and carefully lay the crankshaft squarely in the block. Install the crankshaft and main caps, rotate the crankshaft no more than two times, then roll the block over and rotate it again. Roll the block back over and carefully remove the caps. At least 80% of each bearing-insert surface should be evenly coated with Prussian blue. But if you find the top or bottom inserts at the ends are not blued opposite of the center inserts, the bore is not straight. Similarly, bluing should be consistent over most of the insert surfaces except at the parting lines. There should be no bluing within about 0.25 in. to each side of the bearing insert parting lines. Any closer would indicate a distorted or undersize bearing bore.

After making one of the above checks, use your bore gauge to measure each main bearing housing diameter with caps installed less bearings and bolts torqued. The housings should be round and the correct diameter.

Refer to your bearing catalog for the correct bearing housing specification. As an example, if the main bore spec is 3.1922 in. minimum and 3.1930 in. maximum diameter, or more simply 3.1926 +/-0.0004 in., each bearing bore housing should be no smaller than 3.1922 in. and no bigger than 3.1930 in. Also check out-of-round. Each bore should not vary more than 0.0005-in.

You'll need a dial bore gauge for checking bore diameter and out-of-round. Using a setting fixture, set bore gauge to the desired bore diameter. Check each bore vertically, then rotate it 45° to each side of vertical. If the dial doesn't swing past the published limits for your engine, diameter and out-of-round are OK. Check and record numbers for each bore so you can reference them later so you can make a decision as to what you should do.

Should you line hone or line bore? First, you shouldn't line hone if more than 0.003 in. must be removed from the main bores. Removing 0.003 in. from the bores would move the crankshaft up in the block 0.0015 in. This is because align honing removes an equal amount from the block and cap sides of the bearing housings because the honing mandrel is guided by the bearing housings. Therefore, the bar removes equal amounts from the block and cap sides of the bearing housings. As for align boring, the boring bar is supported outside the block and between the main webs rather than by the main bore. This allows you to set up the bar to remove a minimal amount from the block

Prior to align boring or honing mains, cut caps to reduce the vertical bearing housing diameter.

side of the housings, or just enough to straighten the bore without the danger of raising the crank and loosening the timing chain. Boring is also faster than honing.

Grind Main Caps First—Before align boring or honing, the main bearing cap parting faces must be ground. If stepped caps are used, the same amount of material must be removed from both surfaces. Remove enough material to correct the misalignment. For example, if you're align honing the block, remove 0.0015 in. from the caps. With a cap having a single plane parting face, do this in a cap cutter that holds the cap square to the grinding wheel. Stepped caps must with done in a mill. Position the cap—caps if you can gang them—in a vise, level and clamp it tightly. Using an end mill, cut the high and low surfaces the same amount. After cutting the caps, deburr the edges with a stone or fine flat file. Clean them, and then check how caps fit to the block. They should fit tight in the registers, or with about a 0.002-in. interference fit.

Install all the caps as you did when checking and note if any are

Block girdle/main cap assembly for Donovan Top Fuel block must be surfaced full length before align honing or boring.

Classic Tobin-Arp align boring machine. Align boring limits amount the crankshaft moves up in block.

Support at center of boring bar limits flex.

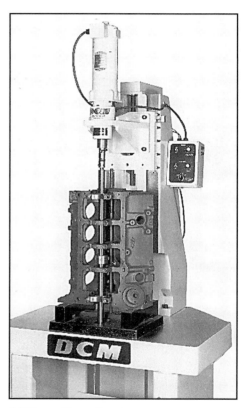

DCM machine align bores block vertically with block secured on rear face. Photo courtesy DCM.

loose. If one or more is, use a hammer and blunt chisel to stake the block adjacent to the register on each side of the cap. This will move block material slightly and tighten the register against the cap. Because you can't use this method with a stepped cap, measure across the stepped portion of the cap with a dial caliper. Measure the block register. It should read 0.002-in. less than the cap. Remeasure register width. If it's close, recheck cap fit. Repeat the process until the cap fits snuggly.

Again, remove at least enough material needed to restore the main bores to the correct size plus 0.0015 in. when align honing or

boring. So if the bores are 0.002 in. out of alignment, remove 0.0035 in. from the caps. The extra 0.0015 in. will ensure all bearing-bore housings will clean up when you've achieved the desired size. However, to make sure all bores will clean up when boring, remove 0.040 in. from the caps. If you have it, use Sunnen's cap checker to determine how much to remove from the caps. As for sizing main bearing bores, aim for a diameter that's at the low to middle end of the tolerance, or 3.1922—3.1926 in. using the above example. This will ensure sufficient bearing crush and retention without the danger of distorting the bearings.

Align Boring—To align bore the block, support it firmly with end plates or bar through the cam tunnel and bar centered with pins or pilots. If you have a DCM 2500 Vertical Align Boring (VAB) machine, set up the block vertically on its rear face. As you did when checking the mains, main bearing caps should be torqued in place. Slide the boring bar through the main bearing bore. Support the bar at both ends and at center. Check

that the bar is on center and at the correct distance from the main bearing bore. Shown at top is Sunnen's PLB-1200 boring bar that positions bar at the correct main bore-to-cam bore distance. BHJ's fixture also positions bar to the cam bore center.

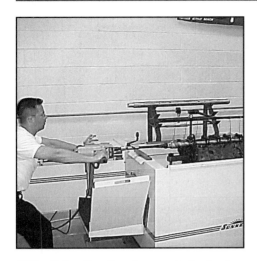

With oil flooding the stones, stroke honing bar back and forth between stops to size main bearing housings.

To prevent honing mains oversize, stop frequently and check diameters. Set bore gauge so it reads 0 when desired size is reached.

The cam tunnel must be straight and parallel to the main bearing bore.

Bearing housings must be enlarged to accept needle roller bearings as was done with this Ford Busch block.

Adjust cutting bits to take a light cut to check your setup. Readjust if necessary before going further. When all is OK, readjust the bits to take an intermediate cut that's within 0.005 in. of the final cut. Check each bearing housing with your dial bore gauge and adjust bits to take the final 0.005-in. cut or whatever will give the desired bearing-bore size. Some engine machinists leave some material for align honing after boring, say 0.0015 in., even though align boring to the final size is acceptable.

Align Honing—To align hone the main bearing bore, slide the correct mandrel into bore. Center bar with the aligning pins and double-check with a dial indicator. Set up the honing stones for each bore and adjust stops so that bar will travel the full length of the stones while honing. For a cast-iron block, use harder stones. A softer 150-grit aluminum-carbide stone for aluminum blocks with steel or cast-iron caps works best. Adjust oil flow to flood stones to flush away metal and abrasive debris as you hone. Stop honing and check each bore frequently with a dial bore gauge. Adjust stones accordingly until you've obtained the desired size. Typically, less material is removed from a wider bore and vice versa.

Cam Bearing Bore

A cam bearing bore will need to be machined to straighten it, return it to its position relative to the main bearing bore, enlarge bores so they will accept needle or babbit bearings, allow use of larger cam bearing journals or raise cam bore to provide clearance for an extreme stroke increase or for bulkier aluminum connecting rods. As with the main bearing bore, cam bore must not only be straight, it must be parallel to the main bearing bore and split the angle between the two cylinder banks. Needle roller bearing outer races have a larger OD than original sleeve-type bearings, which requires that bearing bores be enlarged. Straightening the bores can be done by honing, but enlarging the bearing housings and machining the entire cam tunnel requires boring.

Unlike a main bearing bore, there are no caps that can be cut to close up the cam bearing bore prior to machining it. Consequently, any machining enlarges the bores, preventing the bearing housings from being returned to their original diameter/s without sleeving. This is no problem when machining for installing needle bearings, but what do you do if the original sleeve bearings are to be installed? First, check the

REDUCE POWER LOST IN CRANKCASE

It's a given that oil tossed around by a spinning crankshaft robs power. Additionally, all of this oil from a top-sealed engine comes from the cam journal oil clearances and lifters. For an engine that doesn't have a sealed upper end, additional oil comes from lubricating rocker arms and valves.

To minimize oil flowing onto the crankshaft, some methods used to seal the top end include using an enclosed cam tunnel, using a roller cam, converting to a dry sump system and replace sleeve-type cam bearings with needle bearings. The combination of roller cam bearings and roller lifters receive sufficient lubrication from the little bit of oil from the lifters and oil mist created by the crankshaft, so oil can be restricted to the lifter galleries. But check the recommendations of your camshaft manufacturer before you restrict oil to these passages. Note, too, that you must use a cam with hardened bearing journals when installed on needle bearings.

Caution: Oil must not be restricted to the lifter galleries with a flat-tappet cam. Such lifters need to be drenched with oil for proper lubrication, otherwise the cam lobes and lifters would be destroyed in short order. Consequently, it would be a wasted effort to install needle cam bearings without using a roller cam.

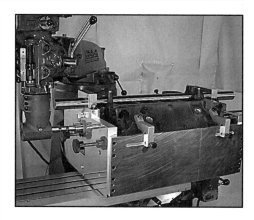

With slight tooling changes, the BHJ cam tunnel boring fixture will set up on a milling machine to align bore the cam tunnel or main bearing bore. Bar is driven by milling machine spindle through 90° adapter.

The oil groove in the front cam bearing housing must be restored to original depth in Chevy block if bores were enlarged for needle bearings. BHJ offers regrooving tool for this purpose.

availability of cam bearings with oversize ODs, typically 0.030 in. over, but with standard IDs. If you can't find such bearings, your only option is to sleeve the bores.

To make things easier, the BHJ cam tunnel boring fixture supports boring bar at both ends at specified distance from main bearing bore centerline. If you have such a fixture, use it. Otherwise, set up your bar at the desired crank bore-to-cam bore distance. Adjust cutters at each housing to provide the desired cut. You should make at least three cuts; one to check your setup, a rough cut and a finish cut. If you're installing needle bearings, provide a 0.0022-in. press fit. Measure bearings, and then refer to the bearing manufacturer's recommended housing diameter. Note which bearing housings are grooved. The grooves will be removed or greatly reduced in cross-sectional area from the boring operation, so they will have to be regrooved.

If you're using needle bearings and the cam tunnel is smaller than the bearing housings, sections of the cam tunnel between the bearing housings must be machined about 0.050-in. larger than the housings so you can install needle bearings. If the cam tunnel has ledges along both sides of its length, you'll first need to provide an opening for each cutter to swing into the tunnel so it can start its cut. Do this by grinding a notch at each cutter with a die grinder, then check the swing of the cutters until there is sufficient clearance. Take a number of cuts on both sides of the notches until you've achieved the needed clearance.

If you enlarged the bearing housings for needle bearings, it's time to regroove the ones you noted. This is a must so oil won't be restricted to connecting passages. BHJ has come through again with a regrooving tool that makes the job easier.

Lifter Bores

Now that you've checked or corrected the main bearing and cam bearing bores, next on the list

BHJ fixture pilots special ream at top with bar across end plates and at bottom with bar through main bearing bore to true lifter bores.

Assortment of lifter bore bushings; material, length and ID. Photo courtesy BHJ.

Bronze keyway lifter bore bushings for Jesel roller lifters in Toyota NASCAR truck block. Bushings must be installed in line with cam bore to ensure rollers track straight on cam lobes. Jesel offers a keyway checking tool to check that bushings are correctly aligned.

is to check or align the lifter bores to the cam bore. This is critical because power and lifter durability will be compromised if the lifter bores are not square with, don't intersect the cam-bore centerline or are not at the correct angle.

True Lifter Bores—If you have a CNC machining center with programming for your engine, truing the lifter bores is relatively easy. On the other hand, BHJ offers a kit that you can use to align the lifter bores to the cam-bore centerline. Their Lifter-Tru Kit is designed to be used on a Bridgeport-type mill. Precision end plates mounted to each end of the block are positioned by mandrels through the main bearing bore and cam tunnel. Used with a special cutter that's part end mill and ream, it is supported at both ends to ensure the cutter stays true to the cam bore and doesn't wobble. The top support, or cutter guide, is mounted between the end plates above the lifter bores. The bottom guide, which doubles as the cam tunnel mandrel, supports the cutter below the bores. End plates support the block and are

positioned one way or the other on the mill bed so lifter bores in each bank will be vertical.

Included in the BHJ kit are 0.8437-in., 0.875-in. and 0.906-in. cutters for standard lifters. A 1.000-in. cutter is used to enlarge lifter bores so they will accept bushings. If you're building a Chevy, you can use the larger Ford lifters. Simply open up the stock Chevy 0.8437-in. lifter bores to the Ford 0.875-in. lifter-bore size. Likewise, you can bore out the Ford 0.875-in lifter bores to the 0.906-in. Mopar size. Caution: Before doing either, check lifter availability and suitability. The other option is to enlarge the lifter bores to 1.000-in. diameter, then sleeve, or bush, them to the desired size.

Install and Size Bushings—If you've decided to install bronze bushings, choose the correct ones—diameter and length—and install them. Check with the lifter manufacturer on which bushings to use. For example, you need to check height of lifter bosses and bushing length if using some tie bar roller bushings. A tie bar could hit a long bushing, even the lifter bore boss, when the lifter is on the

cam lobe base circle. This being the case, the bushings or bosses must be clearanced.

Oil Holes—Lifter bushings may or may not have oil holes as delivered. If they aren't predrilled you can either do it now or drill the bushings after you've installed them. To drill bushings, reference the oil galley size and its position from the top or bottom of the lifter bore, then drill the bushings. You can drill the bushing oil hole oversize, say 1/2 in. in the bushing with a 7/16-in. oil gallery hole. If you decide to drill the bushings after installation you will need a long drill bit. This is the best method, particularly if you plan on enlarging the existing lifter oil galleries. For one thing, you will be certain the oil holes in the bushings align with the oil gallery holes. Be aware that this will generate a lot of shavings that must removed from the oil galleries. Remember to chamfer the holes.

Installing Bushings—Before installing bushings, lightly chamfer the top of the lifter bores to

Hone lifter bore bushings to size. Drill motor drives honing mandrel while oil floods stones. Photo courtesy BHJ.

Allan Powell makes initial check of deck height with digital readout calipers. This reading added to one-half main bore diameter is deck height.

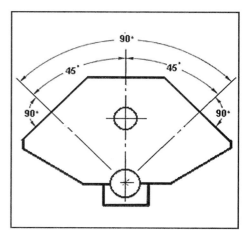

Drawing illustrates correct relationship between main bearing bore and deck surfaces on 90° block.

provide a lead in. Bushings must be aligned if they are slotted for guiding roller lifters. And if the bushings have predrilled oil holes, index them so they line up with the oil gallery hole. Finally, if the bushings are scalloped on the bottom, they need to be oriented so when they are installed, the scalloped will match the curvature of the cam tunnel. Otherwise, the bushing needs to be pushed through the full length of the lifter bore, then trimmed to match the cam tunnel curvature. Using a tool similar to a cam bearing tool, or one that pilots in the bushing and has a flange that butts against the edge of the bushing, drive in each until it is flush with the bottom of the lifter bore. Slotted bushings for Jesel keyway lifters must be installed in perfect alignment.

The lifter bores should now be honed to size. BHJ and Sunnen have dedicated hones for doing this. Each consists of honing stones, mandrels and a u-joint and shaft assembly that is driven by a 3/8- or 1/2-in. drill motor. While honing, flood stone with oil and check lifter bore size frequently until sized to give a 0.0015—0.002-in. lifter-to-bore clearance. Clearance for an aluminum block can have 0.0005-in. less clearance, but check with block manufacturer for his recommendation.

Groove Lifter Bores—The small-block Chevy is susceptible to wiping flat-tappet (lifter) cam lobes and lifters, particularly during break-in. To reduce the risk of this happening with a SBC or any engine using a flat-tappet cam, groove lifter bores on the lead side of the cam lobe. This would be the right side of the bores as viewed from the rear face of the block on an engine with normal—counterclockwise—crankshaft rotation. This vertical groove directs oil to each lobe as it rotates into the lifter, providing additional lubrication. A groove about 0.100-in. deep should extend up about

3/4-in. from bottom of bore. Sources for grooving tools include Comp Cams, Goodson, Mondello and Powerhouse.

A more positive way of providing lifter-to-lobe lubrication is from a small hole "drilled" in the center of the lifer foot using electrical discharge machining, or EDM. Holes such as this in lifter foot routes oil directly to the lifter/lobe contact point. This direct lubrication with flat-tappet followers allows the use of much stiffer valve springs in high rpm engines normally reserved for roller followers.

Block Deck Surface

Unlike a grocery getter, nothing but flat decks are acceptable for a racing engine. In addition, deck surfaces must be square, true to the main bearing bore, have the correct finish for the head gasket and be at exactly the same height. To accomplish this, the block must be decked in a machine that supports the block off the main bearing bore on a mandrel and block plate rather than on the pan rails. Shown is the RMC-1000 boring and

Block with rollover fixture is ready to be installed on V-blocks in boring and milling machine.

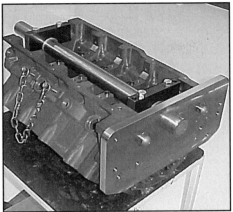

Mandrel and end plate fitted to block is ready to be installed in CNC machining center.

Deck plugs (arrow) should be installed before decks are surfaced.

Knowing the distance from the center of the main bearing to 45⁰ flat on end plate, deck height is checked with dial indicator mounted to precision bar held flat on deck and with plunger against end plate.

BHJ uses a special micrometer fitted to the precision bar for measuring distance to the end plate for determining deck height.

CNC machine touches off deck surface at one point and in several other locations to establish location of the block for the computer.

milling machine with block supported on a universal rollover fixture. The fixture includes a mandrel with collars that adapt it to the main bearing bore, another mandrel centered in the cam tunnel with cones and an end plate that has two 45° precision surfaces with a 90° included angle that represents the deck surfaces. These 45° surfaces accurately position

block rather than using a level on the deck surface with the hope the decks started out at 90° or 60° from each other.

With the rollover fixture fitted to the block and with the main caps torqued to specification, set the block in the boring and milling machine on the 90° V-block. Note: It's critical that all surfaces are clean, particularly the main bore and cam tunnel mandrels and V-block mating surfaces so errors aren't introduced into the block.

Once in place, roll over the block to the right or left on the main bearing bore mandrel against the cam tunnel mandrel. This positions the block to the precise angle for ensuring the decks will be surfaced square to the main bearing bore and at the correct angle.

Clamp block at both ends and support it at the center, then measure deck surface-to-end plate distance. You can do this with a dial indicator, depth gauge or special micrometer. If you use a depth gauge, this measurement

Make first cut across deck, then make a speed or feed change if roughness isn't as specified.

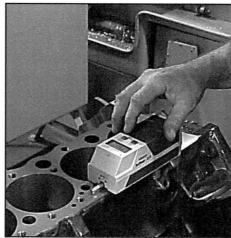

Check surface roughness with an optical profilometer and compare to specifications for roughness supplied by gasket manufacturer. The finish cut shown resulted in a 25 RMS finish.

plus the distance the flat surface the end plate is from the main bore center is deck height. Or, if you're using a dial indicator as shown and you already know deck height, zero the indicator. You can now determine from the dial indicator how much material is removed each time you take a cut. Once both decks read the same, deck heights will be equal.

When using deck plugs, install them now if they aren't already in place. This will ensure they will be at least level with the deck.

Check Deck Condition—Start by checking your setup and the condition of the deck. With the milling head mounted to the spindle and lowered close to the deck, attach a dial indicator to it, positioned so the indicator plunger is compressed. With the indicator at one end of the deck and zeroed, traverse the block the length of the deck and observe the indicator. The dial may fluctuate slightly, but should remain at zero. Any other reading indicates a warped or twisted deck. Check the opposite deck. If readings are

extreme on both decks and in opposite directions, check your setup. Otherwise, firmly clamp the fixture and make a light cut to determine deck surface finish. Do this as shown with a profilometer and compare reading to the Ra or RMS value specified by the head gasket manufacturer. There are visual comparators, but the accuracy is not adequate considering the object is to achieve a finish within such close tolerances.

Surface Finish and Gasket Concerns—With modern laminated head gaskets, surface finish is critical, particularly when sealing dissimilar metals, specifically an aluminum head on a cast-iron block. This is due to the difference in thermal expansion rates of the two materials. Aluminum expands and contracts at a higher rate than cast iron when heated and cooled, causing a shearing or tearing action between the two mating surfaces separated by the head gasket. As a result, the rougher surfaces we used to live with, or were necessary to

grab the head gasket, cannot be used. Gaskets used with aluminum heads on iron blocks must be allowed to "slide" as the engine goes through its heating and cooling cycle.

To solve the problem, gaskets have been developed that conform, notably Cometic's MLS, or multi-layer steel—gasket. Both sides are similar to steel shim-type gaskets sandwiching a compliant layer in between. The steel layers move with the head and block, and the sandwiched section absorbs the shearing action. The gasket surfaces must have a near-polished finish. The problem is there must be some tooth to retain the gasket. It's a fine balancing act. Regardless of surface finish, expect to see some brinnelling—indentation—from the gasket fire ring that surrounds the combustion chambers of an aluminum head.

Surface finish is critical to head gasket sealing, particularly if you're using aluminum heads on a cast-iron block. Expect to see the roughness spec in the 54–100 Ra (60–110 RMS) range when using cast-iron heads on a cast-iron block. For aluminum on cast iron, expect surface finish to be a lot lower, or as low as 10–30 Ra (11–33 RMS).

Assuming you've sharpened and set your tool bits correctly, change roughness by adjusting spindle speed or feed rate. A faster feed rate will produce a rougher finish and vice versa will produce a finer finish and vice versa with spindle speed.

Make speed or feed adjustments until you've achieved the desired finish, then take a final cut. Measure

SURFACE FINISH

A machined surface looks like a mountain range with repeated peaks and valleys when viewing a cross section of it through a microscope. Surface finish is specified by averaging the arithmetic average height differences in these peaks and valleys in micro-inches, or 1/1000000 in. Surface finish can be specified four different ways, but the two common methods is by Ra or RMS value where the average roughness Ra is the most common. For example, if the finish of a surface has a 100 Ra value, the average difference between peaks and valleys over the length of the surface is 0.0001 in., or 100/1000000 in. RMS (root mean square average) values are approximately 11% higher than Ra values due to the mathematical formula used to determine each. Ra uses a straight averaging method whereas RMS uses a squaring system as follows.

$$Ra = \frac{Y_a + Y_b + Y_c + \cdots + Y_n}{n}$$

$$RMS = \sqrt{\frac{Y_a^2 + Y_b^2 + Y_c^2 + \cdots + Y_n^2}{n}}$$

Y values are peaks and valleys measured vertically **N** number of times over a given distance.

To determine the roughness of a surface you will need a profilometer. These operate by dragging a diamond stylist a short distance across the surface being checked. The small diamond tip follows the contour of the surface and does the math to provide a Ra or RMS value. This type of profilometer is very expensive. Fortunately, less expensive optical scanners are available. These don't actually touch the surface, but use reflective mirrors and bounce light off the surface to determine surface contour or roughness.

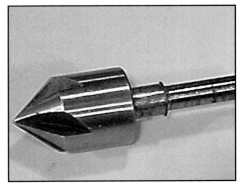

Chamfer tops of bolt holes with 45° countersink or ball nose burr.

deck height and reposition the block for milling the opposite deck to the same height and finish. For the block shown, we've taken off 0.005 in. + 0.0005 in. from each deck with a finish of 25 RMS according to the gasket manufacturer's specification. Final deck height along with stroke, connecting rod length and gasket thickness, will be used to make calculations needed to obtain the deck clearance and compression ratio for specifying pistons when ordering.

Chamfer Bolt Holes—Using a tool like that pictured, chamfer the tops of all head bolt holes. Sharp edges should be chamfered to ensure they won't be pulled above the deck surface when bolts are tightened.

Cylinder Boring

If you don't want to take bores out more than 0.010 in. or just want to clean them up, go directly to the honing step. Otherwise, you need to bore first and follow up with honing.

At this point you should have the condition and size of the bores recorded in your notebook. Additionally, you should know the size you want to take them out to, so it's time to set up the block to be bored. Gone are the days when you could clamp a VanNorman boring bar on the deck surface or block on its pan rails. Instead, machines now position the block on the main bearing bore and use a rollover fixture to ensure cylinders are machined square to and on center with the mains.

As shown, a V-block supports the block for decking. It is also used during the boring operation. The same rollover fixture is fitted to the block, then the block is set on the fixture and rolled over so one deck surface is up. To make sure the bore

Indicate bore to find center. Dial indicator at top of RMC-100 indicates when bore is on center with spindle. Plugs in lifter bores keep out cuttings.

Bob Curl uses dial indicator mounted to a spindle for checking that the block is square to machine.

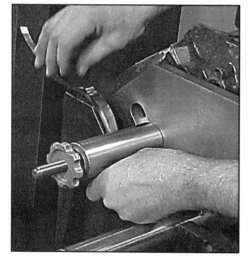

A shim between the V-block and cam mandrel is used to make adjustments until indicator reading is zero. Double-check that the bore is on center.

is straight and square to the deck and centered on the main bearing bore, dial indicate the deck surface with a level. Expect that slight adjustments may have to be made.

Measure Bores—With a dial indicator mounted on the boring bar spindle, lower the spindle to the deck as shown until the plunger compresses slightly, then zero the dial. Rotate the spindle with the dial indicator to the opposite side of the block and check the indicator reading. It should be zero. If not, slip a shim

between the cam tunnel fixture and the V-block that's about 1/2 the reading. For example, if the indicator shows the deck is 0.002-in. low on the lifter valley side, try a 0.001-in. shim. Check indicator reading and readjust as necessary until you achieve a zero reading. To make sure the deck is level end to end, move the block with the machine bed so the indicator is at the opposite end of the deck and read it. Again, the indicator reading should be zero. Swing indicator as you did at the front as a double check. If it doesn't indicate level, the deck is either twisted—not uncommon—or something is wrong with the setup. If you suspect a problem with your setup, lift block off the V-block and check for dirt between the main bearing bore mandrel and the V-block. Make sure mandrels in the main bore and cam tunnel are secure. It doesn't take much to throw the block out of alignment. Wipe off the contact surfaces, set the block back in place, and recheck deck alignment.

Find bore size and bore wall thickness in your notebook or thickness form for this engine. If

there's a serious variation in bore wall thickness side-to-side, the bore can be shifted parallel to the main bearing bore away from the thin side and toward the thick side. Side refers to the thickness of the edge of the bore if you would cut the cylinder in half lengthwise parallel to the main bearing bore. In the case of siamesed bores, use thickness figures measured adjacent to the siamesed section.

Center Boring Bar—Using your dial bore gauge, remeasure bores in this bank to confirm your figures. With that information, center boring bar to the first bore. With a dial indicator fitted to the end of the bar or machine's centering indicator as shown, center boring bar to the bore as best you can and bring bar down so the dial indicator probe contacts the bore wall. Observe the needle as you rotate the boring bar spindle to the lowest reading. At this point, zero the indicator, then rotate the spindle and find the maximum needle swing. Move the machine bed or boring bar half the distance of the indicator reading. Recheck the bar centering by rotating the spindle

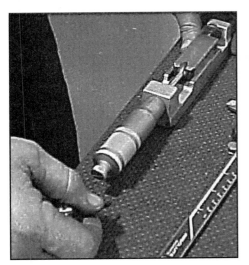

Adjust tool/holder to remove desired material from bore.

Install cutter tool/holder in boring bar.

Make first cut, then check bore with dial bore gauge. Bore out cylinders to size that will leave sufficient honing .

and make adjustments as needed until the needle remains steady. At this point, the bar will be centered.

Correcting Bore Wall Thickness Difference—To correct the difference in bore wall thickness from side-to-side, shift block or bar so the bar will be centered to the water jacket side of the cylinder. For instance, if one side is 0.300-in. thick and the other is 0.310 in., make a 0.005-in. shift, or half of the 0.010-in. difference. Now, if you enlarge bore by 0.010-in.—0.020-in. oversize—0.005 in. less will be removed from the thin side and 0.005 in. more from the thick side. Both walls will be 0.0295-in. thick from side to side. When you do this, keep in mind that you need to leave sufficient honing stock in the bore, or no less than 0.005 in. This will ensure all torn surface material from boring will be removed during honing.

With the boring bar positioned over the bore, check the setup by adjusting cutter so there will be minimal material removed from the bore, say 0.001 in. Adjust cutting tool/holder to remove this

amount and install it in the boring bar. Bring bar down to the top of the bore with spindle running until it makes a light cut around the top of bore. If all is OK, feed bar automatically until it cuts the full length of the bore. Measure using your bore gauge and adjust tool/holder to take a bigger cut. Take out bore to within 0.005–0.006 in. of final bore size if you'll be using diamond honing stones and 0.003–0.004 in. if using conventional stones. Leaving more honing stock than not enough will ensure metal torn from boring will be removed during the honing process. Finish boring cylinders on this bank, then roll block over to other bank and repeat the process.

Cylinder Honing

Caution: If you had to sleeve block, check the other cylinders with a bore gauge before honing them, particularly the ones adjacent to the sleeved bore. Stresses induced into block by the sleeve will distort adjacent cylinders similar to main cap and cylinder head bolts. Honing will correct them, providing you do it

after installing the sleeve.

Preparation—During the honing process it's important that the bores are stressed in a manner similar to how they would be when the engine is assembled and running. This will ensure the bores are deformed as they would be when in use. To accomplish this, install deck plates—cast iron for iron blocks and aluminum for aluminum blocks—with gaskets and main bearing caps installed and with bolts torqued to specification. Likewise, the block should be at a temperature similar to when it's running. To accomplish this, the block can be hot honed so bores will end up straight when at operating temperature.

Installing torque plates and main caps is easy, but not hot honing. The process is expensive and time consuming, so it is not done except where cost and time is not an issue, like with a well-financed race team. Consequently, some engine builders without the capability to hot hone are finishing selected blocks so the bottom of the bores

33

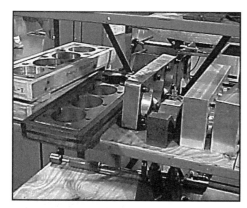

Assortment of deck plates to choose from for installing on block when honing bores.

Install deck plate with gasket and torque bolts to spec. Use aluminum deck plate to simulate aluminum head.

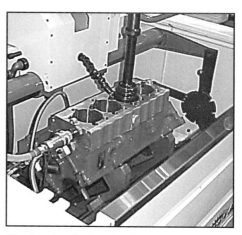

Block setup for hot-honing bores.

are 0.001-in. bigger than at the top to compensate for heat expansion.

Choosing Honing Stones— Recommending what type of honing stone to use and how to use them for finishing your cylinders is virtually impossible. This book is not big enough. There are just too many methods, opinions and factors to deal with. Besides, technology is constantly changing. What I would tell you now would likely change tomorrow. But that doesn't keep us from looking at the basics.

You need to start with components that operate against the bore surface—the piston rings. Dealing mainly with the top ring, ductile cast-iron moly-filled rings or plasma-sprayed moly rings have been preferred for years, but other ring types are available. These include chrome-plated, stainless-steel and nitride-titanium rings. Each requires a different finish. And even though ring material is essentially the same, manufacturers' recommendations on honing and finish can be different. Another variable to consider is block material and bore coating, if used. Modern racing blocks are not manufactured from gray cast-iron, as was once the case, but from

high-nickel cast-iron or compressed graphite. Then there are combinations of aluminum, sleeves and coatings. Then there is the coating NiCaSil, page 38, which is very hard. All need special consideration. So you must work with the ring manufacturer and honing machine supplier to determine the best honing procedure for your particular application. But, even with these complications, there is a given.

It is universally accepted for virtually all applications and ring combinations that plateau honing provides the best bore finish. A two- or three-step process, plateau honing typically involves using coarse honing stones to remove the majority of material from a bore, then a very fine stone is used to smooth the tops of the ridges formed by the coarse stones. Sometimes this process uses diamond-impregnate abrasive brushes or cork hones with light pressure. A plateau-honed finish does two things: It provides channels in the bore surface to act as a reservoir to store lubricating and sealing oil and smooth the surface, much like that achieved from a break-in. This eliminates

premature ring wear that would result from the old break-in process. So one of the main advantages of plateau honing is the rings/bores are essentially broken in on initial startup. But the major advantage with a plateau-honed bore is being able to use low-tension rings, reducing ring drag—the great power robber—while maintaining ring sealing. This makes for a more efficient engine, resulting in more power at the flywheel and reduced fuel consumption.

Although not major, there are differences in the type of honing stones to use and how to use them to achieve a plateau-honed finish. Ask ring manufacturers or veteran engine builders and you'll get different, although similar, answers. Most racing engine builders use vitrified aluminum-oxide or silicon-carbide stones whereas production engine builders are more apt to use diamond stones. As for what you should do, go with the ring manufacturer's recommendations on finish regardless of the stones you use to achieve that finish.

Regardless of the stone used, it's critical to use a good honing

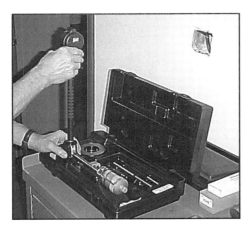

Calibrate your bore gauge to read zero at final bore size. Shown is bore gauge being calibrated with Sunnen CF-1126 setting fixture.

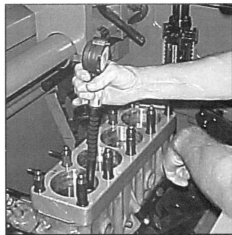

Before you begin honing, check bore size.

Flood stones with oil during honing.

Check bore size frequently.

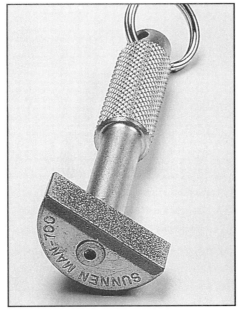

Clean honing stones frequently with diamond dressing stone to ensure smooth cutting and a good finish.

Plateau-honed bore with 45° crosshatch.

oil/coolant such as Sunnen's MAN-30 or MAN-845. Flood stones with oil to wash away abrasive grit and metal particles, and cool the cylinders. Flow should be directed into the cylinder bore before you start stone rotation and continue during the honing process.

Dressing the Stones—Maybe this will come as a surprise, but stones should "break down" during the honing process. This exposes a continuous supply of sharp, clean cutting edges. To back up this process, you should dress the faces of the stones periodically to be sure they cut effectively. Sunnen's diamond stone dresser works well for this. Honing oil flushes loose abrasive and metal particles from the stones and cylinder wall to keep stones clean so they can cut freely. Surface temperatures will also be controlled. This keeps the stones from loading up, which would otherwise cause bore-finish problems such as deep scratching, fragmenting and burnishing the bore surface. Not only should the stones be kept clean, they should be expanded gradually to avoid overloading. Overloaded stones do bad things; slow stock removal, increase stone wear, remove material in a non-uniform manner and burnish the bore surface.

CYLINDER BORE HONING METHODS

After building several engines, talking with many racing engine builders, engine machine suppliers and high-performance parts suppliers, I've come to the conclusion that the one engine building operation that involves an abundance of opinions is how to hone a bore. Regardless, most methods are successful. With that said, you need a starting point. Following are two procedures for honing bores, one from a successful stock car engine (Powell Motorsports) builder and the other from a top piston ring manufacturer (Speed Pro). You can develop your own method. Consider these recommendations and what you read as starting points, then go from there.

Allan Powell of Powell Motorsports devotes considerable time and attention to honing his blocks. Allan uses a power-stroke hone using vitrified stones with firm pressure to size the bores and finishes with diamond-impregnated nylon brushes. While flooding the stones with honing oil, being careful not to overload the stones and checking bore size frequently, Allan starts with 70-grit stones to true bore while removing 0.001 in. He then switches to 220-grit stones to remove 0.003 in. and follows with 280-grit stones to remove 0.001 in. Final bore size is achieved with 400-grit stones, stroked several times with a light load to give a very smooth finish. To obtain a plateau finish without increasing bore size, Allan uses diamond-impregnated nylon brushes. A Ra 8 surface roughness results from using this method.

The Speed Pro recommended procedure for plateau honing is a little different. Using the same precautions by flooding the stones with honing oil, monitoring stone load and checking bore size frequently, the bore is roughed out with 70-grit stones to within 0.003 in. of final bore size. Using 200-grit stones, bore size is increased further to within 0.0005 in. of final size. The last 0.0005-in. is taken out with 280- or 400-grit stones. If a smoother finish is desired, they recommend using 400-grit stones. Up until now, firm pressure should have been used, but once final bore size is reached the stones should run free of heavy drag for several strokes to provide a "polishing" affect to produce a roughness of about 12 Ra for moly rings. For chrome rings, roughness should be about 16 Ra. If it's a super smooth surface you want, Speed Pro recommends using 600-grit stones, but with caution. It is easy to burnish the bore, which will diminish the effect of the crosshatch and slow ring seating. Use a profilometer to confirm surface roughness so you can make adjustments.

Sanding cone fitted to 1/4-in. drill motor is used to chamfer top of bores to provide lead-in for rings.

Die grinder and stone is used to chamfer bottom of bores.

Not only should the finish be correct, the crosshatch should be between 40° and 60°. Higher angle crosshatch provides maximum oil retention to the bore wall, but with slightly higher oil consumption. When it comes to bore sealing and lubrication versus slightly more oil consumption, I go for sealing and lubrication.

Chamfer Bores—There will be sharp edges at the top and bottom of each bore. Put a small chamfer at the top of each bore to provide a lead-in for installing the pistons/rings. Although a half-round file will work, a drill motor and abrasive cone is faster. You'll

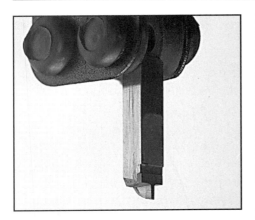

Portable O-ring groove cutter. Photo courtesy Goodson.

For positive retention of one-piece rear main seal, install six evenly spaced No. 4 x 0.375-in. long hexagon-socket buttonhead screws with flat washers. Drill and tap holes so screw heads will overlap seal bore as shown.

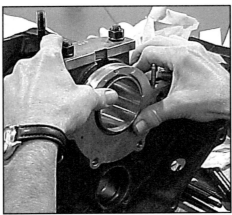

Fit seal adapter over centering mandrel installed in rear main bearing bore. Bolt adapter to block, and then drill two holes to match diameter of dowels through adapter and into block 1/4-in. deep. Apply masking tape to drill bit to match hole depth.

Remove adapter and install dowels with red Loctite. You can now be assured adapter will center seal on crankshaft center.

find it does a much neater job. A die grinder and stone works best to remove the sharp edge at bottom.

O-Ringing—If your engine will be supercharged or turbocharged, consider O-ringing the block or heads. Do this with a portable cutter or tool holder and O-ring cutter for your boring bar. Use 0.0403-in. copper or 0.032- or 0.0410-in. stainless-steel wire. Cut groove depths one-half the diameter of the wire plus 0.001-in. and width to match wire diameter. Overall groove diameters should match the diameter of the head gasket fire rings measured at the center of each ring. Speaking of fire ring, they should not be irregular in shape, but be a perfect diameter. Otherwise, cutting O-ring grooves will be extremely difficult.

Clean Bores—It's hard to overstate the need to clean the bores until they are spotless. Abrasive grit and metallic particles in and on the bore surfaces must be removed—totally. To say it would be bad not to do so would be an understatement. Honing debris is an engine killer.

To do a proper bore-cleaning job, you'll need hot water, bucket, strong detergent, a roll of white paper towels, a stiff bristle brush similar to that used for cleaning toilet bowls, compressed air and some water-dispersal oil. A steam cleaner would be helpful, but not necessary. Starting with one bore, scrub it vigorously with the brush using hot, soapy water. Rinse it out with clean water and check cleanliness by dragging a paper towel over the bore surface. Don't expect it to come out clean the first time. Keep on scrubbing, rinsing and checking until the towel comes out clean. Without hesitation, blow-dry the bore with compressed air and rustproof the bore by coating it with water dispersant oil. Proceed to the next cylinder and the next until they are all clean using the same procedure. If the block will sit for more than a week, let the water-dispersant oil work for a while, then wipe out all bores. Rustproof bores by generously coating them with engine oil and store the block in a plastic bag to keep it from collecting dust and dirt.

REAR MAIN SEAL

Modifications can be made for adapting or retaining rear main oil seals. A popular one is to install rear main seal adapter kits to 1987-and-later Chevrolet blocks. This will allow them to accept earlier crankshafts and oil pans that use two-piece seals. When using one of these kits, the adapter must be centered on the main bearing bore. This will prevent the seal from being eccentrically loaded and leaking. Another modification is to

Sliding wet sleeve into Donovan aluminum block. Flange at top of sleeve keys into adjacent sleeves at top and fits snugly in bore at bottom, sealing at both ends.

Dry sleeve with flange at top. Open up bore to achieve a correct press fit. Leave 1/4-in. step at bottom and, if sleeve is flanged, counterbore at top.

provide positive retention for one-piece oil seals that are driven in from the back. See accompanying photos for how to do both, page 37.

SLEEVING

There are two basic sleeve types; wet and dry. Just as the names imply, a wet sleeve is in direct contact with engine coolant and the dry sleeve is in direct contact with a cast-in cylinder. Wet sleeves are frequently used with aluminum blocks and dry sleeves are used with cast-iron blocks. As for sleeve material, ductile and high-nickel alloy cast iron is the most popular, but steel and aluminum sleeves are sometimes used. As you may guess steel is very strong, but very expensive because coatings such as hard chrome or NiCaSil, a nickel and silicon carbide matrix, commonly known as Nikasil, is used to prevent piston-ring abrasion. As for aluminum, it is suitable for dry sleeves only. And with steel, aluminum sleeves must be coated with NiCaSil or cast from a special aluminum alloy that incorporates silicon and carbide.

NiCaSil coating provides high wear resistance and excellent oil retention, much like a plateau-honed finished bore. Originally used for coating diesel cylinders and aluminum and cast-iron aircooled motorcycle, snowmobile and jet-ski aircooled jugs, Nikasil was used by Porsche for the 917/935 engines, then for liquid-cooled Formula 1 engines. Because of the low-wear and low-friction qualities of Nikasil, the coating has found its way into engines with integral cylinders such as stock car and road racing. Coating integral

BLOCK	SLEEVE	INTERFERENCE	TEMP DIFFERENTIAL
Iron	Iron	.001 - .003	50° F
		.003 - .005	100° F
		.005 - Above	250° F
Iron	Steel	.001 - .003	100° F
		.003 - .005	200° F
		.005 - Above	Not Recommended
Iron	Aluminum	-	Not Recommended
Aluminum	Aluminum	.001 - .003	100° F
		.003 - .005	200° F
		.005 - Above	Not Recommended
Aluminum	Cast Iron	.001 - .003	100° F
		.003 - .005	Not Recommended
Aluminum	Alloy Iron	.001 - .003	100° F
		.003 - .005	200° F
		.005 - Above	Not Recommended
Aluminum	Ductile Iron	.001 - .003	100° F
		.003 - .005	150° F
		.005 - Above	250° F

Press for sleeves is based on diameter, block temperature and block material. Chart courtesy Darton.

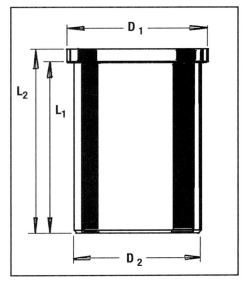

Counterbore should be deep enough to allow approximately 0.060 in. of sleeve to project from top of deck.

cylinders with Nikasil is expensive.

Dry Sleeves

If you found a damaged or oversize cylinder in an expensive race block, it makes sense to save it by installing a repair sleeve. Purchase a quality high tensile-strength, centrifugally cast sleeve from a reputable manufacturer such as Darton or L.A. Sleeve. When ordering, specify sleeve bore size, wall thickness, length, material and, in some cases, coating. The sleeve should be slightly longer than the bore.

To prepare the damaged cylinder for installing the repair sleeve, measure sleeve OD at 90° from each other in about three evenly spaced locations from one end to the other. Record readings, then add them up. Divide the result by the number of measurements to find average sleeve OD. This is the size to use in determining how far to take out the bore less a small amount for a press fit. Press fit must be based block material, sleeve material and temperature difference

between the block and sleeve.

Follow the recommendations of the sleeve supplier. If there are none, allow a 0.0005-in. undersize for every inch of bore size. So for a 4.000-in. bore, the bore should be 0.002-in. smaller than the sleeve OD in a cast-iron block. For example, Darton recommends a 0.002—0.003-in. press fit for like materials, or iron sleeves in iron blocks and aluminum sleeves in aluminum. For other combinations refer to the accompanying chart. Note that the amount of press is affected by temperature. Heat block to about 200°F and chill sleeve to expand block and shrink sleeve to allow for more press. Using standard practice, subtract 0.002 in. from the average OD of your sleeve to determine how far to open up the bore. Be aware that an interference fit is not so much for sleeve retention, but to ensure maximum heat transfer between the sleeve and the original cylinder.

Set up block as previously described. Illustrated in the photos is the process of installing a flanged dry sleeve in a cast-iron block. After determining over-bore size, determine when to stop short of going through bottom of bore so step will be left for sleeve to bottom against. Step should be no less than 1/4-in. thick at its narrowest point. Be aware that sleeve will extend past scallops that may have been provided for rod clearance. Blend sleeve into these scallops after it is installed. Set up cutting tool so a clean cut is made down the bore and finishes with a square cut at the top of the step.

If sleeve is flanged, you'll need to provide a counterbore at the deck.

It should be deep enough so when sleeve is installed the flange will stand 0.060 in. above the deck. This will allow the sleeve to be surfaced flush with the deck after installation. Measure flange OD and its thickness. Cut counterbore 0.001-in. less than flange OD, 0.060-in. less than its thickness and square at the bottom.

Note: If you are installing a dry cast-iron sleeve in an aluminum block, Darton recommends that you lightly hone the bore prior to installing the sleeve with a Brush Research flex-hone. This is to improve heat transfer between the cast-iron sleeve and the aluminum cylinder.

Shorten Sleeve—When installed, the sleeve should bottom at the flange and against the step simultaneously. To make sure this happens, measure the distance in the bore between the top of the step at the bottom to the bottom of the counterbore at top. The depth-gauge end of a long dial caliper is handy for making this measurement. You now have the information to shorten the sleeve. Next, measure the distance from the flange to the bottom of the sleeve. Subtracting these two measurements will tell you how much to shorten the sleeve.

Chuck up sleeve at the flanged end lightly in a lathe, squaring it in the process. You can't tightly chuck on the sleeve without damaging it. To prevent tool chatter, install foam in and around the sleeve as shown. Set up tool bit so it will make a square cut, then, with the chuck and sleeve rotating, touch the bottom of the sleeve with the tool and note carriage position on the lathe bed. Retract the tool with

Bottom of sleeve is trimmed in lathe so distance from bottom of flange to bottom of sleeve will match measurement from bottom of counterbore to top of step. Note foam inside and outside sleeve to damp vibrations. Chamfer edges of sleeve.

After heating block, apply Loctite to chilled sleeve. Start sleeve into block...

...then drive, press or pull it into place.

the crossfeed and move the tool/carriage up the sleeve toward the headstock the amount you found it should be shortened.

With great care, run the tool bit in until it touches the sleeve and make a light cut. Stop lathe and measure the distance from the bottom of the flange to the cut as a double-check. If all is OK, slowly and with great care, run in the tool to cut off the sleeve, but be very careful. The tool bit can catch the sleeve as it cuts through, grabbing it and tossing sleeve out of the lathe. Because of this, remove the sleeve from the lathe and finish trimming it using an abrasive cutoff tool. Deburr cutoff end of the sleeve, putting small chamfers on inside and outside edges.

Install Sleeve—It is common to install a sleeve by driving it in, but I don't recommend using this method. Rather, press in the sleeve. You'll have more control and there will be less chance of damage. A portable press is best for doing this,

particularly a portable type that will pull in the sleeve against a mandrel in the main bearing bore.

Wipe down the inside of the bore and outside of sleeve with a paper towel and solvent such as brake cleaner. Heat block and cool cylinder to the needed temperature spread, checking temperatures with a pyrometer. Coat sleeve with Loctite Sealant 518, concentrating at the flange, then position sleeve square over the bore. Start it in by lightly tapping the sleeve with a hammer—dead-blow type pre-ferred—using a soft block such as a short section of 2x4 over its end for protection. Once sleeve has started square in the bore, press or pull it in until it bottoms.

Now that the sleeve is in, there are four steps left to complete the sleeving operation: bore/hone to size, surface top and trim bottom. Starting with boring, set up block as discussed, page xxx, and bore out sleeve. Leave 0.006 in. honing stock. With the sleeve bored, change bit and face top of the sleeve so it is flush with but not below the deck surface. Remove block from the boring bar and

place it upside down on a bench or stand so you can access the bottom of the sleeve. Using a die grinder and burr, blend the bottom of the sleeve to the original bore, paying particular attention to scallops for rod clearance. Finish sleeve in-stallation by honing the sleeve. Check adjacent cylinders, too. As cautioned earlier, they may require honing because of the possibility of distortion.

Wet Sleeves

Not only are aftermarket manufacturers producing alum-inum blocks, OEM manufacturers are going this direction as well. Most of these blocks are incorporated into overhead cam engines, however the LS1/LS6 GM pushrod engine uses a cast-in, dry-sleeved aluminum block. If a cylinder is in need of repair, follow the procedure I describe for installing a repair sleeve. On the other hand, to prepare the LS-

After boring installed sleeve, trim top flush with block. Finish sleeve installation by honing to size and trimming bottom, if necessary.

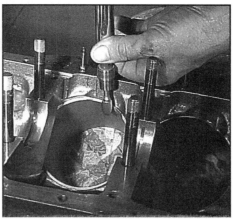

Trim sleeve to match notches for clearing connecting rods. A long-reach die grinder with burr works well for this job. There should be at least 0.050-in. clearance to the crank and rods.

1/LS-6 block for all-out racing, Darton has developed what they call an M.I.D. (Modular Integrated Deck) sleeve. This sleeve essentially replaces the sleeved aluminum cylinder with a cast-iron wet sleeve, allowing a larger bore. In addition, cooling is improved by the way the sleeve is double-flanged and ported at the top. This and heat transfer not being impeded at the interface of the sleeve and original cylinder also improves cooling. In addition to cooling, strength is improved by the way the sleeves are nested, creating a siamesed effect.

Darton provides detailed instructions with drawings and photos for installing M.I.D. sleeves in the LS-1/LS-6 block, so I'll just include the basic procedure. First, machining is best done with a CNC operated machine. Darton worked with Rottler to develop a program to machine the LS-1/LS-6 block to accept the M.I.D. sleeves, but that doesn't mean you must use

a Rottler CNC to do the job.

First, strip, clean, and inspect block for cracks. Mount block in the machine and support it on the main bearing housings with caps installed and torqued to spec. Set up block to machine the left bank first. Deck should be within 0.001 in. front-to-back and side-to-side. If you're using a CNC operated machine, indicate cylinder-1 X axis, the Y axis off the bar and touch off the deck. The 4.4-in bore centers should be maintained within 0.0005 in. of each other. Cylinders in the right bank are offset 0.950 in. to the rear.

Bore out each cylinder in both banks 0.010-in oversize. If you are working with a new block, it should be stress relieved. This is shown being done by vibratory stress relieving. Reinstall the block and finish boring out cast-iron sleeve. Open up bore to 0.0005 in. smaller than bottom of sleeve. Surface at bottom of bore should

have a Ra 32 finish. Complete removing the remainder of the cylinders by boring out to 4.8 in. down from deck 4.3 in. except for number-1 cylinder. Take it down 3.125 in. below the deck.

Machine what's left of the bores at the deck as specified to accept the sleeve flange. Clean sleeve, then measure sleeve OD at the bottom, flange diameter at top and seating depth, or distance from top of flange to the shoulder at the necked-down section at the bottom. Machine flange seat at the bottom of the block so the sleeve will project above the deck 0.005 in. Finish bore at the bottom by sanding it smooth for sealing the three O-rings.

Install Wet Sleeves—Heating the block is OK, but not necessary. Using the lubricant supplied, coat O-rings and coat the flange periphery with the Loctite sealant supplied. With the sleeves organized as to their position in block, slide in each one so holes in the flange and matching flats are oriented correctly. Using a soft mallet, drive in each sleeve. With all sleeves in block, install torque plates with gaskets and torque bolts to specification. It's best to let block sit overnight, or two hours minimum. Finish sleeve installation by align honing the block and boring and/or honing cylinders as desired. Put a 0.050-in. chamfer at the bottom of the bores.

INSTALLING DARTON M.I.D. SLEEVES
Photos Courtesy Darton

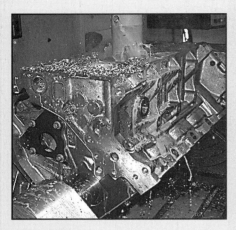

1. Cylinders are then rough cut 0.010-in. oversize to main web.

2. Rough cuts finished in left bank.

3. Set up in Rottler CMC, block is first indicated; right deck, left deck and bores from front to back and side to side.

4. New blocks should be stress relieved prior to final machining.

5. After stress relieving, block is reinstalled in machine and indicated. Cylinder one X-axis is being indicated.

6. Measure sleeve. Bottom diameter is being miked here.

7. Lower area machined to final size. Sand by hand to give it a Ra 32 finish.

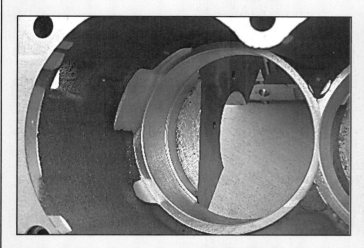

8. Finished bore ready for sleeve. Shoulder at bottom of bore is critical to establish installed sleeve height of 0.005-in. above deck.

9. O-rings installed and lubricated prior to installing sleeve.

10. Sleeve fitted to cylinder-1 is seated by driving in with soft mallet.

11. Once cylinders are all in place, deck plate is installed with gasket and torqued to spec. With both deck plates installed, block should sit for two hours minimum to allow Loctite to cure.

3

CRANKSHAFTS, BALANCING, DAMPERS, AND BEARINGS

Racing engine builders have come to recognize that smaller and lighter pieces made possible through the use of high-strength materials, tighter tolerances, efficient designs and finishing techniques are far superior to the "bigger is better" approach. This is true when it comes to both performance and durability, although the envelope sometimes gets pushed a bit too far in the quest for more power. Results can be an engine will end up with more parts than it started with, some of which end up in the oil pan or on the track. It is a fine balancing act when competitors are doing the same thing. Power is king, but your engine has to be there at the end.

Lighter parts are attached to the crankshaft such as rods and pistons allow the crankshaft to be lightened, too. This and a lighter damper and clutch-and-flywheel assembly results in reduced rotating mass, which allows an engine to accelerate or decelerate quickly, a very important consideration in racing where there are a lot of gear changes such as in drag racing and road racing. Of course overall engine weight is reduced, too.

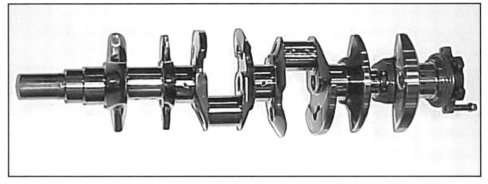

This racing crankshaft is made of 4340 forged steel, fully counterbalanced, coated and nitrided. Counterweights are knife-edged and undercut. Mains are gun drilled and large radius fillets are used at mains and crankpins.

CRANKSHAFT

The typical racing crankshaft is forged or machined from a quality high-strength steel, heat treated to full strength, has drilled crankpins for lightening, is case hardened and mains are cross-drilled. Journals will be finished within close-tolerances, micro-polished and accurately indexed. Balance will be internal and counterweights shaped.

Material

There is only one choice in materials for a racing crankshaft—steel. Although cast iron has superior damping qualities, steel is stronger and tougher. If you are required by rules to use a cast crank, go with nickel-alloy nodular iron rather than a plain cast-iron crank. Otherwise use a steel-alloy crankshaft.

Available steel alloys are 1053, E4340, 5140, 5350, 6415 and EN30B. This can be confusing. Organizations or countries classify steels differently. For example E4340 is SAE, 6415 is AISI and EN30B is British. And 6415 is basically the same as E4340. To make things more confusing, one manufacturer may prefer one alloy for their crankshafts over another. Or they may offer more than one steel alloy to produce the same crankshaft.

Used to replace cast cranks in production cars, 1035 and 5140 are medium-carbon steels. With a smattering of chrome in it, 5140 becomes a medium-carbon, low-alloy steel. Both have similar tensile strengths, or 103,000 psi and 106,000 psi, respectively. Also considered medium-carbon, low-alloy steels, E4340 and 6415 are basically the same. However, they are alloyed with manganese, molybdenum, nickel and silicon, thus increasing tensile strength to over 300,000 psi. Similarly, EN30B is alloyed similarly, but with more nickel, or about 1.8% versus 4.1% as compared to E4340. Similar to 4140, EN30B has a lower tensile strength than E4340 at over 200,000 psi, but its impact strength is much greater because it is less stiff. The bottom line is, the best choices in materials for a crankshaft are E4340/6415 for minimum twist and E30B for maximum fatigue resistance, providing they are chosen from the best stock.

Billet vs. Forged—As discussed in Chapter 4, the fatigue strength of a forged part over one machined from a section of round stock, or a *billet*, page 74, is due to superior grain flow. However, I must admit that even though I prefer forged crankshafts, particularly light-weight models, the shear bulk of a crankshaft makes the advantage of a forged over a billet one negligible.

Then there is the question of twisted versus non-twisted. Both start with a steel billet to forge the crankshaft into a basic shape. The first method starts by forging the crankshaft flat so the crankpins are in the same plane, then they are twisted to the desired angle of the crankpins, or 90° for most V8s, rather than initially being forged in the 90° position. For you, the end user, it doesn't matter much which method is used. Twisted or non-twisted is more of a manufacturing decision rather than which one results in the best crankshaft.

Heat Treating

What really counts after a crankshaft is forged, maybe after some machining, is heat-treating. All involve a process of heating the crankshaft to an established temperature, then cooling at a given rate. Three basic processes are used: *annealing, quenching* and *normalizing*. Annealing softens the steel by heating it and allowing it to cool at a slow rate. This relaxes stresses induced during the forging process. Quenching, which is done after the crankshaft is heated and held at a given temperature for a time, is immersed in oil for cooling at a controlled rate to increase strength and hardness. Normalizing, which is similar to annealing, improves strength and machine-ability of the part.

Case Hardening

After machining, the crankshaft surface is hardened by *carburizing, nitriding* or *induction hardening*. This case hardening process—steel or cast iron—produces harder, better wearing bearing surfaces, but without adversely affecting toughness. Unlike carburizing or nitriding that hardens the full surface of the crankshaft, induction hardening targets only the journals.

Bearing Journals

The bigger-is-better question comes up when considering bearing-journal sizes, particularly the rod journals. A smaller-diameter journal requires less oil due to less surface area and volume that is closer to its centerline, thus reducing friction or drag. Although an incremental gain, material removed from a section that's farthest from the center of the mains also reduces rotational inertia of the crankshaft. This improves acceleration, which is critical in a high revving engine. But consider the tradeoffs. Smaller journals increase peripheral speed at the journal-to-bearing interface and reduce bearing surface area, which doesn't affect crankshaft strength much, but increases unit bearing loads. This tends to increase oil temperature and bearing fatigue. But an efficient oiling/cooling system and planned frequent rebuilds make smaller bearing journals a tradeoff worth considering.

Although bearing journal fillets infringe on bearing width, this is a case where bigger is better. The fillet at each end of a bearing journal blends the journal surface into the cheek at each end. This provides a transition that reduces stress concentration and increases fatigue strength, reducing the tendency for cracks to form these 90° corners. The smoother the transition, the better, so a 1/8-in. fillet radius is better than a 1/16-in. radius even though a slightly narrower bearing is required.

A very effective way to lighten and reduce the rotational inertia of a crankshaft is to drill the crankpins. Not counting bolt-on components such as a clutch and flywheel, this removes weight from about as far from the center of crankshaft rotation as you can get. Additionally, lighter throws allow lighter counterweights, further reducing inertia. Combined with lighter rod-and-piston assemblies, this will result in a significant reduction in rotating mass,

Oil holes are radiused to protect bearings and allow oil to flow smoothly from mains to rod bearings.

Drilled crankpins are effective in reducing the rotational inertia of a crankshaft without reducing strength. Note clearance hole in counterweight to allow room for drilling crankpin.

Fillet radii are critical to maximize fatigue strength of crankshaft. As is evident, increasing fillet radii from 0.0625 in. to 0.125 in. has little effect on bearing width in terms of percentage reduction.

translating to less inertia. Although there will be no negligible reduction in inertia, the crankshaft can be lightened further without serious strength loss by gun-drilling the mains. Material removed at the center of rotation has virtually no moment arm, or leverage. Because it's on center of rotation, it has little effect on inertia.

Shot Peening

Shot peening increases fatigue strength by compressing the surface of a crankshaft.

Oil Holes

Oil holes should be as smooth as possible to prevent stress risers and large enough to allow sufficient oil to flow to the rod bearings. Additionally, the mains should be cross-drilled to ensure one hole is exposed to the pressurized oil supply in the groove of the top bearing-insert, which allows an ungrooved lower bearing insert. The end of each oil hole should be and radiused to prevent the bearings from being scraped and provide for a smooth flow of oil.

Counterweights

Quite a bit of work can be done to the counterweights to affect engine performance. Granted, these are marginal improvements, but if it's worth a second at the finish... For one, counterweights can be shaped to reduce parasitic drag. This is done by radiusing or knife-edging the leading and trailing edges of the counterweights. They can also be undercut on one or both sides and narrowed—so-called *airplane wings* or *pendulum cut*—where sections at the sides and the leading and trailing edges closest to the center of rotation are removed. This concentrates mass toward the outer periphery of a counterweight where it will be the most effective while it reduces overall weight. The use of heavy metal—an alloy made mostly of tungsten with some nickel and copper thrown in—can also be used to reduce the frontal area of a counterweight. This reduces counterweight weight, but is made by the addition of heavy metal. Further, full counter-weighting, or adding counter-weights at the center throws,

reduces bending loads and the size of all counterweights. Finally, the crankshaft can be polished and counterweights treated with an oil-shedding coating to further reduce drag and *windage*, or churning of the oil.

To determine the effect of shaping or coating counterweights on power-loss reduction, an engine can be run on a Spintron, pages 123 and 124. Used mainly for valvetrain testing, the Spintron can also be used to determine the durability and losses or gains of other components. Examples are crankshaft scrapers, crankcase modifications, accessory drive arrangements and oil pump comparisons, all affecting power or durability.

Ordering A Crankshaft

You have a lot of choices to make and information to supply when ordering a crankshaft. Work with the crankshaft manufacturer on this one. He first needs to have basic engine specifications and the racing application. Additional specifications range from material,

Using 2–3-in. micrometer, measure main and crankpin journals. Record results for later use.

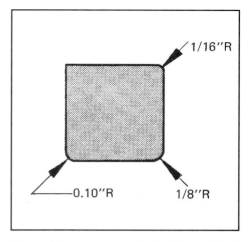

Use radius gauge to check fillet radii. If you don't have a gauge, make one using drawing as reference.

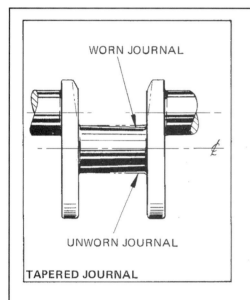 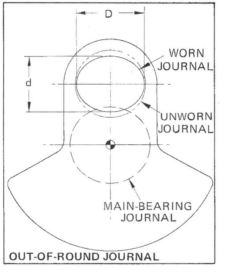

Check journals for out-of-round and taper. The crank needs reground if either exceeds specification.

stroke and bearing journal sizes to counterweight shape, coating and type of balance. This process can be greatly simplified by ordering a particular model crankshaft. These range from OEM-based crankshafts for low-hp drag cars or late-model stock cars to superlight high-hp cranks for low inertia and overall weight for use in unrestricted classes. To make your ordering job even easier, most crankshaft manufacturers supply complete bottom-end packages that include connecting rods and pistons with pins, rings, bearings and retainers.

If you are "parting-out" your order, you need to supply details to ensure your new crankshaft can be installed out of the box. Not only must the crank fit the block and the rods fit the crankshaft, but the complete assembly must be balanced. Consequently, you must also supply bobweight information, page 50. This means you must have in hand the rods, pistons, pins, rings and bearings so you can weigh them. Although this information may be supplied with the rods and pistons, you should confirm it by weighing them.

In special instances you'll also need to supply details on the snout—diameter and keyways—and specifications at the flywheel end. In addition to gun-drilling the mains, the flywheel flange can be machined into a star pattern to further lighten the crankshaft. This is done by removing material from between the flywheel bolt holes. Spending extra time to gather extra information will help to prevent mistakes and save a lot of time later.

Crankshaft Inspection and Reconditioning

Upon receiving a crankshaft, do a visual inspection. If all looks OK, get out your dial calipers and make some measurements. Use your black book, notes or ordering form for reference. Make sure it is what you ordered—and wanted. For a crank that has already been run, look for obvious problems such as burrs, cracks and scored or grooved

Oil holes at journal surfaces should look like these. Run small gun-bore brush with solvent through holes to ensure they are free of abrasive and metal particles.

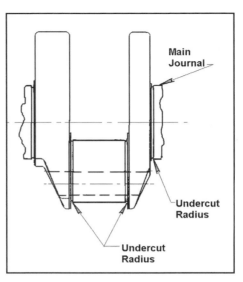

Fillet radii is increased by undercutting journals without reducing diameter.

Front Woodruff keyway in snout of abused crankshaft must be welded closed and remachined.

Check crankshaft alignment. Support crank at front and rear mains on V-blocks or in block with front and rear upper bearing inserts installed. With indicator on center main, rotate crank to determine bend.

journals. Providing all is satisfactory, do a precise inspection.

Using a 2–3-in. outside micrometer and telescoping gauge, measure journal diameters. Reference specifications given in a bearing catalog such as Federal-Mogul's or Clevite's. Measure each journal in several clock positions in the same plane for out-of-round and along its length for taper. Limit out-of round to 0.0002–0.0005 in. and taper to 0.0002–0.0004 in.

Record these numbers for later reference. If the journals are within spec, you'll use the main and crankpin diameters for checking bearing oil clearances. Otherwise it will have to be reground. Be aware, though, the crankshaft will have to recase hardened. Grinding the journals will remove the thin case hardening.

Use radius gauge to check journal fillets. If the radius is too small, or less than 0.125 in., consider

regrinding the crank. And if it's less than 0.0625 in. just do it. To achieve a larger radius fillet without regrinding the crank, undercut the journals. Although journal diameter at the fillets will be slightly smaller, crankshaft fatigue strength will be greatly enhanced. While you're looking at the fillets, check also that the oil holes are not burred and are smoothly radiused. If you find a problem, use a die grinder fitted with a paper roll to smooth the holes.

Crank Keys—Two types of keys are used in a rankshaft snout. A single straight cut is made for a standard key. Two or three radius-cut keyways are made for Woodruff keys. One is used to retain damper, a second is used to locate crank sprocket and a third may be used to position a counterweight for an externally balance engine.

Check that the key is held tightly in the keyway and it's not burred. Remove burring with a file. As for a beaten out keyway, you'll have to weld it closed and remachine it. I would farm out this job to my crankshaft supplier to ensure the

While supported at ends, the yoke is used to magnetize crankshaft. Check for sufficient magnetism with field indicator.

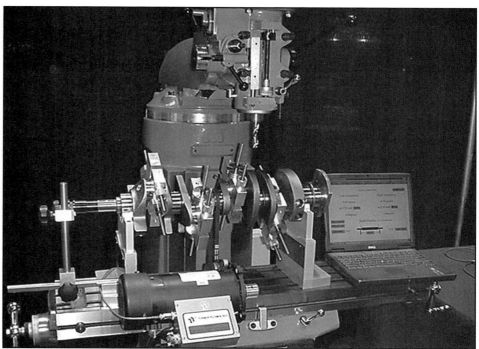

To do a good balancing job you'll need a good balancer such as one from Turner Technology. Balancer mounts to the bed of Bridgeport type mill.

keyway will be correctly indexed.

Check also damper-bolt threads at the front and those for the flywheel in flange at the back. If crankshaft has been run and will be used with a manual transmission, remove the pilot bearing and install a new one later.

Alignment—Check crankshaft for bend. Supported at the front and back main journals on V-blocks or in the block on end main-bearing inserts only, set up a dial indicator so the plunger is preloaded and square to the center main. Check that the needle will miss the oil hole when the crank is rotated, then rotate it to a position that gives the lowest indicated reading. Zero the indicator, and then rotate it to the highest indicated reading, which is bend. If there is any, it shouldn't exceed 0.0001 in. Bend is 1/2 TIR (total instrument reading), or 0.0005 in. maximum.

Check for Cracks—Use the same MPI method for checking the crankshaft for cracks as shown for checking connecting rods, pages 77–78. After you've cleaned it, support the crankshaft at each end so it's centered in yoke. With the machine on, slide the yoke from one end to the other to fully magnetize the crankshaft. Check magnetism with a field indicator. If sufficient magnetism is indicated, flow or sprinkle magnetic particles over the crankshaft. If you're using the Magneglo system, rotate the crankshaft and view each section of it with a black light to reveal any cracks. With dry powder, apply it by sprinkling or with a bulb, then look for the contrasting color of iron particles that align with a crack. Look most carefully at transitional areas from the snout and throws to the flywheel flange.

If a crack is indicated, mark it with a grease pencil or felt-tip marker. Double-check to be sure, as a crack will qualify the crankshaft for the scrap heap. Otherwise, demagnetize the crankshaft and use a field indicator to check that all magnetism has been removed. Clean crankshaft thoroughly.

Balancing

For a crankshaft to be in balance, rotating and reciprocating masses of the connecting rods and pistons must be compensated for at the counterweights. All, or 100% of the rotating mass, and a portion of the reciprocating mass, or 50% in most cases, must be balanced. For 90° V6s and V10s, refer to material that came with your balancer for reciprocating-weight percentages.

Rotating mass spins with the crankshaft. It includes the damper, flywheel, clutch and the big end of the connecting rods, their bearings and a portion of the rod beams starting at the big end and diminishing toward the pin end. *Reciprocating mass* includes pistons, rings, pin and retainers or buttons, and the small end of the rod plus a portion of the beam from the small end and diminishing toward the big end. There is also compensation for

COMMON RECOMMENDATIONS	
All 3 throw V6 (Except GMC 71 & 92 Series	50%
GM 3.3L 90° V6 (Chevy)	46%
Buick 3.2L, 3.8L & 4.1L 90° V6	36.6%
Chevy 4.3L 90° V6	50%
GM 2.8L 60° V6	50%
Capri 2.8L 60° V6	50%
Ford 2.8L 60° V6	50%
Ford 3.8L 90° V6	39.4%
Volvo, Renault, Peugeot 60° V6	50%

Externally balanced — must have flywheel and vibration damper installed along with any spacers & timing gear to position vibration damper correctly.

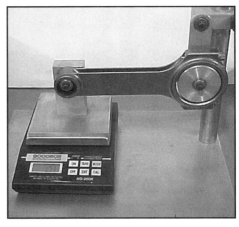

With rod supported at both ends and adjusted so rod is horizontal, weigh small end. Indicated weight is 173 grams.

Use cards such as this one from Winnona Van Norman to record piston, rod, retainer, pin and ring weights in grams for determining bobweight. Weights are organized into reciprocating weight and rotating weights. On back of this bobweight card are recommended reciprocating weights.

oil on and in the rods, pistons and crankshaft.

For engines using cast-iron crankshafts with heavy rods, external balancing may be required. About 6% lighter than steel, the counterweights of a cast-iron crankshaft can't be made large enough in the tight confines of a crankcase to balance some engines. This will require counterweighting the flywheel and damper to complete the balancing job. However, all racing engines using steel crankshafts are internally balanced. This is a big plus because the damper and flywheel can be zero balanced, or be in perfect balance by themselves. This allows a damper or flywheel to be installed on an internally balanced engine without affecting overall engine balance. Not so with an externally balanced engine. The damper and flywheel must be included in the balancing process.

After completing all modifications and machining

operations, weigh each connecting rod, piston and their components, then equalize the weights. You will need a notebook, a *bobweight card* (see above) on which to record weights, and an accurate scale with a trapeze. Weigh pistons, bearing inserts, pistons, piston pins, retainers or buttons and rings. Weigh each of these to determine if their weights need to be equalized. All pistons should weigh the same as should the big- and small-ends of rods.

Weigh and Equalize Connecting Rods—Beginning at the small end of the rod, set small-end fixture on the scale and zero it. Position the small-end of the rod on the small-end fixture and suspend the big end with the trapeze fixture. Adjust the fixture so the rod is level so readings are accurate. Read the small-end weight and record the rod number and weight. Proceed to the next rod, weighing and recording results in the same manner.

After weighing all small ends,

Turn rod around and adjust the trapeze so rod is level. Weights of all big ends were the same at 447 grams.

reposition fixture for weighing big ends—the rotating weight—of the rods. Zero the scale, then install the rod on the fixture and level it. After you've weighed and recorded all big ends, weigh each rod by itself. Compare this to the sum of big- and small-end weights of each. The results should equal total rod weight.

A matched set of race-rods should weigh the same. If they don't, contact the manufacturer and sort it out with him. Above all, don't start grinding on the rods. This will void any warranty. However, if you

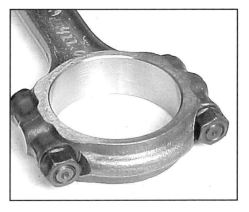 

Note weights recorded on big- and small-ends of rod: 422 grams at big end and 173 grams at small end. Total rod weight is 595 grams, the sum of big- and small end weight.

Use a belt sander to lighten the small end of the rod. The opportunity to reduce total connecting rod weight was taken by first removing most of the balance pad with a bench grinder.

 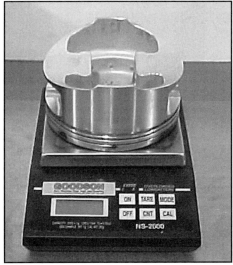

Weigh rod bearing inserts to complete rotating-weight measurements. All of the 45 grams added to 422 grams of the big end of the rod makes up the rotating portion of bobweight.

Piston is weighed separately from pin. All weighed 410 grams.

A rare sight in a racing engine shop is equalizing piston weight. Piston is set on a milling machine, and then an end mill is used to remove material from the pin boss. The skirt must be blended into pin boss.

are working with stock-type rods, find the lightest one and lighten the heavier ones to match. Remove metal from the heavier rods by grinding the balance pads at the top of each small end or bottom of the cap for the big end. Reweigh each rod until you obtain the correct weight. Record big- and small-end weights on the bobweight card. Weigh rod bearing inserts to complete rotating weight.

The major portion of recip-

rocating weight is the pistons. All modifications must be completed prior to weighing them. Once this is done, number pistons with a felt marker for reference, weigh each and record weight. As with the rods, pistons should weigh the same, particularly if they are a matched lightweight set. Again, weigh them just to be sure. If pistons can and need to be balanced, check with the manufacturer for the correct procedure. This usually involves removing material from the

bottom of the pin boss, taking care not to weaken it.

Weigh the rest of the reciprocating components: wrist pin, one ring set and set of retainers or buttons. Record the results on a bobweight card similar to the one shown on page 52. Weigh one or a complete set of each as you won't

51

This piston pin is heavy. It weighs 125% of a typical taper-wall 9310 steel pin or 140% of a titanium pin, all with the same diameter. Weigh the retainers or buttons, too.

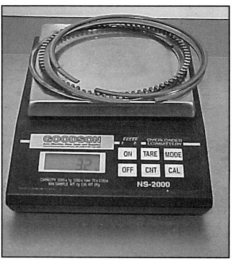

The weight of this ring set is 32 grams. Don't forget to weigh the pin.

Balancing crankshafts such as this with splayed rod journals in 90° V6 block must use one bobweight for each piston-and-rod assembly.

have to equalize weights of these components.

Note that the rotating weights on the bobweight card are listed twice and that 100% of reciprocating weights are listed. A 2-gram oil allowance per rod was doubled. This method minimizes math work needed to arrive at the bobweight figure for a V8. As previously indicated, 100% of rotating weight and 50% of reciprocating weight for a V8 is used to determine what makes up a bobweight—except when connecting rods share a common crankpin such as with a V8. So double the rotating weight and leave the reciprocating weight at 100% to begin with, giving total bobweight for one journal, or 1,697.2 grams in this case. Had it been one rod per journal, bobweight would have been 1/2 that shown, or 848.6 grams less 2 grams for 1/2 of the oil allowance.

Oil allowance is a gray area because of factors that are difficult to establish. Even though oil filling

SYMBOL OF GH QUALITY	CUSTOMER:	V-8
	ADDRESS:	JOB #
	PHONE NO:	DATE

ENGINE MAKE _____   MODEL _____

ROD ROTATING	422	☐ COMPLETE ENGINE
ROD ROTATING	422	☐ LESS FLYWHEEL
ROD BEARING	45	☐ LESS PRESSURE PLATE
ROD BEARING	45	☐ LESS DAMPER
OIL ALLOWANCE	4	
PISTON & PIN	410+142.2=552.2	
LOCKS (1 SET)	2	G & H BALANCER SERVICE
RINGS (1 SET)	32	2919 W. Irving Park Road
ROD RECIPROCATING	173	Chicago, IL 60618-3511
		(773) 509-1988 FAX (847) 559-1120

BOBWEIGHT TOTAL: **1697.2 g**

NOTE: 50% RECIPROCATING, 100% ROTATING

Form 24

Bobweight card completed for V8 components weighed in example photos.

the crank throw passages is finite, a guesstimate must be made for oil clinging to the rods, crankshaft throws and pistons. A rule of thumb is to use 4 grams for a small block and 6 grams for a big block. Or, as Warren Turner of Turner Technologies says, this is an area of opinion, so a majority of those in the industry keep life simple and use 5 grams for everything.

Make up bobweights using your bobweight card as a reference. In the example, four 1697.2-gram bobweights will be used to balance the V8 crankshaft. Steel shot in canisters or washers of varying sizes and thickness are used to make up bobweights. Whichever is used, the end result is the same. Adjust shot or washers until you have achieved the desired weight. Since all

Bobweight assembly is built up using a card as reference. Note the assortment of washers in the background.

Fit the drive belt to the motor and adjust the tension.

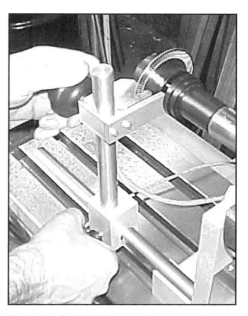

End play is limited on a Turner balancer with adjustable plate fitted to a grooved adapter at the snout end of the crankshaft. Note the trigger wheel and pickup.

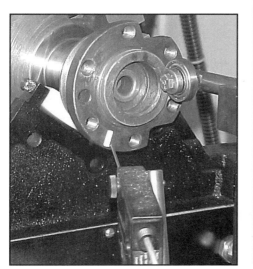

Tape and pickup at the flywheel flange is used to indicate zero-degree position. The bearing limits end play of the crankshaft on Winnona Van-Norman balancer. The degree wheel is adjusted to match zero position indicated at rear. Weighted pointer at the front indicates crankshaft position.

bobweight components are matched, you can weigh the shot or washers separately and match the weights for making up the remaining bobweights. Weigh each assembly to confirm total grams.

Adjust V-blocks so that the distance between them matches that between the front and rear main journals. If the engine is externally balanced, the crank sprocket, damper and flywheel must be installed. Slip the drive belt over the center main, then set the crankshaft on the V-blocks. Fit the drive belt to the motor. Apply a light lubricant such as WD-40 to the mains. Position the endplay limiter/s at one or both ends of the crankshaft. Install the trigger wheel or tape and pickup with a degree wheel and pointer as shown for indicating crankshaft position in degrees. With the degree wheel and pointer, zero the wheel so the needle matches the zero position indicated on the computer screen. Spin the crankshaft by hand and check the computer-screen readout. If all is OK, install the bobweights.

Even though bobweights are the correct grams, they must be positioned precisely on the rod journals to achieve an accurate balance. Kevin Hartley recommends centering them on the journals and rotating them to the same relative positions to the throws. A telescoping gauge is the best tool to use for checking distance from each bearing journal cheek. In addition, the halves must be parallel to each other. Use a dial caliper to check parallelism. Once you've mounted all bobweights, check for clearance by spinning the crankshaft by hand. Double-check for zero position on the readout, then turn on the balancer to check the balance.

Spin the crankshaft, then check the readout. Readout information supplied varies widely, but all readings provide the position in degrees and amount of weight in

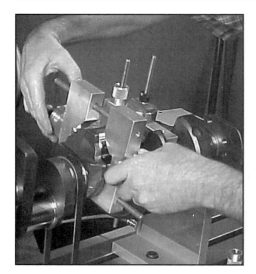

Kevin slides bobweight halves together on the rod journal.

To achieve an accurate balance, all bobweights are centered on the rod journals and halves aligned with the throw.

A split ring that just happens to be the correct thickness is used to check for centering bobweight on journal.

Check that bobweight halves are parallel.

Crankshaft is spun, then amount to add or remove to obtain balance is displayed. From left to right, at 1°, 12.5 grams needs to be added to front counterweight and at 48°, 7.6 grams needs to be added to rear counterweight.

grams that needs to be added or removed from each counterweight and the locations to bring the crankshaft into balance. This will be done in numbers only or will be graphically enhanced. If weight is to be added, confirm this by adding the weight in clay to the positions displayed. Otherwise, drill holes in the periphery of the counterweight at the position, size, and depth recommended.

Using lacquer thinner or brake cleaner, remove oily deposits from the area at the counterweights where you're going to place clay. This will help ensure the clay will stick and not be thrown across the shop or at you. Not that it will hurt, but hunting clay or peeling it off your forehead is inconvenient to say the least. Using scales, weigh a chunk of clay, adding and deleting as necessary until you arrive at the correct amount. Stick this chunk of clay to the position displayed. Do

the same to the other counterweight/s. You can't make one change at a time. All changes must be made to get an accurate reading. Count on doing this several times before you get the crankshaft balanced, or within 0.1 gram.

Mark counterweight in the position weight it will be added, then remove and weigh the clay. Refer to balancer instructions to determine the diameter and length of *heavy metal*, or the Mallory metal, that is equivalent to the

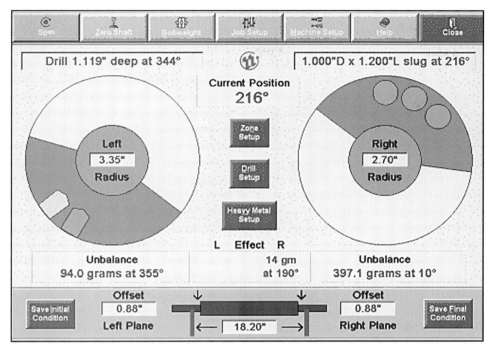

Display llustrates location of heavy metal to add (left) and depth of drilled hole/s (right) to balance crankshaft. Computer takes into account material removed in location/s heavy metal is added. Photo courtesy Turner Technology

After weighing, add clay to the counterweight and re-spin crankshaft. Mark position of clay on side of counterweight before you remove it. Photo by Kevin Hartley

Access hole is first drilled in counterweight at flywheel flange, then through counterweight. Hole is reamed to achieve desire press-fit. Photo by Kevin Hartley

weight of clay you used to achieve balance. The heavy metal will be heavier due to it being installed on a smaller radius, or closer to the main bearing centerline.

Additionally, heavy metal must also compensate for metal removed from drilling the counterweight.

Ideally, heavy metal should have a length equal to the width of the counterweight if the hole is drilled through, so the hole diameter must be sized accordingly.

Remove the bobweights from the crankshaft, then remove the crankshaft from the balancer. To drill and ream the counterweight/s, set up the crankshaft vertically on a mill. Refer to your heavy metal chart for determining the weight versus length and diameter. Also take into account available drill and ream sizes. You may have to turn down the heavy metal to get the exact the length.

A 0.500–1.00-in. diameter slug of heavy metal should be retained with a press-fit of 0.001–0.0015 in. Smaller diameters should have slightly less press. Some engine builders secure heavy metal by welding, but I prefer keeping welders away from crankshafts and depend on the press-fit only unless

Drive in heavy metal so it is flush with sides of counterweight. Photo by Kevin Hartley

Small counterweights require large slugs of heavy metal to achieve internal balance. Note drilled counterweights to correct overbalance.

Weight needs to be added to flexplate for it to be zero balanced. Draw a circle around the clay, remove and weigh it. A washer of the same weight tack-welded to flexplate balances it.

there is no other option.

When adding heaving metal, overbalance the crankshaft slightly. It's much easier to remove weight from the counterweight than add more to achieve final balance.

To remove weight from a counterweight, simply drill a hole to the size and depth using the calculations or as displayed by the balancer. Modern balancers display size, depth and location of the

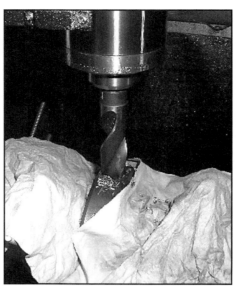

Remove weight from counterweight by drilling with crankshaft rotated to correct position on balancer. Shop towels keep chips off bobweights and crankshaft. Photo by Kevin Hartley.

holes on the counterweight, taking into account even material removed at the drill point. To do this operation you can leave the bobweights and crankshaft in place on the V-blocks. After fitting the chuck with the recommended drill bit, rotate the crankshaft so the counterweight is in the correct position using the readout for reference. Position the drill bit directly over the counterweight. Wrap a strip of masking tape around the drill bit to indicate hole depth. Use your steel rule or dial calipers to measure position of tape on bit. Keep shavings off bobweights by covering them with shop towels.

If yours is a zero-balanced crankshaft, install the flywheel or flexplate and damper with cam sprocket or spacer, bolt and washer to check them for zero balance. Drilling is usually best for balancing a damper or flywheel, but a slug of steel tack-welded works best with a

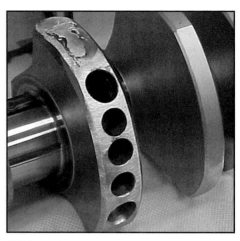

OEM crank matched with lightweight rods and pistons required considerable lightening. Counterweights were ground, then drilled. Excess weight removed was corrected by welding.

flexplate. Secure it with a short strip of duct tape to check balance, then tack-weld it on when balance is achieved. Tape will simulate weight of tack weld. Use a grinder to remove slight overweight.

Polish Bearing Journals—The object here is to put a super finish on the journals without affecting journal size or the fillets. This is best done with a broken-in—worn—400-grit, cloth-backed belt. Use a lubricant such as Goodson's Grind Aid to keep belt from loading up.

DAMPER

The primary function of a crankshaft damper is to absorb—damp—damaging torsional vibrations that cause a crankshaft to twist and untwist, thus the correct name *torsional damper*. Deflections, similar to the linear suspension movements of a car, are due to forces caused by the camshaft and valvetrain through the timing set, accessory drive, drive line and, most of all, forces from the piston-and-rod assemblies. This damping action works similar to two

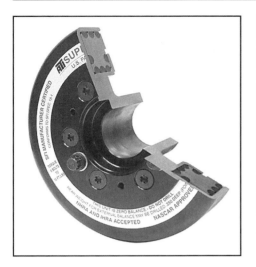

ATI Super Damper incorporates inertia ring encased in housing between large-diameter elastomeric O-rings.

ATI damper can tuned or rebuilt by changing O-rings.

Timing marks on traditional bonded damper. Indicated crank position is 32° BTDC.

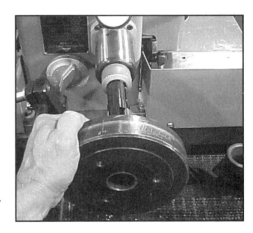

Hone damper hub to provide 0.001-in. maximum interference fit to crankshaft snout.

eggs being spun on a countertop, one raw and one boiled. The boiled egg seems to spin forever while the raw egg won't make one rotation because of the shearing action and mass of the raw egg. Indicating angular crankshaft position is usually another function of a damper. Added to most damper assemblies is a degree scale for setting ignition timing or finding TDC indicated by **0** and other crankshaft positions on both sides of TDC. Finally, there may be a provision for additional engine counterweighting on the damper hub.

Types of Dampers

Three basic styles of crankshaft dampers are used. The most familiar damper consists of an inertia ring bonded to the hub with a thin section of elastomer, or rubber-like material. Next is the Fluidamper. Used extensively in drag racing, it was originally developed for industrial use by Houdaille. Much like the raw egg, the Fluidamper achieves damping from the shear action of silicone gel

encased with the inertia ring in a sealed housing that is attached to the hub. Third is the ATI damper. Used extensively on high-rpm engines for endurance racing, it is similar to the traditional elastomeric-bonded damper. Instead, it uses elastomeric O-rings on all sides of the inertia ring between it and the hub. The ATI damper is easily rebuilt or tuned by changing these O-rings.

The problem with this type of damper is the inertia ring can move if the bond fails, moving the degree scale in the process. A paint daub or matching punch marks on the hub and inertia ring will alert you if this happens.

Check damper fit to the crank snout. The interference fit of many dampers is just too tight. Using a bore gauge, measure the damper bore ID and compare it to the crank-snout OD. If the damper is tighter than 0.001 in., hone it on your rod machine to provide a 0.0008–0.0010-in. press.

BEARINGS

The two basic physical characteristics of sleeve-type engine bearings are material and shape. Material determines bearing strength,

tolerance for debris in the oil to be absorbed and ability for the bearing to reshape itself. Shape ensures the bearing will fit securely in its housing and provide full lubrication to the bearing journal.

Material

Fatigue strength gives a bearing the ability to endure high cyclical loads. *Embedability* allows a bearing to absorb small particles carried by the oil that may otherwise groove the bearing journal. *Conformability* gives the bearing the ability to reshape itself

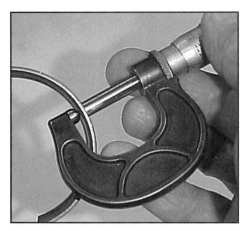

Bearing thickness is measured at center.

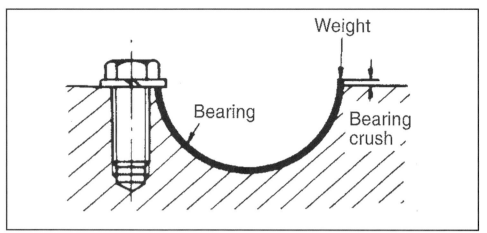

End of insert extending above parting line while other end is held flush represents 1/2 total bearing crush. or 0.0016 in. for rod bearings and 0.0019 in. for main bearings.

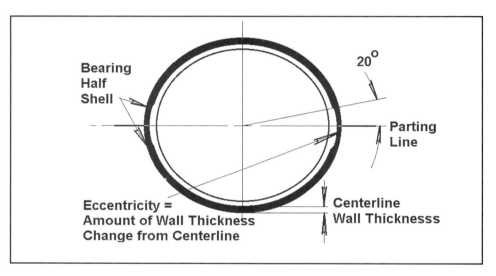

Bearing bore diameter is at parting line due to bearing eccentricity. Reliefs prevent bearing from bulging at parting line when bearing is crushed. Drawing courtesy Clevite.

slightly to make up for slight irregularities in the journal surface. Unfortunately, when one of these characteristics is improved, the other is reduced. As an example, a harder bearing material generally increases fatigue strength, but reduces embedability and conformability and vice versa. For most racing applications it makes sense to go with a high fatigue-resistant material and compromise, but not eliminate, the others. Sacrificing embedability and conformability to gain increased fatigue strength should not be a problem, however. Oil in a racing engine should be well filtered and the journals should have very accurate, highly polished surfaces.

To produce a bearing that incorporates all three of these characteristics, the bearing industry offers a tri-metal bearing. Tri-metal bearings consist of three materials on a steel backing, or shell. Materials include copper, lead and tin or indium. Simply stated, a binary structure, or a cast microstructure of lead pockets in a copper matrix, is first placed on the steel backing. This is followed with the application of a thin overlay of lead-tin-copper or lead-indium, thus the term tri-metal. The tri-metal bearing is preferred for virtually all forms of racing with the exception of blown fuel or alcohol drag-racing engines. In this case a babbitt bearing, a tin and lead-based material, is preferred. Long bearing life is sacrificed for the ability of the softer bearing material to absorb shock.

Bearing Shapes and Characteristics

The shape combines all of the dimensions defining a bearing, size being the most common. A bearing must be sized to fit a specific bore in the block or rod while providing sufficient oil clearance to the bearing journal. Details of bearing shape include:

Undersize—Defined by journal size, a bearing is either standard size or undersize. A journal turned down 0.010 in. uses a 010-under bearing, 0.020-in. smaller shaft uses a 020-under bearing and so on. Bearing thickness will be increased by half the undersize, or

0.005-in. thicker for a 0.010-in. undersize journal.

Crush—The circumference of bearing OD is more than bore ID circumference. This circumference difference forces the bearing—crushes it—into firm contact with its bore, effectively giving the bearing a press fit to lock it into place and prevent spinning. Performance bearings need slightly more crush to provide additional locking. Correct rod- and main-bearing crush is obtained by making sure bearing-housing diameters are correct. As reference, though, crush for the rod and main bearings should be 0.0016 in. and 0.0019 in., respectively.

Eccentricity—Bearing inserts are thickest at the center, or 90° from the parting line, and are gradually thinned on both sides of center toward near lines to create a slight oval, or eccentric, shape. This compensates for bore distortion under high loads.

Parting-Line Relief—Bearings are relieved, or thinned, approximately 3/8 in. back from each parting line to prevent bulging and contact with journal in that area when bearing is crushed.

Spread—Insert halves are slightly wider than housing diameter across the ends. This provides a spring action to preload insert against the bore to help ensure it stays in place during assembly. Typical spread is 0.012 in. for main bearings and 0.020 in. for rod bearings.

Oil Grooves—Bearings are fully grooved, partially grooved or have no grooves at all. Most race-engine main bearings have grooved upper halves only so the area of the higher loaded bottom halves is not

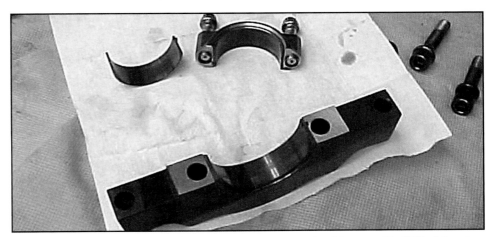

Inspecting bearings during teardown. Contact pattern should cover 60–80% of bearing surface. Backsides of inserts should have clear crosshatch pattern of honed housing bores.

reduced. Bearing manufacturers disagree on the benefits of extending the grooves even partially into the lower insert. Tests have shown ungrooved bearings are best. An oil reservoir provided by a grooved top insert is for supplying oil to the rod bearings. Rod bearings are not grooved. Cross-drilled journals ensure oil is picked up and supplied to the bearings.

Lug or Dowel Hole—The bent-down lug—dowel hole for aluminum rods—is for locating inserts during assembly. Either may delay bearing from spinning, but won't stop it.

Chamfer—Chamfered edge of the bearing provides clearance for large fillet rod- and main-journal radii.

Vertical Oil Clearance—This is basically the difference between journal OD and bearing ID measured vertically to parting line as installed in bearing housing.

Coating—Coated bearings reduce friction and increase heat transfer, an important feature during those critical times of low oil pressure where severe bearing or journal damage would otherwise occur. They also allow less-than-

standard clearance. Clevite cautions that when coated, bearings should not be heated above 350° F for over 30 minutes to prevent blistering of bearing surfaces.

Bearing Suppliers

The best place to get information on choosing, fitting and installing bearings for your specific application is from a bearing manufacturer. Names such as Clevite, Federal Mogul and Vandervell are standards in the racing industry. Depend on them when you have specific questions. One of the first things they will tell you: "Avoid excessive romancing of parts such as polishing the bearings with an abrasive pad such as Velcro." At the least this will do nothing. Instead, it will likely remove the thin 0.0005-in. overlay. But if you are determined to do something, use a paper towel soaked with denatured alcohol or lacquer thinner to wipe down bearings, no more.

4

PISTONS, PINS, RINGS, AND RODS

The piston-and-connecting rod assembly has the job of transferring the force created by the pressure of combustion to the crank pin. To do this efficiently, the piston and rings must seal combustion chamber pressures on the topside and oil and miscellaneous vapors below. This must be done with minimal friction loss as the piston moves in the bore.

Ring sealing and piston durability are aggravated by loads imposed by pressures created during the four strokes, particularly high-temperature combustion-chamber pressures during the power stroke and resulting forces from the connecting rod. Inertial loads are also a major factor. Pressure on top of the piston tries to escape down past the compression rings—blowby—while oil and vapors try to escape up past the oil and bottom compression rings. All of this happens while the piston is heated and cooled, accelerated and decelerated as it travels up and down the bore, thrust against the cylinder wall by the connecting rod and rocked back and forth on the wrist pin. During all this, the piston-and-rod assembly must maintain its integrity. To ensure the rods and pistons in your engine perform properly you must choose the right components. To accomplish this

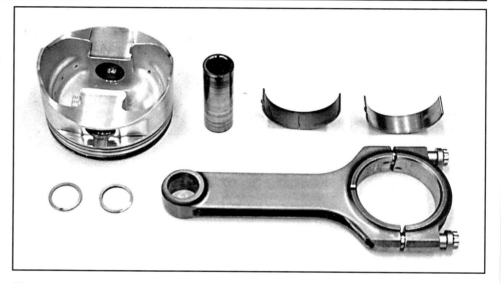

Piston and rod after a 500-mile race. Only things here that may be reused are the rod and bolts. Some components are automatically discarded after inspecting them, such as piston, rings, bearings, and retainers.

you must establish the piston and connecting rod dimensions and materials that will perform adequately within the operating range of your engine. This starts with the pistons.

PISTON VELOCITY

Unless your engine will have pneumatic- or solenoid-operated valves, the valvetrain will limit maximum engine rpm, but piston velocity must not be ignored. High rpm operation causes reduced ring sealing, excessive wear and low durability or catastrophic failure from dynamic loads on the piston as it moves up and down. As a crankshaft rotates, each piston travels up and down the bore at an

average velocity, or *mean velocity*, between TDC and BDC. Directly proportional to stroke and engine speed usually expressed in feet per minute, average piston velocity is found by multiplying engine rpm by stroke in inches, then dividing by six. For example, an engine turning at 7,500 rpm with a four-inch stroke has an average piston velocity of 7,500 rpm x 4.000 in. ÷ 6 = 5,000 fpm. For a stroke of 3.50 in, average velocity drops to 4,375 fpm. The accepted average velocity of a piston was 4,600 fpm, but it is common for race engines to operate at sustained average piston speeds of up to 5,700 fpm. I also am familiar with instances where average piston velocities have exceeded 7,000 fpm,

PISTON VELOCITY & CONNECTING ROD LENGTH

Maximum velocity of a piston occurs when the connecting rod is at 90° to the crank pin. Therefore, the angle of crank rotation from either side of TDC must first be found. To do this you'll need to know connecting-rod length (l_c) and crankshaft throw (l_1), or half of the stroke. A calculator or trig tables will be needed for doing these calculations.

Crankshaft angle $\emptyset_{max} = \arccos 1 \div \sqrt{(k^2 + 3)}$ where:

$k = 2l_c/l_1$

l_c = connecting-rod length

l_1 = stroke ÷ 2

V_{max} (Maximum Piston Velocity) $= 6.283l_1 \, w(\sin\emptyset_{max} + \sin 2\emptyset_{max} \div 2k)$ where: w = engine rpm

Using these formulas to find piston velocity at 7,500 rpm for a 5.25-in. connecting rod used with a 3.50-in. stroke, first find crankshaft angle at which V_{max} occurs. Starting with the 5.25-in. rod:

$k = 2l_c \div l_1 = 2(5.25 \text{ in.}) \div 3.5 \text{ in.} = 3.00$

$\emptyset_{max} = \arccos 1 \div \sqrt{(3^2 + 3)} = \arccos 0.2887; \emptyset_{max} = 73.2°$

$V_{max} = 6.2831(3.50 \text{ in.} \div 2)(7,500 \text{ rpm})[(\sin 73.2° + \sin 2(73.2°) \div 2(3.000)]$

$= 82,465 (0.9573 + 0.0.09223) = 82,465(1.0495)$

$= 86,550 \text{ in./min; or } 7,221 \text{ fpm where average velocity is } 4,375 \text{ fpm.}$

With the engine operating at the same rpm, compare this to the same connecting rod used with a stroke of 4.00 in.:

$k = 2(5.25 \text{ in.}) \div 4.00 \text{ in.} = 2.625$

$\emptyset_{max} = \arccos 1 \div \sqrt{(2.625^2 + 3)} = \arccos 0.3180 = 71.5°$

$V_{max} = 6.2831(3.50 \text{ in.} \div 2)(7,500 \text{ rpm})[(\sin 71.5° + \sin 2(71.5°) \div 2(2.625)] = 82,465 (0.9483 + 0.1146)$

$= 82,465 (1.0629) = 87,652 \text{ in./min; or } 7,304 \text{ fpm at the same } 4,375 \text{ fpm average velocity.}$

See what happens with the same 5.25-in. connecting rod and 4.00-in. stroke at 9,500 rpm:

$V_{max} = 6.2831(3.50 \text{ in.} \div 2)(9,500 \text{ rpm})[(\sin 71.5° + \sin 2(71.5°)/2(2.625)] = 104,456 (0.9483 + 0.1146)$

$= 104,456 (1.0629) = 111,027 \text{ in./min; or } 9,252 \text{ fpm with an average velocity of } 6,333 \text{ fpm.}$

At current accepted maximum piston velocities, an engine with such a setup will not live long operating at 9,500 rpm.

although with 200-gram pistons. Advancements in piston design and development of materials used for them, piston rings and connecting rods have made this possible. Although the envelope has been expanded, basics still apply.

You may have wondered how a Formula 1 engine stays together at 17,000 rpm. Notwithstanding pneumatic-operated valves, *short stroke* is the simple answer. A V10 with a 1.7-in. stroke has an average piston velocity of 4,817 fpm compared to a stock car engine with over 5,500 fpm at 9,500 rpm! More importantly, when a piston decelerates to a stop at the top or bottom of a stroke, it is accelerated in the reverse direction to *maximum velocity*. A matter of dynamics, maximum piston velocity far exceeds average velocity.

An extensive discussion on bottom-end dynamics exceeds the scope of this book. But you need to appreciate the effects of *inertia load*—accelerating a mass—the force on the connecting rod and piston that results from accelerating and decelerating a piston. For example, the load imposed by a piston being accelerated can reach 2,000g. For a 400-gram piston, the resulting inertia load is 2,000g x 400 grams x 2.204 x (10)$^{-3}$ pounds/gram = 1,763 lb on the piston-pin boss! Rather than going into the real piston killer, acceleration, an understanding of maximum piston velocity in relation to average velocity should be sufficient. This is followed up by looking at methods to reduce piston velocities, both average and maximum. See accompanying sidebar for specifics.

Piston Velocity and Acceleration

Maximum Piston Velocity— This occurs when the connecting rod is square, or 90°, to the crank throw. At this point, the angle of the crankshaft throw is typically near 75° from TDC, depending on the length of the connecting rod. Just as piston velocity is highest when square to the crank throw, so are side loads on the piston, particularly when thrust by the lateral vector into the cylinder wall on the power stroke. As pressure on the piston forces the connecting rod down, reaction from the connecting rod pushes the piston

against the cylinder wall. This not only stresses the cylinder wall and piston, it also rocks the piston, which upsets ring sealing. This condition is aggravated by a shorter connecting rod.

A function of connecting-rod length, piston velocity and side load will be highest at lower crank angles, or more so when the crankshaft is at 70° than when at 76°. Ideal rod length would be near to infinity, but that is not practical. In the real world, a connecting rod should be *at least* 1.7 times as long as the stroke of the crankshaft. This translates into a connecting rod-to-stroke ratio of 1.70:1 or higher.

Connecting Rod Length-to-Stroke Ratio—or connecting-rod length measured between big-end and small-end centers divided by stroke, should be established early on because of the effect it will have on the durability and performance of your engine. Although less important is the dwell time of a piston near TDC—less dwell with a short rod and vice versa with a long one. Although shorter connecting rods will result in slightly more torque at lower rev ranges due to dynamics in the intake and exhaust ports from a faster accelerating piston, power will be higher with a longer connecting rod. But any advantage gained with a short connecting rod pales in comparison to the problems mentioned.

As for how long a connecting rod should be, use the longest one possible for your block and crankshaft combination. With that said, you have the distance from the crankshaft throw at TDC to

Lightweight forged Mahle piston for NASCAR cup engine with reinforcing webs make up for pure mass. Reducing reciprocating weight benefits any engine that operates at high rpm.

the top of the block to fit a connecting rod-and-piston assembly, give or take a little deck clearance. Subtract piston compression height from this distance and you have connecting-rod length. As a general rule, rod length-to-stroke ratio is best kept within a 1.7–1.9:1 or higher range. As an example of how important rod length is, high-revving Formula-1 engines use rod length-to-stroke ratios of over 2:1. If you are starting with a raise-deck block, finding a connecting rod that will give a desirable rod-to-stroke ratio should not be a problem. This is not so for a stroker crank in a low-deck small block. Whatever your situation, always work with piston and connecting rod manufacturers to arrive at the right piston and connecting rod package for your engine. Let's start with the pistons.

PISTONS

Choosing pistons starts with the material. Because this is a book on building racing engines, I only discuss forged aluminum pistons. Use cast pistons only if you are

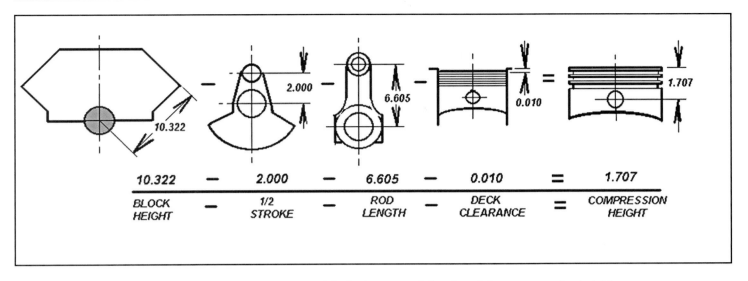

10.322	−	2.000	−	6.605	−	0.010	=	1.707
BLOCK HEIGHT	−	1/2 STROKE	−	ROD LENGTH	−	DECK CLEARANCE	=	COMPRESSION HEIGHT

For a given deck height, stroke, connecting-rod length and deck clearance, determine piston compression height.

forced to do so by the rulebook. In this case use *hypereutectic*—high silicon—Sealed Power or Silv-O-Lite aluminum pistons, companies that supply pistons to OEM manufacturers. But if you are among the majority who has a choice, you will be working with aftermarket piston suppliers who use forged-aluminum pistons exclusively. The preferred aluminum alloy for forged pistons is 2618 except when controlled thermal expansion is a priority. Then 4032 aluminum is used, but the higher silicon content—0.20% versus 12%—reduces the strength of 4032 by 14% compared to 2618.

Regardless of the material used, other choices involve physical features that will ensure the piston stops short of the cylinder head and clears the valves and sparkplug. It also must have the desired volume, fit the bore, accommodate the ring pack, have sufficient strength with minimal weight, move straight in the bore with low friction, retain the wrist pin and

work with the rings to contain combustion pressure. Let's take these one at a time from the top.

Deck Clearance

The location of the wrist pin in relation to the top of the piston establishes piston compression height, or distance from the pin bore center to the flat surface at the top of the piston. Once block deck height, crankshaft stroke, rod length and deck clearance—or distance between the top of the piston and block deck—are established, compression height can be determined. Because deck clear-ance ensures the piston stops just short of hitting the bottom of the cylinder head, great care must be taken when choosing a piston and checking it during preassembly.

Piston-to-Head Clearance

This is the sum of the deck clearance and gasket thickness, and should be minimal, or about 0.040 in. for a steel or titanium connecting rod and 0.060 in. with

aluminum. Give the sparkplug the same clearance. So if compressed gasket thickness is 0.042 in.—make sure of this—and steel rods are used, deck clearance will be 0.040 in. − 0.042 in. = −0.002 in. This piston will stick out of the block 0.002 in. at TDC. With the piston all the way up, deck clearance is measured from the flat surface of the piston to the block deck.

When you're trying to squeeze out every horsepower possible, keep piston-to-head clearance at a minimum with a wedge combustion chamber. As just shown, zero or negative clearance—the piston projects above the block deck at TDC—is not unusual. I'm not suggesting you set up the pistons to run this close to the head, but I've seen pistons that have actually touched the heads without damage during an endurance race.

Running a piston this close to the head creates maximum *quench*. This forces the air/fuel charge from the far side of the combustion

Pin in this JE piston is about as high as it can get before it must be placed behind oil-ring groove. Note thinned bottom ring land at intersection with pin bore.

CP piston with reverse dome, or dish, and valve reliefs. To minimize piston weight, top is kept as thin as possible, requiring shape of underside to mirror shape of top side.

chambers where it can "hide" and otherwise go unburned into the volume closest the sparkplug where it will be burned. This and the resulting turbulence burns the air/fuel charge more efficiently and in less time, requiring less ignition lead, or timing advance. Not only is power increased and fuel consumption reduced, the chance of engine killing detonation—air/fuel mixture exploding—is reduced.

Sparkplug-to-Piston Clearance

This clearance should be 0.040 in. or 0.060 in. minimum for steel or aluminum rods, respectively. Plug clearance is usually not a problem when using wedge heads, but a high-dome piston used with open-chamber or hemi heads frequently require a notch at the sparkplug. Check plug clearance during preassembly with the same type of plug and gasket you will install at final assembly.

Wrist Pin Height

The height of the wrist pin is limited by either the ring package or clearance to the small end of the

connecting rod and bottom of the piston. The primary reason for moving a pin up in piston besides using a longer connecting rod is to reduce weight. Less compression height allows for a shorter piston, thus weight will be less. Ring package height includes the distance from the top of the first compression ring to the bottom of the oil ring or second compression ring, so there's not much wiggle room here. Included in compression height is how high the top ring can be placed in relation to the piston deck. For a naturally aspirated engine, this should be no less than 0.200 in., even though 0.100 in. has been used for drag racing. As for nitrous, blown or turbocharged engines, ring-to-piston deck distance must be substantially more to shield the top ring and ring land from excessive heat, preventing them from being "torched." It goes this way: More manifold pressure equals more heat requiring more ring-to-piston deck distance. Follow the recommendations of your piston manufacturer.

Closest to the underside of the piston is the small end of the

connecting rod. Valve reliefs or reverse dome—dish—force down local areas of the piston top that can crowd the top of a connecting rod. This shouldn't be a problem if you're using aftermarket racing rods, but check them just the same, page 81. Clearance to the rod and underside of the piston should be 0.050 in. minimum.

Piston Tops

The tops, also referred to as crowns or domes, are available in various configurations, from high domes for hemispherical combustion chambers to reverse domes for wedge heads. It begins with combustion-chamber shape and compression ratio. Aftermarket catalogs list pistons according to such specifications as bore diameter, heads used, valve angle, stroke, rod length, cylinder-head volume, compression ratio and weight. There's not much they don't cover. Pistons will usually have a dome or dish and valve relief/s for specific heads. If the one you need is not listed for a valve angle or compression, either purchase existing pistons and machine them to fit your needs or work with the manufacturer to do the machining for you. Not unusual when building a custom racing engine, work may involve increasing dome volume, enlarging valve relief/s or notching for sparkplug clearance, all of which reduce compression ratio.

Valve-to-Piston Clearance

The valve-to-piston clearance should be no less than 0.100 in. in the axial direction with steel or titanium rods. Add another 0.020-in. clearance for aluminum rods.

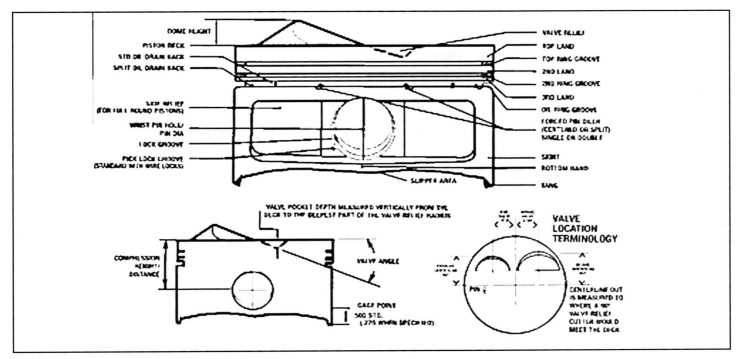

This drawing illustrates just about every piston feature and dimension. Become familiar with these terms and specifications when ordering or using pistons.

Note gas ports in top ring land (arrows). Top ring grooves and adjacent lands are anodized to reduce wear.

You may want to add another 0.020 in. to the exhaust valves for extra insurance for a drag engine in case of a missed shifted. Clearance at the edge of both valves should be 0.050-in. Check valve clearances using a dial indicator—most accurate method—or clay during preassembly. If the valve reliefs need enlarging or re-positioning, use a fixture—piston vise—to secure each piston and a cutter

that's 0.100-in. larger than the valve to give the needed 0.050-in. radial clearance to the valve head. So if the valve in question is 2.125 in., use a 2.225-in. cutter.

Ring Belt

From the top down to the skirt is the ring belt, which is made up of the ring lands and grooves. The outside diameter of the ring belt is slightly smaller than the skirt to ensure the rings and not the ring lands contact the bore. Stating at the top, the ring belt consists of the first ring land, top compression-ring groove, second ring land, second ring land, second compression-ring groove and, finally, the oil-ring groove. Because pressure buildup between the two compression rings tries to unseat the top ring from its ring land and cause ring flutter, an accumulator groove may be cut into the second ring land. This groove adds volume

between the first and second compression rings, creating a damping chamber to slow combustion pressure buildup from blowby past the top compression ring. The damping action also reduces blowby that would otherwise continue past the second compression ring and oil ring.

Gas Ports

Gas ports are used to route pressure directly to the backside of the top ring. These are a must for sealing low-tension compression rings. Gas porting is done one of two ways: Typically 12 or so evenly spaced small-diameter holes are drilled vertically from the top down that intersect the back side of the top ring groove or eight or so slots milled horizontally in the top of the top ring groove. Vertical gas ports are preferred for drag racing and the horizontal, or lateral, gas ports are more common in road

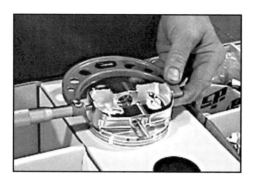
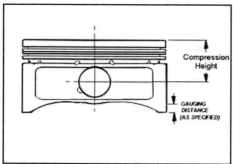

Measure pistons the instant you receive them. Check compression height and volume, too. You won't have any more time than now to get a problem corrected. After checking manufacturer's gage point, Allan checks diameter using specifications supplied by CP Pistons. Drawing courtesy CP Pistons

Ugly things occur such as piston scuffing when an engine leans under sustained full power. A thermal barrier will delay this, but not prevent it under extreme conditions.

and circle-track racing. Gas ports give direct route for a quicker pressure buildup behind the top ring when a tight 0.0010-in. ring-to-groove side clearance is used.

Piston Volume

The piston volume consists of the valve reliefs and dome, which may add or subtract volume. To find piston volume, start with the desired compression to calculate total clearance volume, or total combustion-chamber volume at TDC, pages 157–158. Subtract combustion chamber, piston deck clearance and head-gasket thickness volumes from clearance volume to find piston volume. Order pistons based on this figure. But if you're in doubt, specify a lower volume and expect to do some machine work. You can always remove material from the top of a piston, but you can't add it. This is a good way to go if your goal is to achieve an exact compression ratio. Consequently, check piston volume soon after you receive the pistons to confirm they are what you ordered, particularly if you have to enlarge the valve reliefs, page 158. If you must machine the top of the piston for any reason, check

thickness. Don't go any thinner than 0.200 in. without consulting your piston manufacturer.

Skirt

Piston-to-bore clearance should be that specified by the piston manufacturer or information you've gained through dyno or track testing. Skirts, with help from the rings, stabilize the piston to keep it from rocking in the bore so ring sealing is maintained. This is particularly critical when running low-tension rings. So minimum piston-to-bore clearance is desired, providing there is enough to prevent scuffing. When sizing a bore, measure piston diameter at the gage point, which is usually 0.500 in. up from bottom of the skirt. Refer to the manufacturer's recommendation for exactly where to measure. With the piston sitting upside down on a bench and not in your hot hand, measure the piston at room temperature.

Typical bore clearance for drag, road or circle track racing is 0.0040–0.0055 in. This works out to be approximately 0.0012 in. for each 1.000 in. of bore diameter. As bore size increases, more clearance is needed to allow for expansion of

Coated piston includes Calico's CT-2 thermal barrier up top and CT-3 low-friction coating on skirts.

the larger-diameter piston. Boat-racing engines or those with filled blocks (HardBlok) require another 0.0005-in. clearance for a 4.00-in. bore. Even though you should use minimum clearance, use an initial clearance so final piston-to-bore running clearance will be enough to ensure the piston won't expand beyond the size of the bore and thin hydrodynamic oil film. Be aware, though, clearances can be reduced if pistons are coated,

Casidiam coated pin retained by wire locks must have 45° x 0.040-in. chamfers at ends.

TruArc retainers must be installed with radiused edges against end of pin and sharp edge facing out. Two retainers at each end may be used.

particularly thermal coatings, or are cooled with an oil spray. Work with your piston manufacturer or information you gained through dynamometer or track testing to determine piston-to-bore clearance.

Piston Coatings

Coatings for pistons are used on the tops, skirts and ring grooves. Precoated pistons are available from manufacturers or you can have them coated by a specialist.

A ceramic thermal barrier applied to piston tops has many advantages. It reduces the transfer of combustion heat into the pistons. This improves efficiency, reduces piston expansion, oil temperature and possible piston failure in the event of a cooling or air/fuel mixture malfunction.

For the skirts, piston manufacturers and coating specialists offer PTFE (Teflon), moly (MoS_2), graphite, electroless nickel or anodizing for skirts under various trade names. Coatings and platings are used alone or in combination to reduce friction, scuffing and increase oil retention. Friction reduction is particularly significant because skirt friction contributes

about 7% of power lost from the combined power losses of an engine. Mahle determined this from motoring tests—monitoring power needed to drive an engine. They isolated various engine components and systems to determine power lost from each such as ring drag and pumping losses.

During preassembly, check that there is sufficient crankshaft counterweight-to-skirt clearance. There should be at least 0.060 in. between the counterweights and skirts. I caution you about this because of the numerous crankshaft and stroke combinations. Don't assume there won't be a clearance problem.

Wrist-Pin Bore

The central structure of a piston is the pin boss, which transmits forces between the wrist pin, piston top and skirt. These forces are constantly changing in magnitude and direction during the four engine cycles. Centered in the pin boss of a racing piston is the wrist-pin bore, which typically accommodates a 0.927-in. diameter pin, although they range from lighter

0.912-in. pins and to heavier 1.156-in. pins for blown applications.

Unlike OEM piston-pin bores, racing piston pins are not offset simply because quiet engine operation is not a priority, and for practical reasons. Full-floating pins are the racing standard. Although pressed pins—non-floating pins—are easily installed by heating the small end of the rod to expand it and sliding pin in, it cannot be removed without pressing it out, overstressing the piston-pin boss. Pressed pins also slow piston R&R, which is usually a matter of a convenience, albeit important when refreshing or doing preassembly checks.

Without a press fit in the small end of a connecting rod, wrist-pin retention is done with spiro locks, wire lock or TruArc retainers installed in a groove at each end of the pin. Aluminum buttons can also be used. If you are in a situation where pistons have to be changed quickly, buttons are an alternative to locks. If the pin bore intersects the oil ring groove, you must use buttons or rail supports. Buttons for this application are grooved to bridge the sections of the oil ring grooves removed as a result of high pin-bore placement, providing support for the oil rings. If you prefer using pin locks, then you'll have to use rail supports. In this case the oil-ring groove must be widened 0.030 in. to accept the support.

When ordering pistons, specify the type of locks or buttons so they will accompany the pistons. If you have the option, I recommend you use wire locks because of superior

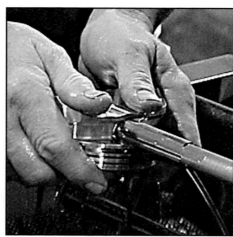

Measure pin bore and hone to size with light pressure and lots of coolant. Check pin-bore size frequently.

pin retention. When compared to spiro locks, wire locks are easier—I didn't say *easy*—to install and remove. As for TruArcs, they are relatively easy to install, but they must be installed in a specific direction against the end of the pin. Also, there are pistons that require two TruArcs be used at each end of the pin.

Oil is drained from the ring groove through a series of evenly spaced holes drilled radially through the backside of the oil-ring groove. These holes drain oil from the oil-ring groove to the crankcase. Two of these holes are drilled at each side of the pin bore so they intersect the top for lubricating the wrist pin. They either join and enter the pin bore at the center top of the pin bore or individually a few degrees to each side. To enhance wrist-pin lubrication, the pin bore may be grooved.

Pin Fitting—Fitted wrist pins may or may not be included with the pistons. Considering the wide array of pins available, you may prefer to purchase pins separately and do your own fitting. This being the case, hone the pin bore to give the wrist pins 0.0008—0.0015-in. clearance or whatever the piston manufacturer recommends.

Using a connecting rod reconditioning machine, measure piston pin-bore diameter on the bore gauge. Compare pin-bore diameter to that of a wrist pin. Once you know how much material needs to be removed, set up the honing mandrel with stones and guide shoes, then hone the bore to size as shown.

While using light pressure and 320 rpm spindle speed, monitor the honing dial as you stroke the piston back and forth. Flood the piston with honing oil to keep it cool and free of honing particles. Check pin-bore diameter frequently. Once you've approached the desired bore size, check wrist-pin fit. If the pin feels tight, recheck bore diameter, continue honing and recheck. When pin feel is good, leave that pin with the piston and size the next piston using the same procedure.

PISTON RINGS
Ring Basics

Although they help stabilize the piston, the primary function of the piston rings is to seal the piston to the bore during all four strokes, the power stroke being the most critical. There are two seals: a dynamic seal at the bore and a static seal at the piston. The top compression ring has the primary job of sealing combustion pressure. The second ring seals pressure that escapes past the top ring and controls oil that passes the oil ring. At the bottom, the oil ring has one job; remove oil from the bore, leaving just enough for lubricating and sealing the compression rings.

Dimensions—The two dimensions describing the cross section of a compression ring are *axial height*, or width, and *radial thickness*. Axial height is the smallest dimension of the ring, or ring-groove width less ring-groove side clearance. A ring with an axial height of 1/16 in. is listed as a 1/16-in. ring. Radial thickness is the distance from the face of the ring—surface contacting the bore wall—to the back side of the ring.

Making up the axial and radial dimensions of an oil ring are the two rails with an expander/spacer separating them. Radial thickness is the portion of the expander that hooks behind the rails added to the radial thickness of the rails. Axial height of an oil ring is made up of the rails and expander/spacer axial heights as installed in the ring groove.

Twist—To improve top ring sealing to the piston, it deflects up when compressed in the bore. This slight bend, or *torsional twist*, is created by chamfering the inside

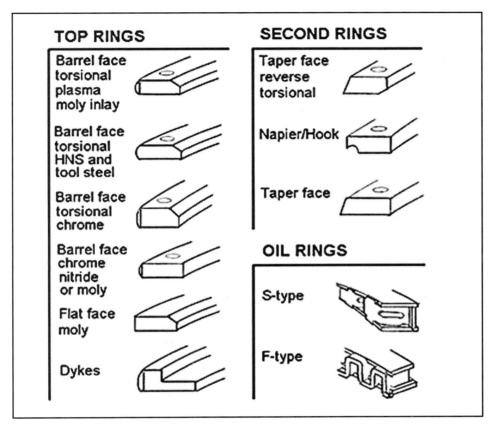

Common ring shapes: Barrel-faced with a torsional twist are most frequently used in the top groove with a bevel with a reverse twist or Napier face in the second groove.

top corner of the ring to weaken it at the top. When loaded from combustion pressure the ring is forced down flat against the bottom of the groove, or ring land, with most pressure being exerted at the inside corner of the ring. This provides a superior ring-to-piston static seal.

The second compression ring, which is really an oil control ring, is chamfered at the bottom inside corner, causing it to deflect down, or have a reverse twist, when compressed. As the piston travels down the bore, the ring is forced up against the ring land, creating a better ring-to-piston oil seal.

Face Shape—The top compression ring typically uses a radiused face. This large radius, or barrel face or D-shape, ensures good ring-to-bore contact as the compression ring flexes during high-speed load reversals. The second ring typically uses a taper face or Napier face. The taper face, shaped similar to the edge of a gasket scraper, removes oil from the bore wall on the down stroke. A Napier face is has a hook shape at the bottom edge to improve oil removal.

Material—The most common base metal used for compression rings is cast iron. Ductile cast iron is preferred for most racing applications because of the higher strength and flexibility compared to plain cast iron. However, with the move toward lighter and thinner rings, steel is the best choice for some applications. For the second compression ring, plain cast iron remains the most popular.

When a ring is listed as a chrome, moly or nitrided, the reference is to the face material and not the base material of the ring. Plasma-sprayed moly—molydenum—filled racing rings have been the standard for years. Molydenum, nickel and a chromium compound in powder form is sprayed in the form of molten droplets onto the edge of the ring, "welding" it to the base metal. But there are applications where moly rings should not be used such as dirt-track and off-road racing. Just as moly carries oil well, the same applies to dirt, causing the ring to become abrasive much like a fine honing stone. Similarly, a moly ring should not be used in a blown or turbocharged engine because the thermal shock would cause the moly filling to flake off. In such cases, a chrome-faced or hardened ring should be used.

Chrome-faced rings have been in use for years, however ring faces hardened by gas-nitriding are becoming the preferred choice. This is particularly true with very thin rings where there's insufficient surface width for sprayed moly to adhere. So expect to see the availability of gas-nitrided rings to increase.

In addition to base material and facing treatment, some applications require coated rings. For instance, top rings for an alcohol-burning engine should be hardened and coated with manganese to ensure lubrication. Likewise, phosphate coated cast-iron ring should be used in the second groove.

File Fit—Pre-gapped rings are available, however it is best to use file-fit rings. By fitting and filing the rings, you will be assured the

RING TENSION & ENGINE EFFICIENCY

Responsible for nearly 10% of the parasitic losses of an engine, *ring drag*—friction created by rings moving in the bore—is worth a reducing, providing ring sealing is maintained. Imagine the effort you would put forth to get a similar power increase? Consequently, methods of reducing ring drag has gotten considerable attention from both OEM and aftermarket manufacturers. Reducing ring drag improves engine efficiency—increased power for the fuel burned. From dyno testing, this translates to a reduction—improvement—in BSFC (Brake Specific Fuel Consumption) expressed in pound of fuel burned per hour per horsepower (lb/hp-hr). So if a back-to-back run on the dyno shows a drop from 0.47 lb/hp-hr to 0.45 lb/hp-hr at peak torque, engine efficiency has been improved.

Ring drag against a bore wall is directly proportional to the force applied by the ring to the cylinder wall. The major contributor to this force is *ring tension*, which is the tangential force needed to compress a piston ring to a specified bore diameter. Second is combustion pressure. Higher tension causes the ring-to-cylinder wall force to be higher. Combined with ring tension needed to seal the top compression ring is combustion pressure. This pressure forces the ring down against the bottom of the ring groove, sealing it to the piston and harder against the cylinder wall.

Top Ring Tension—The beauty of the top compression ring is it is only needed during the power stroke. So by reducing ring tension and routing combustion pressure more directly to the back side of it through the use of gas-porting the piston, ring sealing is achieved during the critical power stroke while ring drag is reduced during the other three strokes. The consequence of this is a major reduction in power loss and bore wear from ring drag.

Tension is reduced by thinning a ring or narrowing its radial width. For example, a standard top compression ring for a 4.00-in. bore is 1/16-in. (0.0625-in.) thick and 0.187-in. wide for a tension of 19—22-lb. To reduce tension, a ring can be backcut, or narrowed. A backcut 1/16-in. ring that may have a 0.160-in. radial width. Ring thickness of 1.5mm (0.59 in.), 1.2mm (0.47 in.), 0.043 in. and, in extreme cases, 0.8mm (0.31 in.) are available, but gas porting is required with light- or ultra-low-tension rings.

Coupled with gas porting, lighter low-tension rings are an important factor in reducing ring flutter, and a lighter ring doesn't make much difference in terms of total reciprocating weight. But a little less weight here and a little less there adds up, allowing an engine to accelerate quicker and, in some cases, produce more power, particularly if ring flutter is reduced or eliminated.

Second Ring Tension—A backcut second ring is usually supplied with a backcut top ring except where the oil ring needs help with oil control. Such is the case when a low-tension oil ring is used with a wet-sump oiling system that has little or no crankcase evacuation. In such a case, it is probably best to use the wider ring in the second groove.

In certain applications it is possible to eliminate the second compression ring, or at least set it up so there is little or no tension if rules require a second ring. If a second ring is required, an oil ring rail is sometimes used. But doing either requires a very efficient crankcase-evacuation system and tolerance to some oil loss.

Oil Ring Tension—These create approximately 60% of total ring drag, so most gain will be made by reducing oil-ring tension. But just as with the second ring, an ultra-low-tension oil ring can only be used with a system that reduces crankcase pressure. How much tension can be taken out of oil ring tension depends on the effectiveness of the oiling/evacuation system. These range from exhaust scavenged wet-sump to six-stage dry sump systems that can pull from 8-in.Hg to 20-in.Hg of vacuum, respectively. The lower the pressure, or higher the vacuum, means more tolerance to lower ring tension.

To choose a ring pack for your engine, work with an aftermarket piston-ring supplier. Before you do, look through ring and piston catalogs to get an idea of what is available and what is recommended, then gather as much information you can glean from fellow competitors. This will give you a general idea of what rings tension to use in your engine.

ring-end gaps will be correct for your engine. Just exactly how much gap a ring should have is covered in pre-assembly, pages 160–161.

Ring Package

The most common racing ring package is a 1/16-in. top compression ring, 1/16-in. second compression ring and a 3/16-in. oil-control ring. The top ring will be a plasma-moly faced ductile cast-iron ring with a torsional twist and a barrel-face. As pictured, the 1/16-in. cast-iron second ring has a taper face and reverse twist. In the bottom groove is a 3/16-in. oil ring, consisting of two chrome-faced steel rails and an expander/spacer. The sole function of the oil ring is to control, or meter, oil needed to lubricate and seal the compression rings. The rest is channeled back to the oil sump.

To illustrate how far the "envelope has been pushed," a typical endurance racing engine such as that used for circle track or road racing uses light, ultra-low-tension rings. These have been developed along with coatings, dry sump lubrication, many hours of dyno and track testing. Be aware, though, that an engine so equipped must be refreshed frequently, or after every race.

A typical ring pack starts with a torsional-twist 0.8mm (0.031-in.) steel top ring with a titanium-nitrided face installed in a gas-ported piston. In the second groove is a reverse-twist 0.8mm (0.031-in.) cast-iron ring with a Napier face. In the third groove is a 2.8mm (0.118-in.) ultra-low tension three-piece stainless-steel

ring oil ring that, along with dry sump oiling, provides adequate oil control with minimum drag. The complete ring pack and piston assembly benefits from Nikasil coated cylinders that has high oil retention and a low friction coefficient of about 0.1.

Low friction and ring drag is dramatic. Typical ring drag for a conventional wet-sump oiling system is 12 pounds. Compare this to low-tension rings for a dry-sump system at 4 pounds drag.

For special applications, Dykes or *headland* rings are used in the top groove. Similar, but different, these L-shaped rings are wide at the face, but have a thin longitudinal thickness for the groove. This lightens the ring while retaining a thick face. Additionally, the thick section behind the face increases the area for combustion pressure to seal the ring. Unique to the headland ring is exposure to the burning air/fuel mixture. The top of the ring at the outer periphery is not covered by the top ring land, but is within 0.0625 in. of the piston top, which nearly eliminates the dead space that would otherwise exist at the outer periphery of the piston.

Gapless rings were first offered by Total Seal. Childs & Albert followed up with their Zero-Gap second ring (ZGS). Used in the second groove only, the feature of a "gapless" ring is obvious: no gap, almost no leakage, or blowby. The debates continue as to whether or not this is an advantage, but some engine builders have shown gains. To achieve the no-gap feature, Total Seal actually uses two rings; a ductile-iron ring fitted with a rail

Wire lock installed with chamfered pin. Chamfer forces wire lock into groove more securely as pin moves in bore. Relief at edge of pin bore allows access for easy lock removal.

in the same groove. One installs on top of the other with gaps staggered 180° to so one ring covers the gap of the other and vice versa, thus no gap. Childs & Albert achieves a similar affect by thinning each end of the ring, one on top and the other on the bottom, so they overlap. This allows the ring to expand and contract without opening a gap.

WRIST PINS

There are a lot of choices when specifying wrist pins. This is best done when you order pistons even though you may choose another source for the pins. Start with pin diameter and length, which obviously must match the piston. Other features include material, coating, end treatment and internal shape. The most popular steel alloy is 9310, a high-nickel alloy steel, followed by titanium. Titanium piston pins must be coated with a diamond-like coating (DLC) to prevent galling, however steel pins

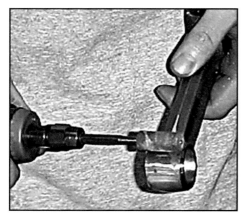

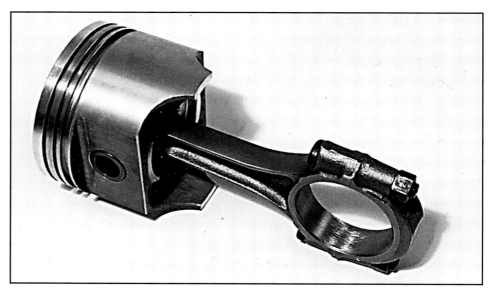

Shot-peened, reconditioned rod fitted with SPS bolts that is assembled to piston is ready for rings and installation into engine. Pin is retained with press-fit.

How racing rods used to be prepared: Beams and small ends were ground smooth, then shot-peened. Ready for shot-peening, cap is secured to rod with hardware bolts.

can be coated if you are using connecting rods *with or without* bushings for reduced pin-to-bore friction. Depending on size, an equivalent titanium wrist pin weighs over 20 grams less than a steel pin, which reduces reciprocating weight significantly.

The ends must have a 45° x 0.040-in. chamfer when retained with wire locks. Square ends are for spiro lock or TruArc retainers. The ID finish can be straight or tapered for lightening—thinned from the center toward each end. Not only should the outer pin surface be super finished to improve durability, so must the ID have a smooth finish for improved fatigue strength.

CONNECTING RODS

Connecting rods don't make horsepower, but if one should fail…! As one driver related when asked what happened after loud noises came from under the hood, smoke out the pipes and a trail of oil spewed down on the track, he said, "Something important broke in the engine." That something important was a connecting rod. Although rare, connecting rods break. For your part, do whatever it takes to keep this from happening. One broken rod bolt can ruin your day.

The wide availability of high-performance connecting rods from the aftermarket or factories at reasonable cost has virtually ended the need to prepare a stock rod for racing. This doesn't eliminate basic inspection and reconditioning processes, but the need to grind, polish, shot peen, drill oil holes, prep the small end for a floating pin and install high-strength bolts has become a thing of the past. Instead, the job boils down to choosing a high-performance connecting rod for your engine.

Rod Length

As detailed earlier in the chapter, connecting rod length-to-stroke ratio can have a significant impact on the durability of your engine. Given that, rod length—the distance between big-end and small-end bore centers—is one of the first specifications you should establish. Using crankshaft stroke, block deck height and piston-pin height, determine rod length that will give a minimum length-to-stroke ratio of 1.70:1. With this information, you can now work with a supplier to find a connecting rod of this or longer length that should work well in your engine.

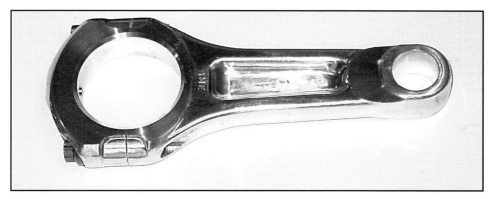

An example of an aluminum racing rod. it's main advantage over steel is lighter weight—up to 64%—but it sacrifices strength. Photo by Larry Shepard.

Material

Although connecting rods are or have been made from as many as six basic materials, you have three to choose from. The most popular is forged steel, followed by aluminum and titanium. For anything but drag racing, aluminum is out. The choice then becomes steel or titanium, depending on racing rules or funds.

Aluminum—Forged from 7075 aluminum and heat treated to the T6 condition, this is the aluminum alloy used for connecting rods. The ultimate tensile strength—point at which it breaks—of 7075 T6 is 83,000 psi. The main feature of an aluminum rod is light weight, or 64% less than steel. But an aluminum rod has about 50% less strength than E4043 steel. This requires that an aluminum connecting rod have a much larger cross section than a steel or titanium rod. Consequently, an aluminum rod must have much more room to clear the crankcase and camshaft. This means the block either has or can be modified to provide needed clearance. Also, 50% more clearance is needed to the deck and valves to allow for additional rod stretch. And although an equivalent volume of

aluminum is much lighter than steel, about half of the weight advantage is lost due to the need to maintain strength by increasing size. There is some weight reduction, although the major advantage is the shock-absorbing quality of aluminum when used with blown or nitrous drag engines.

Steel—The two most popular steel alloys used for forged or billet steel connecting rods is 4130 and 4340. The most common material for racing rods is E4340 steel, a high tensile-strength chrome-moly steel. Chromium and molybdenum content is 0.9% and 0.3%, respectively. E4340 also contains 0.4% carbon and 1.78% nickel. Obtained by oil quenching and tempering, E4340 steel rods will have tensile strength of up to 186,000 psi. This is the key. Any problem with a steel rod is usually due to improper heat treat. Because hardness has a direct relationship to tensile strength, an excellent way to determine strength is to check hardness. Using a Rockwell hardness tester and specifications that accompanied the rods, check hardness of your rods. Expect 29—36 Rc with an E4340 steel rod.

The 4130 rod is perfectly

adequate for lower horsepower classes. It is also less expensive. With a content of 1.0% chrome, 0.2% moly, 0.3% carbon and no nickel, a 4130 rod will have a tensile strength of 132,000 psi, or about 8% less than a 4340 rod. After water quenching and tempering, hardness will be approximately 27 Rc.

A third steel alloy used to manufacturer steel connecting rods is Carillo's proprietary Carrilloloy. Similar to E4340, this steel is alloyed with vanadium to increase hardness, strength and toughness. To what degree I can't say, however the success of Carrillo rods speaks for itself.

Shot-peening increases the fatigue strength of a steel connecting rod by about 35%. This involves impacting the surface with cast-steel shot to compress it, reducing the chance surface cracking and eventual failure. The procedure for shot-peening connecting rods is based on the Society of Automotive Engineers' (SAE) standard J442/J443. Here, #230 cast-steel shot is blasted with 95% minimum coverage on a smooth surface using the Almen arc-height of 0.012—0.015 in. Almen arc-height is a standard that refers to the height shot bounces off an Almen test strip, or 0.012—0.015 in. in this case.

Titanium—About 35% lighter than steel, titanium connecting rods are worth your consideration given the performance advantage they have. With a content of 6% aluminum and 4% vanadium, Ti-6AI-4V is an Alpha-Beta alloy, meaning it is heat treatable, an important factor with any forging.

FORGED VS. BILLET

The term billet has been used as a marketing tool for years to sell performance parts. But a billet this or that is simply a part produced by machining it directly from steel, aluminum or titanium round, square or flat stock, be it a crankshaft or connecting rod. The process is much like a sculptor chipping out a figure from a chunk of granite until all material that doesn't look like the finished product is removed. Forging, on the other hand, is a two-step process. It also starts with a billet. But the billet is forced into the basic shape of the intended part. The forging is then machined where necessary to produce the finished part. The primary purpose of forging is not done to reduce machining time and waste stock, but to produce a part where grain flow follows the shape of the part, allowing it to withstand higher stresses. This is critical when a highly stressed part is reduced to the lightest weight possible. An example is a bolt with rolled threads compared to one with cut threads of the same size; rolled threads are stronger. So when comparing parts, particularly those considered to be lightweight, the forged part is superior to the billet part.

One downside to titanium connecting rods is cost. Both the material and manufacturing techniques are more expensive. Secondly, titanium doesn't have the fatigue strength of steel, so they

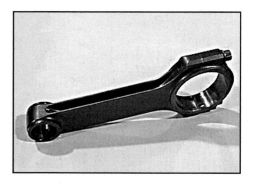

Classic H-beam from Carrillo. The H-beam design is made possible by turning the beam 90°, making it a wide-beam flange.

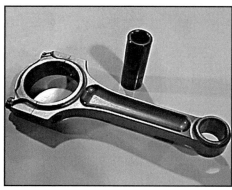

Lentz A-beam rod is a variation of the I-beam rod. Matte finish is from shot peening. Note lack of bushing in the small end and Casidiam coated titanium pin.

Failure wasn't fault of connecting rod, but oil starvation that led to bearing and rod seizure. Note journal galling from spun bearing in adjacent rod.

have a shorter service life. But if you are willing to replace the rods periodically in trade-off for improved performance gained from lower rotating and reciprocating inertia, titanium is the way to go.

Beam Shape

There are two basic types of connecting rods: H-beam and I-beam. The classic H-beam connecting rod introduced by Carrillo was the recognized race rod. I-beam rods were considered to be OEM pieces. However, aftermarket I-beam rods are now used with equivalent success. As a result, quality H-beam and I-beam rods are interchangeable in racing engines, making the one you choose a matter of personal preference.

The connecting rod is basically a column with pivoting ends, one at the big end and one at the small end. So it makes sense that the beam should have a section modulus that is stronger—resistant to bending—in that direction, which the I-beam satisfies. Providing the connecting rods are correctly inspected and assembled, the only time a connecting rod beam fails will be due to some

other failure occurring first such as a seized rod bearing or dropped valve. Also, claims have been made that one beam shape has less drag in the crankcase, but this has yet to be proven. Any power advantage one beam shape has over the over is less than the repeatability of dyno-testing. So concentrate on choosing a quality connecting rod rather than a particular beam type.

Small End

How you treat the small end depends on whether you are using a pressed pin or a full-floating pin. For whatever reason, if you must

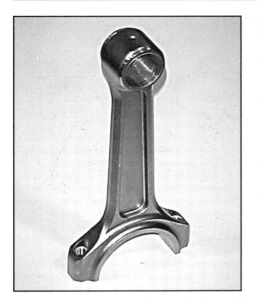

Carrillo A-beam rod with bushed small end and chamfered oil hole for pin lubrication.

H-beam rod uses one hole per side drilled at about 45° from bottom for pin oiling.

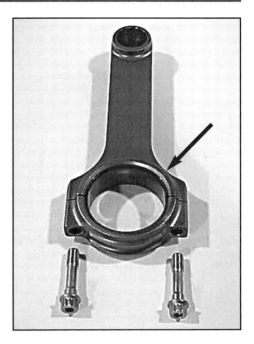

Cap fitted to dowels of H-beam rod. Note ARP rod bolts and large chamfer needed to clear 1/8-in. rod-journal fillet (arrow).

use pressed pins, a 0.0010-in. + or − 0.0005 in. press fit is required in the small end. For example, for a pin measuring 0.9270 in., pin bore ID should be 0.9260 in. But if you're among the majority that uses full-floating pins, the small end should be bushed and honed to provide about 0.001-in. pin-to-bore clearance. The exception is when DLC-coated pins are used with steel rods. Unbushed rods can be used without the danger of galling when fitted to DLC-coated pins. This is not so with titanium because of the tendency of the material to galling. Titanium rods must be bushed.

As for small-end diameter, match it with the piston-pin bore, They must be bushed. Spec your rods accordingly.

Oiling—Different methods are used to lubricate full-floating pins. One is to depend on splash lubrication and a hole drilled in line with the rod and chamfered at the top of the small end with an I-beam rod or one hole drilled 45° at each side between the flanges of an H-beam rod. The second method uses a hole/s drilled from the big end to the small end that routes pressurized oil from the big end to the pin bore. Which way you go depends on how dry the crankcase will be. If wet-sump oiling or a dry-sump system with piston-cooling squirters will be used, splash lubrication may be adequate. If you are in doubt, though, go with connecting rods that provide pressure lubrication to the small end.

Big End

In this imperfect world, the big end of the connecting rod must be split in order to assemble it to the crank pin. This means the separate cap must be held securely to the rod, requiring more than your average off-the-shelf Grade 8 bolts, rather highly specialized aircraft-grade bolts. Positioning the cap is done by either the bolts or hollow dowels fitted to counterbores in the rod and cap that are concentric with the bolt holes.

Both ends of the big-end bore are chamfered, but one with a much wider chamfer. The larger chamfer

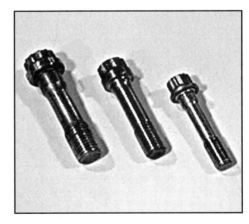

Twelve-point head 7/16-, 3/8- and 5/16-in. rod bolts, or cap screws. Necked-down ground sections provide stretch for accurate tightening and reduced stress at the transition point between the head and threads.

provides clearance to the large bearing-journal fillet radius. At the cap parting line are bearing-tang reliefs, one in the cap and one in the rod. As you receive the rods, they will be honed to size. Check them to ensure they are what you specified and that bore size matches specifications for retaining the bearings.

Rod Bolts

Other than the valves and valve springs, the most critical components in an engine are the connecting rod bolts. Failure of either one of these usually means catastrophic engine failure. For rod bolts, this typically occurs when the rods are stressed in tension to the maximum, or just after the piston goes over TDC during the intake/exhaust overlap period. The crank pin pulls the rod-and-piston assembly down against the inertia of the whole assembly when pressure in the cylinder is lowest, creating maximum tension load on the rod. Failure is signaled by that dreaded puff of blue smoke out the exhaust as the car enters a turn and a rod bolt snaps.

You can prevent the above from happening by choosing rod bolts wisely, then being relentless as a Marine Corps DI during in-spection. Rod manufacturers provide information and support necessary to ensure inspection and installation are done correctly. They know from experience that if a rod failure occurs, it will be rod-bolt related due to an error made during inspection or installation.

Other than a minor bending stress that occurs when the rod is in tension and compression as the big-end bore distorts to a slight oval shape, the only additional load a rod bolt should see is static tension from tightening during install-ation. This makes it critical that rod bolts are preloaded as accurately as possible, or about 80% of yield strength. This

> ### HYDROGEN EMBRITTLEMENT
>
> Sometimes referred to as *corrosion stress,* hydrogen embrittlement is an evil thing that happens to the surface of some high-strength steels, titanium alloys and aluminum alloys. When a part made of one of these materials is subjected to high tensile stress under adverse conditions such as high temperature, hydrogen enters its surface. The resulting reaction causes the surface to become brittle, thus the term hydrogen embrittlement. This reduces the fatigue strength of the part, which leads to cracking and eventual failure if it remains in service. Because it is not fully understood, hydrogen embrittlement is hard to detect. Consequently, the only way to prevent such a part from failure is to replace it periodically or use a material that's not susceptible to hydrogen embrittlement.

eliminates cyclical stress, which also eliminates fatigue stress and ultimate bolt failure. So a bolt that is not tightened enough will break before one that is over-tightened providing the bearing doesn't spin first. This is caused by bearing crush being relieved as the bolts stretch, allowing the cap to separate from the rod.

Bolt and/or Nut—ARP and SPS are the recognized connecting-rod bolt suppliers to the racing industry. They maintain minimum aircraft/aerospace-industry or better standards, apply these standards and needs to the needs of the racer. They know what it takes to hold things together in the most adverse conditions.

The two basic rod-bolt config-urations are bolts and nuts or just bolts. Bolts with nuts are used with OEM-style rods, however the OEMs are moving toward bolt-only type rods. With the nut-and-bolt setup, the bolts drop down through holes in the rod, into the cap and are secured by nuts. Racing rods use bolts only that are inserted up through the cap into threaded holes in the connecting

rod. This setup allows a smoother transition from the rod beam to the big end by eliminating flats on the rod, which eliminates two stress risers. Another advantage: Without two nuts and additional bolt length needed to engage them, rod-assembly weight is reduced.

If you must use a connecting rod with bolts and nuts, ARP and SPS offer high-strength bolts. These 8740 chrome-moly bolts are available in tensile strengths ranging from 176,000 psi to 220,000 psi. You also have a choice between the stock-type knurled shank or ARP's Wave-Loc design. Both have heads designed for the specific rod and shanks formed so they fit tightly in the bolt holes to position the cap to the rod. The Wave-Loc shank reduces stress risers introduced by knurled shanks. ARP and SPS bolts are dimpled at each end to accom-modate a stretch gage to check for correct bolt tightness.

Bolt-only configurations are available with several high-strength materials, but are similar in design. Twelve-point flanged heads are used with reduced shanks, rolled

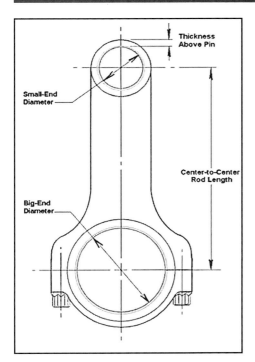

Three main dimensions of a connecting rod to be concerned with are overall length, big-end and small-end diameters. Others are widths at big and small ends.

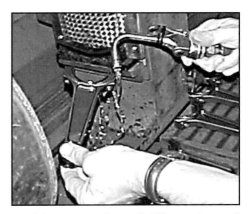

Magnetic-particle inspection begins with magnetizing connecting rod. When using wet technique, flow fluorescent magnetic particles suspended in liquid over the rod. Particles will be attracted to any cracks.

threads and dimpled ends. Materials include the popular SAE class H-11 high-strength bolts with up to 260,000-psi tensile strength. These bolts need to be changed periodically due to their tendency to stress corrode—become hydrogen embrittled—when operating at or above 250°F.

To reduce stress-induced hydrogen embrittlement, SPS developed Multiphase bolts for use in gas-turbine engines. These bolts can operate in temperatures of up to 1,100°F. Resistance to stress corrosion was accomplished through age hardening and the use of 36% cobalt to block hydrogen from entering the surface of the material. The Multiphase alloy also includes nickel, chromium, molybdenum and iron, resulting in a bolt that is capable of 260,000-psi tensile strength.

Rod Inspection and Reconditioning

As with all parts that go into the building of a racing engine, both new and used connecting rods should be inspected. If an engine comes apart because you installed a flawed part that you neglected to inspect, it's your fault. So take every piece you install in an engine through every inspection and, if needed, reconditioning. If you find any new connecting rods that aren't "perfect" while making the following checks, work with the manufacturer to determine how to resolve the problem.

Upon receiving a set of connecting rods, make sure you got what you ordered. Thoroughly clean the rods and bolts, then do a visual inspection. Check that the small end is bushed, if required, pin-oiling holes are where they should be and the bolts are correct. Check color, too. A used rod that has been blued from a spun bearing will probably be in the annealed condition and the big end badly scored. Such a rod requires heat treating, shot blasting, big end honed and bolts replaced before it can be reused.

Don't be concerned about ten thousandths at this point, so use dial or digital-readout calipers to measure big-end and small-end diameters. You can check the big-end diameter across the parting line, so the cap doesn't have to be on for this measurement. Check also the distance from the bottom of the big end bore to the bottom of the small end bore. Add this figure to one-half of each bore diameter to get rod length. For example, if the distance between the bottom of the bores is 4.774 in. and the diameters measure 0.928 in. and 2.225 in., half of each bore is 0.464 in. and 1.112 in. respectively. Rod length is 4.774 in. + 0.464 in. + 1.112 in. = 6.35 in. If you ordered a 6.35-in. rod for a 0.927-in. pin and a 2.100-in. bearing journal and all other things are OK, you have the correct rods. In case you are wondering, the 2.225-in. big-end bore allows for the bearing and oil clearance for a 2.100-in. journal, which is how a connecting rod is specified.

Check big-end width with your micrometers. Using a telescoping gage and micrometers, measure the distance between the thrust faces of a crankshaft bearing-journal throw.

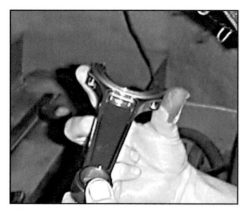

View rod in darkened area with a black light. Fluorescent particles will highlight cracks on or slightly below the surface. A cracked rod or bolt is useful only as a paperweight. Toss it in the junk bin or, in the case of a new one, back to the manufacturer.

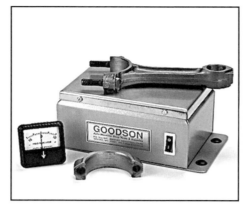

After putting rod through the MPI process, demagnetize it. This prevents it from collecting metal debris that would otherwise be filtered out by the oiling system. Field indicator is used to check for magnetism.

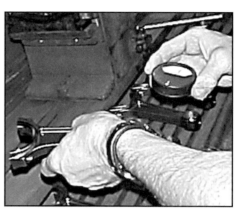

Check that the part is demagnetized. If magnetism is indicated by swinging needle, demagnetize parts again.

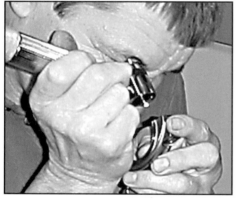

Allan checks cap closely using magnifier and light that looks like something the doctor would use to look in your ear.

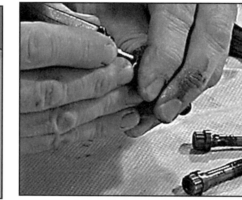

Mark all parts so you can keep a record of them in your notes, even the bolts. Bob etches numbers on the heads of these bolts.

Double the reading you got for rod width and subtract it from bearing-journal throw width. The result should be rod side clearance, or 0.0015—0.0020 in. for steel and titanium rods and double that amount for aluminum rods.

Crack Inspection—Check the rods and bolts for cracks. The best method is by magnetic-particle inspection, or Magnafluxing. Pressed-in rod bolts will have to be removed. If you can't tap out the bolts with a plastic mallet while holding the rod in your hand, use a rod vise to hold it.

Using either the dry or wet method, first magnetize the rod or bolt, then sprinkle colored magnetic particles or flow liquid-carrying magnetic particles onto it. Dry particles with a contrasting color to the part are more visible in exposing cracks. With the wet method, view the part under a black light to expose cracks. Fluorescent particles light cracks. It's best to view the bolts through a magnifying glass. Using zero tolerance, discard any rod or bolt

that is cracked. Otherwise, wash off the magnetic particles, set the part aside with the good rods or bolts and continue checking. When finished crack checking, demagnetize the parts. Make sure the magnetism has been removed by checking with a field indicator, which is nothing but a special compass. Number each rod bolt on the head 1, 2, and so on using an etching tool.

Reinstall rod bolts or dowels in the big end. Align bolts so their heads will seat correctly to the rods as you press them in. The shaped bolts head must be positioned to the rods so they will fit firmly against the flat or spot face. Using a plate as a backup with a clearance hole for bolt, press in bolts.

Recondition Big End—Use a bore gage to check big end bearing bore diameter. A portable bore gage or one such as that on the rod-reconditioning machine should have 0.0001-in. accuracy. Once you've checked bores, check rod length and parallelism of the big- and small-end bore axis. They must be parallel to each another.

Fit cap to rod so the chamfers and bearing-tab reliefs match.

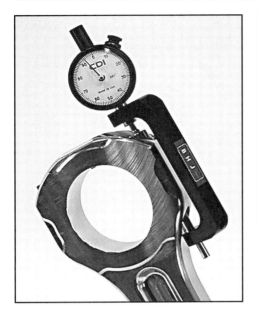

Rod bolts should be tightened to about 80% of their yield strength. Use a stretch gage to tighten bolts. Photo courtesy BHJ

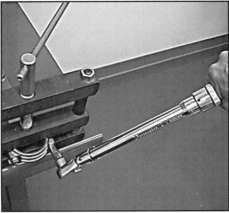

When installing cap on rod for checking and reconditioning bearing housing, always use a rod vise to hold rod. In this instance it is OK to tighten lubricated bolts with torque wrench.

If big-end bore is round, needle will not fluctuate much, but just wiggle.

Using a soft mallet, tap cap into place over dowels or bolts until parting surfaces are hard against each other. Never pull a bearing cap down with the bolts. Clamp the rod firmly in a rod vise and tighten bolts. Following the manufacturer's instructions, lubricate bolt threads and underside of the bolt heads or nuts. Use the lubricant supplied with the rods or the type recommended. If lubricant wasn't supplied, use a mixture of motor oil and moly. Install bolts or nuts, snug them down, and then back them off so you can turn them with your fingers.

Install a bolt-stretch gage so the centers engage the dimpled ends of the bolts. Set up the gage so the dial swings at least 1/2 turn. Zero the dial. Using the manufacturer's recommendations, tighten each bolt to the recommended stretch. A stretch of 0.006–0.007-in. give or take a few 1/10s is typical. Loosen bolt and recheck stretch.

Gage should read **0** when tension load is off bolt. If it indicates 0.0001 in. or more, replace bolt. It has exceeded its yield point, indicating the bolt has weakened. If all is OK, retighten bolt to spec. When you're finished with installing all caps, number the rods. Coat one side of each big end with machinist's dye and scribe number on each side of parting line. Numbers should coincide with position rods will be installed in engine. Number rods permanently after resizing them.

Refer to bearing catalog for recommended bearing-housing diameter. Specified housing diameter for rod used in the previous example is listed as 2.2247/2.2252, where 2.2247 in. is the low limit and 2.2252 in. is the high limit. Overall tolerance is 0.0005 in., allowing a 0.0003-in. smaller and 0.0002-in.-larger than a nominal bore size of 2.2250 in. Another way of listing this specification is 2.225 in. +0.0002 in./-0.0003 in. Regardless, you should use a total tolerance of ±0.0001 in., or 2.2249/2.2250 in.

in this case, to ensure precise bearing crush.

Measure big end with your bore gage and record results. Set aside rods that need resizing. Chances are all or no rods will need it. Measure bore in line with the beam, across parting lines and at a few points in between. A bore that is oval—not likely with a new connecting rod—is usually big in the vertical direction and pinched across parting lines.

Resize Big Ends—Before honing big ends, close up bore by "cutting" the cap and rod parting surfaces. You'll need to remove the bolts or dowels. Caution: Removing and replacing a rod bolt or dowel will reposition cap, albeit slightly. Regardless, this will require the big end be reconditioned even though it didn't need it in the first place. With that said, don't take off any more than what will be needed to achieve the correct bore size. After checking that you're using the right stone, set cap or rod squarely on the stone, clamp it firmly, back it

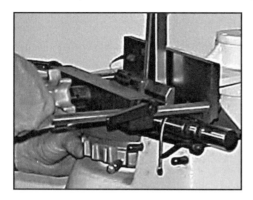

Clamped securely in Sunnen CRG-780, rod is traversed across stone to square and remove a small amount of material from parting face prior to resizing. Different machine, cap is cut in same manner.

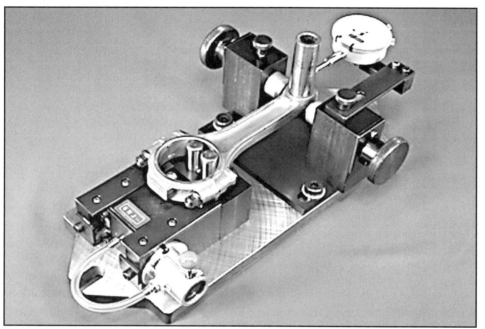

Rod-length checking fixture uses air clamp to support big end while small end is centered. Pin installed in small end is gauged with dial indicator to check rod length based on standard. Any deviation from 0 indicates how long or short a rod is from preset length. Photo courtesy BHJ

It is best to size two rods simultaneously to keep big ends square to honing mandrel. Rest rods against support bars staggered as shown to prevent wider small ends from butting.

Check for Twists and Bends— Big- and small-end bore centers must be parallel or not twisted relative to one another to ensure piston traverses the bore without a gyrating or moving with a twisting motion. Check pistons if you're refreshing an engine. A twisted or bent rod will show up as a skewed wear pattern on the skirts. Use checking fixture to check rods for this condition. Either install a pin in the rod or a piston and pin as shown in the nearby photo. Twist and parallelism should not exceed 0.001 in.

Check and Correct Length— The object here is to achieve a set of connecting rods that are all the same length. This will ensure that deck clearances for all pistons will be consistent in a trued block with pistons of the same compression height. Rod-length checks can be made with a dedicated fixture or one you've devised using dowels at either end and a dial indicator set up at the other. Use a master to zero the dial indicator with plunger square against the center of the pin. This can be a known rod you have

off, turn on machine, then feed the cap or rod down until it touches the stone. Take off no more than 0.001 in. from the cap or rod...just enough to clean up the surfaces and pull the top and bottom of the bore closer by no more than 0.002 in.

Set up rod-machine mandrel with the appropriate stones and guide shoes. Use CR stones if yours is a Sunnen machine. Starting off with

zero cutting pressure and honing oil directed at the stone, hone two rods at a time with the small ends staggered. Pairing rods in this manner helps ensure bores will be square. Stop and check your progress frequently using the bore gage until you've achieved the desired size. If one rod reaches the finished size before the other, finish honing the second by itself. Take extra care to keep it square to the mandrel.

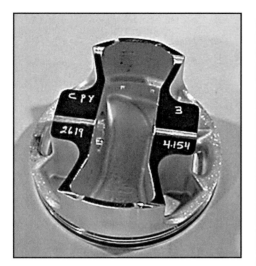

Match rod and piston, then number them accordingly. Piston has a lot of information etched on pin bosses; part number, bore size and piston number.

After bluing underside of piston, fit rod to piston, then swing and slide rod to limits of travel.

or a master supplied with a store-bought fixture. Remove master and check rods. The indicator will zero if rod is the same length, or positive or negative if it is longer or shorter, respectively. As you continue checking, record rod numbers and readings. Organize rods according to length. Hopefully, they will all be the same. If any aren't, you'll have to rebush and bore the small end with an offset that will give the desired center-to-center length.

Follow the procedure described below to remove and replace the bushing. With new bushing in place, fixture rod so it is level, square and secure to the table of a mill. Indicate center of the big end and center it under spindle. Run table down to the small end a distance equal to the desired rod length. Indicate the small-end bore as a double-check. Bore out the new bushing smaller than finished bushing size, then hone to size in rod machine.

Replace Pin Bushings—Press out old bushing in arbor press with piloted punched. Punch should fit bushing bore and clear housing in small end of rod. Chamfer bushing bore lightly with taper reamer or paper roll in die grinder, then press in new bushing. There should be enough clearance between punch and bushing that it won't lock punch as bushing size reduces. Use tapered mandrel to swage bushing at edges to lock it in place. Drill oil hole/s, using holes in rod as a drill guide. Hone bushing as described above.

Size Small End—You'll only need to replace the pin bushing if it's undersize or you need to offset the small end to correct rod length. Check diameter of each rod with bore gage set up for a smaller bore. Rock gage or rod gently to find the smallest reading. This diameter should equal wrist-pin diameter plus oil clearance, or 0.0008–0.0015 in. As an example, if you're using a 0.927-in. pin, pin-bore-bushing diameter should be 0.9278–0.9285-in. Make this clearance larger if you're using unbushed pin bores—steel on steel—with DLC coated pins. In this case, give the small-end bores 0.0008–0.0015-in. clearance to the pin. For pressed pins there should be a 0.0010–0.0015-in. interference fit.

If a bushing is oversize or needs offsetting, press it out. Back up the small end so there is clearance for the bushing as it comes out, then use a drift and to press out the bushing. Using the same setup, press in the new bushing so it's flush with the end of the pin bore. If the bushing is longer than the bore, trim the opposite end so it's flush, too.

Complete pin-bushing installation by honing bushings to size using the manufacturer's recommendations or as recommended above. Install a KL mandrel of the appropriate size or equivalent to your rod machine. Using wrist pin for reference, hone bushings to size. Use very light pressure with a lot of coolant, check often with the bore gage until you reach the desire bore size.

Piston-to-Rod Clearance

Check clearance between small end of each rod and underside of piston. This can be very tight with low compression-height pistons. Coat underside of piston with machinist's blue, then assemble rod to piston less retainers so piston and rod are correctly oriented. This is where full-floating pins come in handy. The piston and rod will now be a matched set. Etch number on piston-pin boss to match rod number.

Swing rod from side to side and back and forth on pin the full travel of the rod. Remove rod and

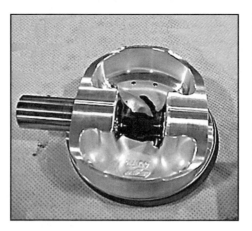

Remove rod and check for interference. Note two bright spots at pin bosses. Clearance should be 0.050-in. minimum.

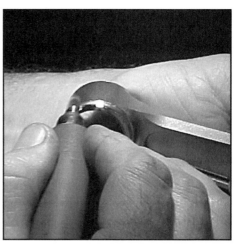

Rod is chamfered at small end to provide clearance to piston.

check for any rod-to-piston interference as indicated by bluing that is wiped away. Clearance should be 0.050 in. minimum. How you provide clearance depends on location of the interference. If it's at the center area of the piston, remove material from the piston with a die grinder and paper roll. For interference at the

edges of the rod, it would be better to chamfer rod at the small end rather cutting a sharp corner at the pin bosses and create stress risers. Double-check clearance with a feeler gage.

CYLINDER HEADS

5

It would be an understatement to say that cylinder heads contribute to the power and efficiency of an engine. To be more specific, they have the most effect on power output than any other component. That's not to say the camshaft, carburetion/fuel injection, intake manifold and exhaust system aren't important. They are. But your objective should be to end up with the best set of heads possible and use all other systems to optimize the power potential of these heads. Start with a bad set of heads and your engine will never get close to its maximum potential. Conversely, start with a good set of heads and you'll be way ahead in the power output game.

With the exception of R&D port work, CNC machining has replaced tedious and dirty cylinder head porting work. Shown is DMG Maho Gildemeister 5-axis DMU 80 machining center.

CHOOSING CYLINDER HEADS

What with the explosion in the number of aftermarket heads, things have gotten much easier for engine builders. There are choices we wouldn't have dreamed of 20 years ago. In the '60s, '70s, '80s and well into the '90s, we moved valves, installed bigger valves, welded, added filler here, ground material there—spent hours on the flow bench and performed all sorts of surgery to OEM heads with the single goal of increasing airflow, mostly to cast-iron heads. The flow bench is still a huge factor, even more so. But we now recognize that turbulence, swirl and the resulting combustion efficiency is critical when it comes to squeezing the last bit of power and, particularly, efficiency out of an engine. These, along with the machining methods and materials used to produce modern racing heads, has resulted in a quantum jump in cylinder-head technology, so much that the prediction that the days of the pushrod engine were numbered has been "put on the trailer." So we now have the modern problem of choosing a head rather than spending hours reworking an existing OEM head.

Additional choices are rocker arms, valve guides, valve seats and of course, valves. Throw materials and coatings into the mix and you have to make a lot of decisions. And don't forget cost, racing rules and intake-manifold availability.

It's easy to get into the trap of choosing a cylinder head based only on maximum airflow. Mid-range flow, or flow at 0.300–0.500-in. valve lift, is critical. You must then decide where power is best produced; higher or lower in the rpm range. Burn efficiency is a factor not to ignore. It is affected

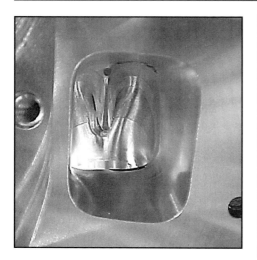

Viewed from the intake side, this CNC'd intake port needs little, if any, additional work to improve flow.

Before the days of CNC'd racing heads, engine builders used to spend hours on the flow bench as I am doing here to squeeze more flow from cast-iron production heads.

greatly by combustion-chamber shape, quality of the flow into the combustion chamber and sparkplug placement. The more confined combustion chamber, with a higher velocity and swirl of the air/fuel mixture entering the chamber combined with a centrally located sparkplug, gives a superior burn, or one that is faster and more complete. That's why a hemi-spherical combustion chamber with its centrally located sparkplug typically outperforms other configurations. The challenge with other designs is to duplicate the performance of the hemi head. And don't forget compression ratio. It's all about volume at TDC above the piston—less volume means more compression; more com-pression means more horsepower. Then there are the ports; their shape and path. Whatever the port shape, it should have the straightest possible path into the valve pocket.

A very practical matter you must deal with is matching components to the heads. In the case of radical heads, it's not unheard of that the intake manifold will have to be fabricated. However, chances are you will have a choice of manifolds that will fit. This is not so with exhaust headers. Plan on fabricating all or part of the exhaust system. There are too many engine and chassis combinations.

A good way to judge the importance of cylinder heads is the security at a race-engine-builder's shop. Some areas may not be restricted. Not so with cylinder heads. They stop just short of sealing off the cylinder head shop with barbed wire and guard towers. And questions about cylinder heads are typically met with silence. This is not to say race teams aren't secretive about components such as camshafts, pistons, exhaust systems and carburetion. They are, but not like heads. Unless a builder is among the few that does his own porting, usually by CNC'ing them, he buys the heads already CNC'd to his specifications and sometimes to specs required by rules. Even then, he will typically flow the heads for verification, then make allowable

modifications—sometimes not allowable—in an effort to improve flow. The good news is there's no black magic here, but the devil is in the details—small details that yield big dividends. Keep in mind that details can also hurt.

Pay careful attention when choosing cylinder heads and the work you do to them. Particularly port size and swirl features. They are critical. Generally speaking, a smaller intake port with higher velocity fills a cylinder with a superior air/fuel charge mixture. Combine high velocity with high swirl and it will have a very efficient burn. Such heads are better power producers at the low end, but will cause an engine to peak quicker. On the other hand, larger ports are superior at the higher rpm ranges. But an engine so equipped will be flat at the lower end because of lower velocity, poor mixing of the air/fuel charge and the resulting poor burn efficiency. You have to reach a balance, but always err by choosing higher velocities, or smaller ports, over larger ones. The challenge is to find a combination that has a little of both, particularly a two-valve head. And once you have chosen a particular head, maximize flow efficiency by paying particular attention to the valves, valve seats and areas in and around the valve pockets as you recondition or make modifications.

Cast Iron or Aluminum?

This is a no-brainer. Use cast-iron heads only if they are required by the rules. Aluminum has too many advantages, such as ease to work with, lightweight and availability. An

Begin head work by cleaning them. Bob secures heads to center post in preparation of jet spraying them. He follows up by a vigorous scrubbing in the wash bin.

aluminum head is much easier to weld and machine, which is very important if damage repair is required. Pictured on the following page are examples of such damage caused by a dropped valve. Welding, grinding, machining and new seats fixed these heads.

In virtually all racing situations, it's helpful to reduce the weight of the engine, which also lowers the center of gravity of the engine. This allows you to put the weight somewhere else in a car if it has a minimum weight requirement. Finally, the availability and cost of aluminum heads are a big advantage, making a nice problem—simply choosing the one you want. Did I mention aluminum cylinder heads are a lot easier to carry around the shop? Wouldn't you know that there is a downside to aluminum heads; they are more easily damaged than their tougher cast-iron counterparts. So treat them with more care.

The cylinder heads you will be working with will range from bare heads straight from the manufacturer to heads right off an engine you will be refreshing. Except for a major amount of cleaning, the work is basically the same. Just leave out steps that don't apply to your situation. So let's get started with refreshing a set of used heads.

CLEANING AND INSPECTING

Before you clean and inspect heads, strip them. Remove the plugs, rocker arm stands and valve-guide seals. If used, remove the valve cover studs, too.

Cleaning

Using a hot tank (except for aluminum), jet washer, pressure washer, steam cleaner and/or a parts washer, clean heads. When cleaning used heads, pay particular attention to the combustion chambers and ports. Remove all carbon. Some jet spray solutions are effective at removing carbon, but a mechanical cleaning method such as wire brushing is required for final cleanup.

Dry Soda Blasting—Fortunately, an option that works well at removing carbon is dry soda blasting—it almost makes this job easy. As with glass bead or sand blasting, dry soda blasting removes baked-on carbon, paint, grease, grime and rust, but without the risk of damaging machine surfaces. Additionally, the non-toxic soda residue can be rinsed off with water. Further, soda particles will dissolve in oil and not damage the engine in the event that all soda media is not completely removed after blasting.

Remove all gasket material, but look carefully at the head gasket. It will tell a story, sometimes a bad one. Concentrate on the fire ring. A blowout at a fire ring indicates there was a compression leak. The head may be warped. Remove any gasket material by scraping and wire brushing. Be careful with aluminum. Don't use a carbide or steel scraper, but one designed for use with aluminum. The same goes for a wire brush. It should have copper bristles, not steel. As for cast-iron heads, a carbide scraper and wire brush works great without the danger of damaging the surface.

Inspection

Once heads are clean, do a quick visual inspection. Just because they may be new, don't get caught in the trap of thinking they can be installed as is. You don't need any surprises. Identify each head by marking with an engraver or number stamp. Have your notebook ready to record during the inspection and machining processes. Check heads for cracks, warpage, thread damage, brinnelling, burning, valve guide wear, damaged valve seats and valve guides. Do an overall visual inspection, first. Some problems will be obvious, such as those pictured. More detailed inspection requires measuring and crack-detection equipment.

As previously described, check for cracks using magnetic-particle inspection or dye testing. Concentrate on the combustion chambers, particularly around the valve seats. Welding can be used to repair cracks in an aluminum head fairly easy. Welding cast iron is not so easy, but pinning is an option. I

Leaned-out air/fuel mixture did obvious damage to aluminum cylinder head. Specks of aluminum on intake valve are from the piston. Repair was made by welding, machining and installing new valve seat inserts.

Exhaust valve head broke off to cause this damage. Head was repaired.

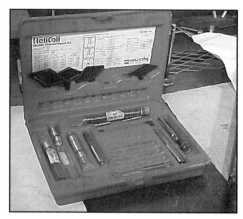

Every engine shop should have a HeliCoil repair kit.

wouldn't use a head repaired in this manner in durability events.

Combustion Chambers—Check around combustion chambers for fretting or brinnelling—indentations in the metal—caused by the head-gasket fire ring. This problem was common with aluminum heads fitted to cast-iron blocks, but has been reduced significantly through the use of MLS—multi-layer steel—gaskets. Also look at each combustion chamber for signs of compression leaks where a fire ring may have failed. This is more likely to occur between the center combustion chambers due to cylinder-head warpage.

Check for warpage with a precision straight edge and feeler gauges. The gap between the straight edge and gasket surface shouldn't exceed 0.00156 in. for a V6 or 0.002 in. for a V8. Check with the bar positioned lengthwise in several positions and diagonally across the head. Pay particular attention to surfaces around the center combustion chambers. You must repair any irregularities on the

gasket surface so the gasket will have a new surface on which to seal.

Valve Seat Inserts—The valve seat inserts in aluminum heads need special attention. These can loosen and actually fall out due to the difference in thermal-expansion rates of the seat material and surrounding aluminum. Aluminum cylinder heads, just as pistons, can melt from a leaned out condition or detonation. The area around the exhaust valve seat in the photo above at left melted due to leaning out during a restrictor-plate race.

While you're looking at seats, look into the valve pocket and check the end of the valve-guide inserts. It's not unusual for this end to break off, especially if guides extend unsupported into the valve pockets. Replace a broken guide.

The last item to check are threaded holes. These include those for the sparkplugs and rocker-stand bolts or stud threads. If you have any experience with aluminum heads, chances are you have used HeliCoils. Unlike cast iron, it's fairly common to find damaged threads in an aluminum head. If you find such damage, use

a thread insert to make the repair. To prevent such damage to an aluminum head, install thread inserts in holes such as those used to mount rocker-arm stands.

CYLINDER HEAD MACHINING

Now that you've completed a visual inspection, the next steps are measuring and machining. Precise measuring equipment and machining go hand in hand. You don't do any machining without making accurate measurements and vice versa. With that said, there is a definite sequence to follow when doing cylinder head work.

Make Repairs First

Start cylinder head work by making repairs such as installing HeliCoils or smoothing and welding damaged combustion chambers. With that done, start with the valve guides for the same reason block work begins with checking main-bearing bores —the valve guides must be in good condition before you do any valve-seat work. This is because valve seats center off the guides. Valves are checked and faced at this point. Turn your attention to combustion

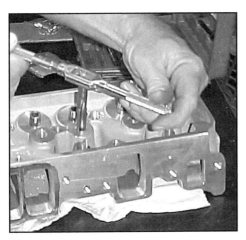

Begin tread insert installation by drilling out damaged thread and rethreading oversize.

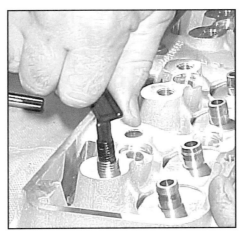

Thread inserts being installed in rocker-stand bolt hole.

Tapered guide pilot can be used to check for guide wear quickly.

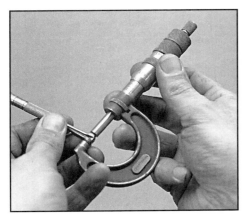

Small hole gauge and 0–1-in. mike are good tools for checking valve-guide wear.

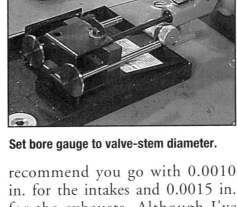

Set bore gauge to valve-stem diameter.

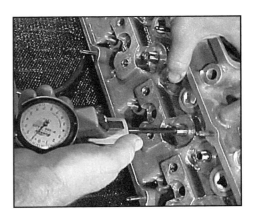

With gauge inserted in guide bore, the gauge reading will be stem-to-guide clearance.

chamber related work, such as cc'ing and surfacing. You'll need to do some flow testing, providing it is in your plan Combine this testing with work done on the valve seats, in the ports and combustion chambers. Then, attention must be paid "up top" to the spring seats, valve-stem seals, rocker-arm mounts and pushrod-clearance holes.

Valve Guides

Check valve guides for wear. Valve stem-to-guide clearance specifications and preferences seem to be all over the map, or in a range of 0.0010–0.0020 in., but I

recommend you go with 0.0010 in. for the intakes and 0.0015 in. for the exhausts. Although I've even seen intake clearances as low as 0.0005 in. and exhausts at 0.008 in., too little clearance risks valve stem seizure in the guide. On the other hand, too much clearance means the valve will not hit the seat squarely when closing.

Start guide work by measuring valve guide bore diameter. The difference between this figure and valve-stem diameter is stem-to-guide clearance. Measuring valve guides is best done with a small-hole bore gauge, however you can use a small-hole C-size gauge and 0–1-in. micrometer. When using

the dial bore gauge, zero it as shown in a setting fixture using two valves as reference.

Brush out each guide, and then insert gauge, moving it from the top to the bottom while watching the dial. Concentrate on readings at each end of the guide where maximum guide wear occurs. With the dial set to zero, it will read stem-to-guide clearance. To check with the small-hole gauge, expand the end of the gauge in the guide until there is slight drag, withdraw it from the guide and measure it with 0–1-in. micrometers. Measure both ends and in the middle of the

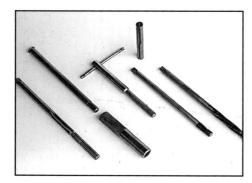

Thin-wall bronze guide insert installation kit includes everything from coring to final reaming or broaching tools.

Driving in thin-wall bronze guide insert. Insert is then expanded and reamed or broached to size. Follow instructions supplied with kit.

Use core drill that is slightly smaller than guide OD to relieve press fit of thick-wall guide insert.

Drive guides out from port side.

guide to find point of maximum wear. Using the above figures, if clearance exceeds the specified clearance plus 0.0002 in. for allowable wear, or 0.0012-in. maximum for intake guides and 0.0017-in. maximum for exhausts, replace or sleeve guide.

Repairing Valve Guides—You can repair valve guides by sleeving with thin-wall—0.030-in. thick— or thread-in, bronze-wall. HeliCoil-looking guide inserts have been used successfully. But you may be required to use replaceable cast-iron guides to make guide repairs in cast-iron heads with integral guides. If the rules allow, install thick-wall bronze-alloy guides for maximum durability.

To install thin-wall, phosphor bronze sleeve-type inserts, follow the detailed instructions in the installation kit. Use Bronze Bullet guide liners for best performance.

The basic installation procedure starts with coring out each guide. Use centering cone to align ream to seat. Next, chamfer guide at top, brush out guide, lubricate it and drive in liner with a punch and guide so sleeve projects equal amounts from both ends of guide. To lock insert in place, expand it

by running a spiraling (knurling) tool or lubricated tungsten carbide sizing ball (broach) through the guide to lock insert in place. The broach should be 0.001-in. smaller than the finished guide size. You can also size the guides using a well-lubricated ream, but broaching is faster and yields superior results. Trim both ends of liner flush with the guide using trimming tool, then chamfer both ends using a taper reamer or chamfering tool. If you used a knurling tool to expand the liner, size it with a ream that will leave the guide 0.001-in. smaller than the finished size. Use plenty of bronze lubricant. Final sizing and honing will be done after you've finished doing any seat work.

Install thread-in Bronze-Wall insert in a manner similar to installing a HeliCoil. First thread the old guide bore with a sharp tap. Using a special drill guide, drill notch into top of guide. Run a

brush through threaded guide to make sure threads are free from all debris, then thread insert into guide inserted from top using a slotted tool engaged to the tang at the bottom. Once threaded in so insert is flush with bottom of guide, break off tang. Cut off insert at top by bending it over into the notch, leaving a short tang to bend over so it can be clamped to top of the guide. Size guide with a ball broach or ream as previously

Measure guide and compare to bore size in head.

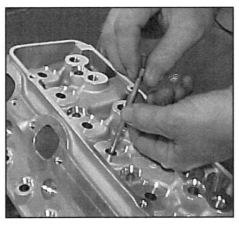

Using small-hole gauge and 0–1-in. mike, measure guide hole in head. Subtract this from guide OD to see if there will be adequate press, or 0.0017 in. for aluminum and 0.0012 in. for cast iron, plus or minus 0.0002 in.

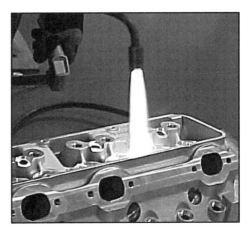

Use rosebud tip to heat head evenly.

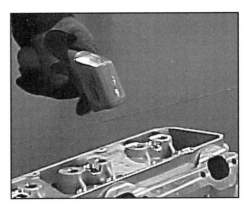

Check temperature frequently with pyrometer. Aluminum head should not exceed 270°F.

described. When reaming a bronze wall insert, use a reverse rotation ream. Remove clamp and chamfer top of guide to finish the installation.

Installing New Thick-Wall Guides—The first step in installing non-integral guides is to remove the old ones. Be it integral or non-integral, drill out each guide using a core drill. If it's a non-integral guide, the core drill should be slightly smaller than the guide OD. This will relieve the press fit, allowing you to remove the remainder of the guide with light pressure and without damaging the bore in the head. This is critical with an aluminum head. Damage may result if you drive out the guide before relieving the pressure of the press fit. Drive out shells that are left from port side.

Choosing Replacement Guides—When choosing replacement guides you have some choices. Thick-wall phosphor-bronze, manganese-bronze or silicon-aluminum-bronze alloy guides are preferable to cast-iron guides because of durability and heat-transfer considerations. You can go one step further and install copper beryllium guides for

superior heat transfer. This is critical if you'll be using titanium valves, particularly on the exhaust side. The first thing to do when ordering guides is to determine which ones were originally used in your heads, providing you're reconditioning them, or the manufacturer's recommendations if you're working with new heads.

Guides may project into the bowl area. This is usually different for intake and exhaust guide inserts. At the other end, check height projecting from the spring side to ensure there will be sufficient retainer-to-seal clearance There should be 0.050-in. minimum from the retainer to the top of the guide at full valve lift. Although no machining should be required with aftermarket high-performance guides, check to make sure. Machine the top of the guides if necessary. This is best done after guides are installed. Check also the guide bore diameter in the head. Measure guide OD, then subtract the amount of press to determine guide bore ID. You can also do this

the other way around and size guides to fit the head. Whichever way you do it, allow for 0.0015–0.0020-in. press minimum for an aluminum head and 0.0010–0.0015-in. for cast iron. Also, double-check the heads for size and condition of guide holes. If you removed old guides, you may have to ream holes and install oversize guides if bores in the head are damaged. Check insert diameters and ream the head to achieve the desired interference fit.

Install Guides—You'll need some press-fit lubricant, a piloted driver and a pneumatic hammer to install new guides. Heating heads will make guide installation easier,

Lubricate guide OD and start guide straight in from spring side by lightly tapping guide driver with hammer.

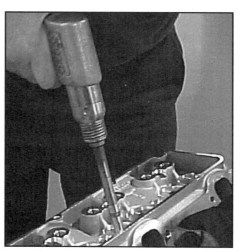

Once started, drive guide in to shoulder with pneumatic hammer. Use free hand to feel for guide as it comes out on port side.

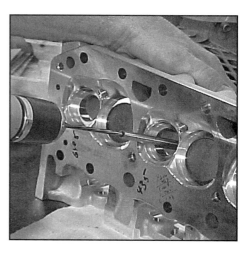

For now, ream guides 0.0005-in. smaller than valve stem. Use plenty of cutting oil when reaming bronze guides.

so you'll need an oven or an acetylene torch fitted with a rosebud tip. Although a temperature-indicating crayon can be used to indicate maximum temperature, it won't tell you temperatures above or below its melting temperature. So use a pyrometer, or temperature gun, for checking temperature.

Heat a cast-iron head to 400°F or an aluminum head to 250°F—don't exceed 270°F. Heating will reduce the interference fit, making guide installation easier. It also reduces the chance of galling an aluminum head. Heating is relatively easy with an oven because it heats evenly to the desired temperature. More skill is required when using a torch.

If you're installing several guides, lay them out within reach in an organized manner so you don't waste time hunting for guides as the head cools. Set head on wood blocks so steel table won't draw heat from the head. Don't forget your hands. Wear heavy leather gloves for handling the hot cylinder head. Play the flame evenly over the head to increase temperature

evenly. Check head temperature frequently, but don't allow it to exceed 270°F if it's aluminum or 400°F for cast iron.

As soon as head is up to temperature, fit insert to the end of driver, coat it with an anti-galling lubricant and insert tapered end of guide into the bore from the spring side. With driver in the guide and aligned with bore in the head, drive in guide with the air hammer until shoulder on guide bottoms in the head. If you're fast you may not have to reheat the head before installing all the guides. But if you do, check temperature with the pyrometer. When you've installed guides in both heads, turn your attention to the valve seats.

Size Valve Guides—What do the valve guides have to do with valve seats? Everything. Just as the name implies, they guide the valves onto their seats. With this in mind, the guides should be semi-finished at this point. This is because all valve-seat finishing systems are piloted off the guides. For example, fixed pilots in the guides are used for grinding or cutting; a live pilot is used when

finishing seats in a seat-and-guide machine. Therefore, final sizing should be done after all seat work is done to ensure imperfections introduced into the guides during seat work are removed.

Determine whether guides need sizing at this point. Some may not. Check guide diameter as you did when inspecting them. Accurate results are best achieved by comparing valve-stem diameter with a dial bore gauge in a checking fixture. At this point, semi-finish guides by reaming the guide to 0.0005-in. smaller than valve stem diameter. Final-size the guides by honing after you complete the seat work.

Replace Valve Seats

Inspect Valve Seats—First check the valve seats for damage such as burning, beating out or other physical damage. Valve seat inserts can loosen, particularly those in aluminum heads. If heads use large valves, the exhaust-valve-seat inserts are probably cut into the intake inserts. Check the proximity of the intake and exhaust inserts.

After clamping cylinder head securely in seat-and-guide machine, level it in relation to guide.

With the cutter set to bore slightly smaller than the OD of the insert, cut out damaged seat.

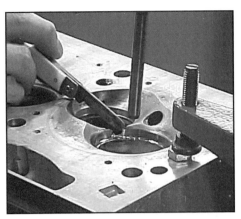

Bob removes remainder of seat with pocketknife.

The diameter of the seats may be so large that the adjoining exhaust-seat insert may be cut into the intake insert, possibly to the extent that the OD of the exhaust insert extends into the intake valve seat. The line contact under the intake valve can open up, causing an intake valve leak. Seats with this or similar problems just mentioned must be replaced.

Rather than using the traditional method of prying out an insert or welding on it to shrink and loosen it, cut out insert on your seat-and-guide machine to relieve the press fit. This will avoid the risk of damaging the head when removing. Use this method to provide a counterbore for installing seat inserts in a cast-iron head with integral valve seats.

Set up head on seat-and-guide machine, combustion chamber side up. Level it both ways using a valve guide as reference. Remove seat by counterboring. Check and note seat thickness so you don't cut deeper than necessary, or no more than the depth of the valve seat. It's best to use an adjustable counterbore for precise final sizing. I also address a situation where the

inserts need to be turned down to obtain a precise press fit. Press, or an interference fit, is required. For cast-iron heads it is 0.003–0.005-in. and for aluminum, 0.005–0.007-in. Keep in mind that a press-fit creates stress that can cause cracking in the combustion chamber and too little press may allow an insert to loosen or fall out, particularly with aluminum heads. Do not stake a seat insert to retain it. This has the potential of deforming the seat and creating gaps between the stakes, reducing heat transfer from the seat to parent material.

If you're counterboring integral seats in preparation of installing inserts, cut to a depth that matches the thickness (depth) of insert. When removing the insert, don't cut any deeper than the original counterbore. If you are in doubt don't go any deeper than 0.190 in. An insert that stands proud after it's installed is one you can blend in when you're finishing the valve seat, but cutting into the water jacket is not good. It's best to err on the safe side. Bring the spindle down with it rotating so cutter just touches the seat. Zero the dial

Allan uses a Bowers/Sylvac bore gauge to make accurate check of valve seat counterbore diameter.

indicator. Using a spindle speed of 500 rpm with lubrication for aluminum or 200 rpm for cast iron, gradually cut counterbore to the desired depth. To remove an insert, set up the cutter to cut seat a few thousandths smaller than the existing insert diameter. Check counterbore diameter as you make the cut. The insert may rotate if it loosens. If not, remove the seat after you make the cut just short of going through the bottom. Be careful not to cut through side of the old insert.

Check availability of oversize seat inserts, then open up the counterbore to a diameter that

Bob Curl made a collet chuck from bar stock and pipe plug at center to hold seats for turning down to size in lathe.

matches the insert OD less the press fit. It's best to use an adjustable cutter to enlarge the counterbore to within 1/2-thousandth of the final diameter to provide the desired press-fit for the new insert. The fresh counterbore should have smooth walls for maximum heat transfer to the parent metal. Likewise, the bottom of the counterbore should be flat. However, if you can't open up the counterbore for an oversize insert, you may have to turn down the insert to achieve the desire press-fit. Such a situation is illustrated. In this case, the exhaust insert actually extended into the intake valve seat, meaning the counterbore could not go any larger.

Seat Inserts—You have a wide range of materials from which to choose. Regardless, use the same as you removed or whatever is recommended by the valve manufacturer for new heads. The most popular high-performance seat insert is ductile cast iron. Many sanctioning organizations require this material to be used, so check the rulebook first. For durability and applications where there will be extreme heat, such as

with a nitrous-injected, super-charged or turbocharged engines, use stellite seats under the exhaust valves. Other valve seat insert materials are nickel-chrome, stainless steel, and tungsten carbide. But for maximum heat transfer—required when using titanium valves—use copper-beryllium inserts. For example, Del West and Xcelydene recommend Alloy 25 copper-beryllium inserts for use with titanium intake valves and Alloy 3 for use with titanium exhaust valves provide additional heat conductivity.

Machine Valve Seat Inserts—If you have no other option than to size the valve seat inserts to the counterbores, turn down the inserts to give the required press fit. Holding a valve seat insert firmly so it can be turned down accurately requires that it be held with an internal collet chuck. So to do this you'll need a lathe and at least two internal collet chucks, one for the intake inserts and one for the exhausts. You can either purchase these or fabricate the chucks. With the prospect of this being a one-time situation, fabricating is attractive. Collets are relatively easy

to machine from cold-rolled steel round stock. Start with a 6-in. long section of 2-in. diameter round stock. Most insert IDs range from 1.345 in. to 1.970 in., but if you are working with larger inserts, use bigger round stock.

After cutting off a 6-in. length of round stock, chuck the piece in a lathe. Leave about one-half of it sticking out, then check for runout. Adjust as necessary, then turn down the diameter of that end to about 1 3/4 in. Deburr the end, then turn piece around and re-chuck it on the turned-down section. Check that there's no runout. Turn this end down no more than 0.002-in. smaller than the insert ID, 0.500 in. from the end, and face it. Smooth surface and deburr it with a flat file. Check that insert slides over the new surface with little effort, but with little play. Center-drill the end and drill it for a 1-in.pipe thread 3-in. deep using a 1 1/8-in. tap drill. Chamfer hole. Tap drilled hole for a 1-in. pipe plug to a depth that plug will begin to tighten when it is flush with the end of the bar. To finish your collet chuck, remove pipe plug and make three evenly placed cuts, or 60° apart, the length of the tapped section with a bandsaw.

Chamfer edges of cuts, reinstall the pipe plug and fit the insert over the end of your new chuck. Tighten the plug to expand collet chuck to hold insert firmly in place. To be sure, remeasure counterbore diameter with a bore gauge, then turn down insert to a diameter that will give the desired press fit, or 0.003–0.005 in. for cast iron and 0.005–0.007 in. for

Again using rosebud tip, expand seat bore by heating head aluminum/cast-iron head to 250°F/400°F.

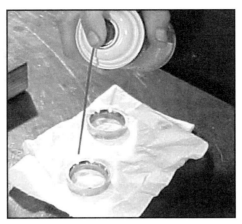

Cool seat inserts in freezer or as shown with CO_2.

If intake and exhaust seats need replacing and they overlap, install intake seat first, then counterbore for exhaust insert as shown.

Install pilot in guide…

…then position cold insert on hot head with driver centered on pilot.

Drive in insert so it bottoms firmly in counterbore.

aluminum. Chamfer bottom of insert OD to provide a lead-in to the counterbore.

Install Valve Seat Inserts— Similar to installing valve guides, you'll need a pneumatic or manual piloted driver, driving heads and hammer or pneumatic hammer to install seat inserts. The driver pilots over a mandrel in the valve guide, fits to the insert ID, and shoulders against it. Although some don't expand the head by heating, it's best to do so when installing valve-seat inserts. Use an oven or torch with rosebud tip to heat head. Check temperature with a pyrometer, or temperature gun.

Don't forget gloves.

To heat with a torch, position the heads with combustion-chamber side up on wood blocks. Heat one head at a time evenly while increasing temperature gradually. Check temperature frequently. Don't heat aluminum over 270°F or over 400°F for cast iron. As soon as the head is up to temperature, install pilot in the guide. Place insert laying on a block of ice to cool it. Another method to cool insert fast is to use CO_2, such as Goodson's Fast Freeze. Once cooled, quickly fit insert to the end of the driver with seat side against the driver and chamfered side

down. Coat insert with an anti-galling lubricant and slide driver over the pilot until insert is firmly against the counterbore. Drive seat insert in until so it bottoms solidly in the counterbore. Repeat procedure until you have all inserts installed.

If inserts are so big that intake and exhaust insert counterbores cut into each other, such as shown in the photographs above, install the intake seat inserts first. Take head/s back to your seat-and-guide machine and cut out the section of intake inserts that project into the exhaust insert counterbores on the

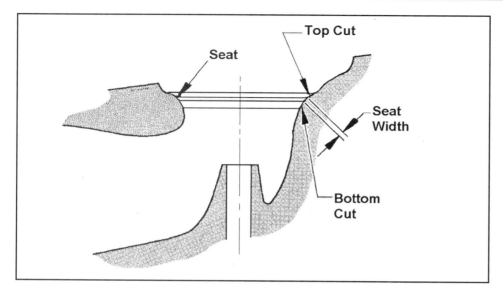

One of many valve seat profiles. Off-the-shelf blades with many profiles are available. You can also have blades custom-made for your specific valve seat.

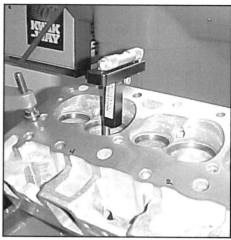

Level and secure head in seat-and-guide machine using guide as reference.

Cutter blade cuts seat to specific angle and width while cutting top angle and throat angle simultaneously. Use chart to cross reference blade to width and angles it will cut.

same exhaust counterbore diameter. Proceed with installing exhaust inserts.

Machine Valve Seats

At this point you should know what intake and exhaust valve seat profiles to use. You are either accepting the head manufacturer's recommendations or have come up with what you want through flow testing, possibly backed up with dyno or track testing. Regardless, it's pretty well accepted that the three-angle valve profile formed around a 45° or 30° seat performs best, all things considered.

Grinding valve seats will give adequate results. The same goes for another popular method, the Neway valve seat cutting system. It uses four or more tungsten-carbide cutting blades installed in bodies centered on a fixed pilot for cutting different angles similar to grinding. But it's hard to beat finishing valve seats with a seat-and-guide machine. Compared to grinding, it's cleaner and doesn't require dressing grinding stones and

finishing each angle separately. Although expensive, the seat-and-guide machine is faster, more accurate, gives a smoother seat and is decidedly cleaner than grinding. Repeatability is another plus.

Seat-and-Guide Machine—Set the head in a fixture with the combustion-chamber side up. Level it fore and aft and side to side, using a level installed in the guide. Position the level in line with the head and adjust head until level indicates 0°, then turn level 90° to the head and rock it until it is level in that direction. Clamp head in place, and then check it again both ways. Makes adjustments as necessary until you've established that the guide is square to the machine.

Here's where the seat-and-guide machine shines: Valve seat cutters will do all three angles with the correct seat width simultaneously; or seat, top angle and throat angle. You'll probably be doing a 45° seat, but some heads work better with 30° seats. Regardless of the angle, what should the seat width be? I like 0.060 in. for intakes and 0.090

in. for the exhausts. These widths can go a little smaller if you're willing to give up some durability, such as for drag racing where durability is not a major factor. But make sure airflow increases with a narrower seat. It may not.

You'll need a chart for matching cutter blades. Without such a chart to compare blades, it's nearly impossible to determine blade angles and seat width. Once you've installed the correct pilot and chosen a cutter blade, mount it in a tool holder and set it to cut the proper seat OD. Use a valve to establish seat OD by fitting tool-

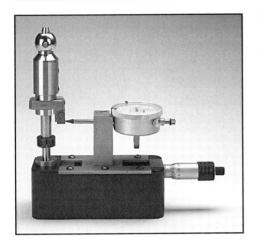

Cutting head is set on fixture. Shown is Goodson's 3-D Fast Cut setting fixture.

Zero indicator reading when finishing cut. Cut remaining intake or exhaust valve seats to same depth.

Deck bridge is handy for checking height of valve head. Check valve head at highest point. Check other seats using same valve. All intake valves should end up at same height. Same for exhaust valves.

setting fixture to one of the intake or exhaust valves.

This brings up a question: How far back from valve margin should the seat contact area be? First, both intake- and exhaust-valve faces should overhang the seat slightly to ensure full contact and sealing with the seat. This is critical to durability for both valves and cooling for the exhaust valve as the seat grows. For an intake valve, this distance can be less. But because moving the seat out on the valve face improves flow, the temptation is to "push the envelope" as far as possible. I recommend you maintain at least 0.010 in. with intake valves and 0.040 in. for exhaust valves. Adjust the cutting fixture accordingly.

Fit the cutting head to the setting fixture and position cutter blade to the pointer. Install the cutting head in the seat-and-guide machine spindle. Brush out guide to ensure it's clean, then lubricate guide. With a bounce spring over it, move pilot into the guide to check that it moves freely, but without any slop. If all is OK, zero dial indicator when cutter touches the seat, then bring cutter

down to make a light cut.

With dial indicator on the spindle positioned to contact the head, note its reading at bottom of cut. As a precaution, double-check seat diameter with dividers set to the valve. Make another cut so there's sufficient top cut. Note dial-indicator reading and record this on head with a felt-tip marker. Install valve, then using a bridge and dial indicator, check valve-to-deck surface height with valve firmly on the seat. Note reading for later reference. Check valve-seat concentricity with accurate gauge. Seat should be within 0.0005 in.

Finish remaining intake valve seats to the same depth, then change your setup and finish exhaust valve seats, or vice versa. Reference dial indicator readings as you go. Readings for intakes should be the same as should exhaust valve seats. As you go, periodically check that seat runout is within the 0.0005-in. limit. Likewise, install valve to check that valve heights are consistent. Once both heads are finished, turn you attention to the top side of the head.

Grind Valve Seats—Grind valve

Check seat with concentricity gauge. Hall-Toledo gauge is accurate to 0.0001 in.

seats on the bench. Use roughing and finishing stones that are sized for the intake and exhaust seats. Install the correct tapered pilot in the guide and slip a bounce spring over the pilot. Cut seat first, using a set of dividers set to the valve to determine seat OD as described above. With stone fitted to the holder, dress it to the desired seat angle. Take out 45° or 30° seat to about 0.060-in. larger than the seat diameter. Wipe off seat and install valve. Check valve-to-deck surface distance with your bridge and dial indicator. Record this dimension—

Three valve seat grinding stones freshly dressed and ready to go—60°, 45°, and 30°.

Install pilot in clean guide, slip bounce spring over guide followed by holder with stone.

Use a light touch when grinding.

Mark across all valve seat angles with felt marker to highlight the cut. Shown is throat cut on intake seat.

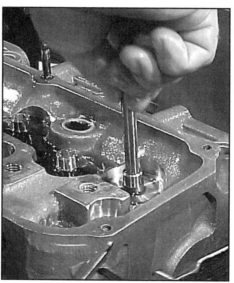

Tapered pilot works well for checking guides as you hone. A 0.0010-in./0.0015-in. intake/exhaust stem-to-guide clearance should work well.

it will be used to set the other intake or exhaust valves at the same height. Use a fine grit stone for making the finish cut on the seats. Dress stone frequently to ensure you get a smooth, accurate seat.

Switch over to the top-cut stone to establish seat OD, or typically 30° and 15° for 45° and 30° seats, respectively. Coat the seat with machinist's blue to make the seat visible after you make the top cut. Check seat OD with dividers. Once you've established seat OD, switch to the bottom-cut stone. Typically, this will be 60° with both seat angles. This angle will establish seat width. Check valve heights.

Cut Valve Seats—Use Neway valve seat cutters in a manner

similar to grinding. Install cutters in the correct diameter and 45° or 30° holder. Install pilot in guide, fit cutters over pilot, then cut seat as described above. Wipe off seat, install valve, then measure and record valve height. Coat the seat with Dykem blue or a marker and switch to a top-cut holder to establish seat OD. With the seat OD established, make bottom cut to narrow seat to the desired width. Mark the seat with Dykem blue or a marker to highlight the cut. The

final cut can be difficult to make, as the cutters tend to wedge, so use light pressure as you turn the cutters. Finish the remainder of the intake and exhaust seats using the same process, checking valve height as you go.

Note: When grinding or cutting seats with a fixed pilot, don't remove it until you've made all three cuts. You can never be sure a tapered pilot will end up in the same exact position once removed, then reinstalled. The result will be a seat that varies in width, narrow on one side and wide on the opposite side.

Hone the Guides

With the seat work done, hone the guides to the final size. This removes any damage that occurred from inserting and removing pilots during seat work. Start by rechecking guide size as described earlier, pages 87–88. For convenience, use a tapered pilot that will indicate when guide is to size. You will also need a 3/8-in. drill motor and valve guide hone set, or everything from the driver to the mandrel with stone.

With head set where you have a supply of honing oil, such as used in a rod-reconditioning machine,

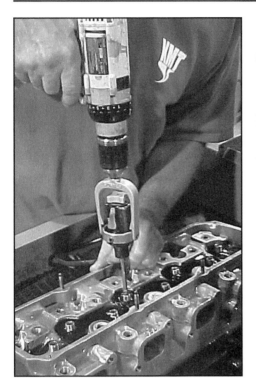

Hone guides from spring side…

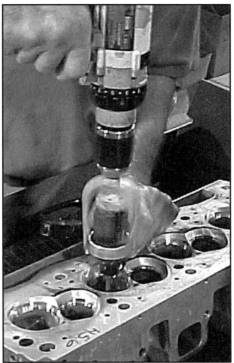

…then hone from opposite side to ensure guides are straight. Use plenty of oil and check size frequently.

Apply thin line of 600-grit lapping paste to valve face.

check the guides with a tapered pilot. Hone some material, then recheck as you go. Run hone the full length of the guide, then flip head over and hone from the opposite side to ensure guide is straight. Continue honing and checking until all guides provide the desired stem-to-guide clearance. Tight is best, but too tight can be disastrous. Again, shoot for 0.0010-in. clearance on the intakes and 0.0015 in. on the exhausts.

Lap Valves

There's some controversy as to whether valves should be lapped. Some engine builders do it and others don't. The bottom line is, if the valve seats and valve faces are done correctly, lapping is not necessary. It's is a waste of time. This is particularly true if you've finished the seats on a seat-and-guide machine. On the other hand,

lapping is a security measure. It confirms the valve face has full contact with the valve seat. Additionally, lapping ensures a valve seals to the seat the first time it closes. But the valve will seal the first time the engine is fired, unless the seat and valve face are grossly out of alignment. In this case it wasn't a good valve job in the first place. So if you question the valve job for some reason, double-check by lapping the valves.

Caution: Don't lap valves with coated faces. It will remove the coating.

You'll need some valve lapping paste and a stick. Some fine compound such as 600-grit. You don't need a fancy lapping stick. A wood stick and suction cup at each end will do the job. Have your engraving tool handy for marking the valves, too. This will ensure you lap, check, and assemble each

valve on the same seat.

Line up both heads on your bench, combustion chamber sides up. I set them on short sections of 2 x 4, one under each end so the intake sides face me. Slip valves in the guides and onto the seats. Now is a good time to mark them with your engraver, 1–8 for the intakes and 1–8 for the exhausts for a V8. Mark the head, too, so you'll know which one they go with.

Start with the first valve. Apply a fine line of lapping compound on its face. Slip valve in guide and onto its seat. Apply some moisture to a cup on the stick and push it against the center of the valve head. While applying light pressure against the valve, work it back and forth by rotating the stick back and forth between the palms of your hands. You will notice the gritty feel will smooth out, meaning the valve is lapping in. At this point, pull out the valve and wipe the compound off the valve face and seat.

Check pattern on the valve face and seat. There should be a continuous gray satin-finished pattern the same width around the face and seat. If there's not, it's not concentric with the guide. Do likewise with the valve face.

Using lapping stick, spin it back and forth while applying light pressure off and on to the seat. You'll feel a change when the valve is lapped in.

Lapped surfaces on valve and seat are indicated by satin finish.

Arrows point out engraved numbers on the valve heads in #3 combustion chamber.

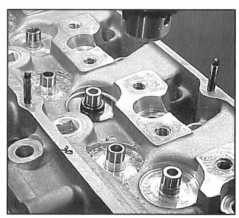

Check that the spring seat fits over the valve guide and down against the pad. If not, recut the guide and spring pad.

Find valve spring seat cutter of correct size and cut seat on valve guide-and-seat machine.

Otherwise, something is wrong. Make and note so you can correct the problem. If all looks good, make sure all lapping compound is off the valve and seat, then replace valve on its seat and continue lapping the remainder of the valves. Engrave a number on each valve head corresponding to the seat. The valves should stay with the seats on which they were lapped.

Spring Pads and Guides

On the spring side of the head, make sure spring pads will accommodate the springs. Also, check that top of guides will accept the valve-stem seals and spring retainers will clear top of seals by at least 0.050 in. at full valve lift.

Spring Pad—Use the springs you'll be using to check fit to the spring pads. If heads are aluminum, also check steel spring cups or locators. They should fit over tops of guides and seat firmly against spring pads.

If there's a fit problem with the springs, spring cups or locators, check with the head manufacturer before you do any machining. With things so tight in a racing head, ports and water jackets have minimum clearance that restricts machine work in this area. Enlarge spring pads by removing too much material and you risk cutting into a port or water jacket. If all is OK to enlarge the spring pads, use a spring seat spot facer and pilot to do so. You can do this with a cutter and drill motor, however use a seat-and-guide machine if you have one.

Guides—Check tops of guides. Diameter and height must be correct for the seals and camshaft you'll be installing. If guide diameter is too large, use the correct OD machining tool. Diameters range from 0.415 to 0.625 in., but chances are you will need a 0.500- or 0.530-in. cutter to accommodate a PC seals. Check also that spring cups or locators fit over guides, particularly the type shown that locates to the guide rather than spring-pad OD.

As for guide height, it should be short enough to allow at least 0.050-in. clearance from the spring retainer to valve stem seal at full lift. To check retainer-to-seal

More aggressive valve-spring-seat work can done with this type of cutter.

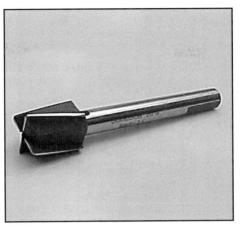

If clearance from spring retainer to stem or seal at full valve lift is less than 0.050 in. or 0.100 in., respectively, use spot facer in your seat-and-guide machine to shorten guide.

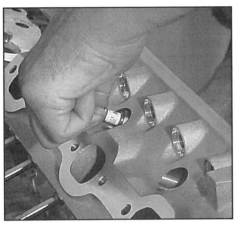

To check combustion chamber volume, first install a sparkplug.

Bob Curl applies thin line of grease to valve seats with needle-tipped grease gun.

Install valves with checking springs and apply thin line of grease to periphery of combustion chamber.

clearance, install a valve with its retainer and locks without the spring. Hold the valve firmly up against its seat and measure between the bottom of the retainer at the valve stem to the top of the guide. Now push the valve open so retainer contacts top of guide and remeasure. The difference between the two measurements should be no less than full valve lift plus 0.100 in. to provide the needed retainer-to-seal clearance. If it's not, spot-face and chamfer tops of guides and recheck clearance.

Combustion Chamber Volume

After valve and seat work is done, check combustion chamber volumes. You'll need this figure for calculating compression ratio. Even though the heads are new, check them. This is a must. I've seen new out-of-the box "quality" performance heads that vary as much as 2cc from one combustion chamber to the next. They must be equalized.

CC'ing Procedure—To cc heads, you will need a 100cc burette, clear acrylic plate, low-viscosity fluid such as solvent or alcohol, two checking springs and some light grease. Instead of the plate, you can use a bridge with a threaded pointer, but you'll have to have a level. You'll also need a sparkplug, valves and retainers with locks. Have your notebook and pen or felt marker ready for recording volumes. It's convenient to record each chamber volume on the head with a Sharpie, then transfer these figures to the notebook.

Install the type sparkplug you will use. To ensure positive sealing, apply a thin line of grease to each valve face, then install and retain them with checking springs and retainers/locks. Wipe off excess grease. If valves aren't marked, do so on their heads with an engraver. Note neat mini grease gun being used in the illustration.

If you're using a pointer, level head. Otherwise, tilt head up on side away from you. Apply a thin line of grease around combustion chamber. Lay acrylic plate over chamber so fill hole is at the high side. While slightly wiggling it, push down on plate to seal and force it flush with the head-gasket surface. If you're using a pointer,

Position plate over combustion chamber with fill hole at one side.

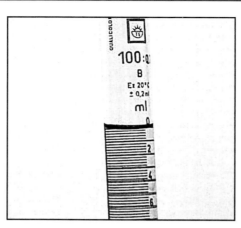

Fill burette until meniscus is level with 0 mark.

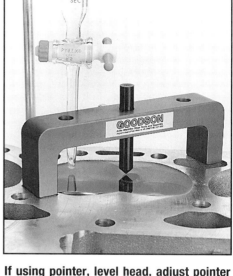

If using pointer, level head, adjust pointer down to gasket surface, position pointer over combustion chamber, then fill chamber until liquid just touches pointer.

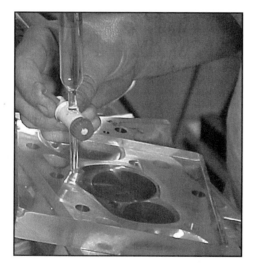

When using plate, tilt head slightly so fill hole is at highest position. Add liquid through hole by opening burette valve until all air bubbles have been purged and liquid is even with bottom of hole, no more.

Reading from bottom of meniscus, chamber volume is 70.5cc. Each division is 0.2cc. Record volume on head with felt marker.

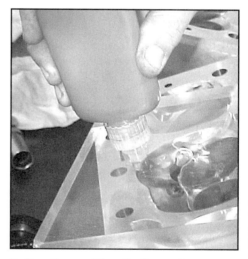

Rather than spilling it all over bench and floor, Bob uses empty Loctite container to draw fluid from combustion chamber and return it to burette.

position it on the head and run pointer down until it touches the gasket surface, then move it over the combustion chamber.

Fill burette with liquid so the meniscus lines up with 0 mark as shown. When using a pointer, adjust it until it touches the gasket surface, then move it over the combustion chamber without disturbing the adjustment. Add liquid until it just touches the pointer. Hold burette and check combustion chamber volume.

Be patient when using a plate. Fill chamber through hole in plate until all air bubbles are gone. Purging air bubbles can be frustrating. If you're not sure of your reading, empty chamber and recheck. Read burette and record value on head or note pad. Remove plate and wipe off grease from the gasket surface, valves and valve seats. Install a new set of valves in the next chamber and repeat procedure until you've checked all combustion chambers. Compare

results.

If you find that chamber volumes are equal, great. Too big is another plus, providing you can achieve the desired clearance volume by reducing piston volume or surfacing the heads. Too small a combustion chamber requires that you increase piston volume by increasing dish volume or compression height, or opening up

Level head front to back and side to side in resurfacing machine using precision level as reference.

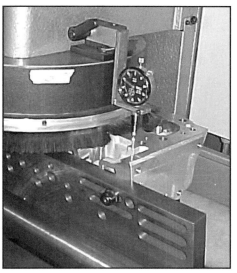

Double-check your setup by traversing table length of head and indicating it with a dial indicator. Check that plunger will clear all holes and combustion chambers. Make adjustments as necessary.

Adjust machine to take initial 0.005-in. cut.

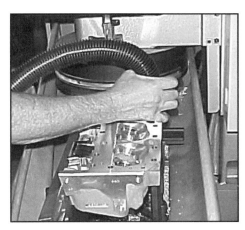

Shop vacuum is handy for cleaning head after each cut.

Bruce Jacobson of Glendale Machine & Balance sets up to mill head in a Block Master machine. Make sure machine will provide surface finish specified by the gasket manufacturer.

the combustion chambers. Don't sink the valves to increase combustion chamber volumes, though, due to the damaging effect it will have on flow. A head gasket that is too thick would not be good either.

Mill the Heads

Set head level on fixture in the machine. Check it from end to end and front to back, making adjustment in both directions. Secure the fixture and jack screws. With a dial indicator mounted to cutting head and zeroed while touching head, traverse the table or swing cutting head to check that it's level with the machine.

Transfer chamber volumes you recorded on head to your notebook. You will need them.

As discussed in the block chapter, it is critical to achieve a surface finish as recommended by the gasket manufacturer. Roughness is normally 54–100 Ra (60–110 RMS) when using cast-iron heads on a cast-iron block. It's much smoother for aluminum heads on a cast-iron block. For example, Fel-Pro recommends 10–30 Ra (11–33 RMS) when using their MLS gaskets with aluminum heads on a cast-iron block.

Using sharp tool bits you've set correctly—this is critical—change roughness by adjusting spindle speed or feed rate. A slower speed or faster feed will produce a rougher finish; the opposite gives a smoother finish. Make speed or feed adjustments until you've achieved the recommended finish, then take a final cut. Check roughness with a profilometer.

In addition to roughness, keep a record of combustion chamber volumes. As an example, we needed 63cc to get a 12:1 compression ratio. Starting with 70.5cc combustion chambers, we needed to reduce volume by 7.5cc. Knowing from the manufacturer that 0.0065 in. milled off the head reduces chamber volume by 1.00cc, we needed to remove 0.049

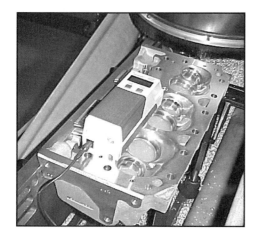

Optical profilometer is used to check surface roughness. Make adjustments if necessary to achieve the finish specified by gasket manufacturer.

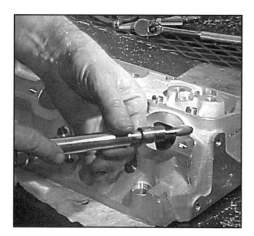

While you're at it, clean up the rest of the head.

Using 45° deburring tool to chamfer holes.

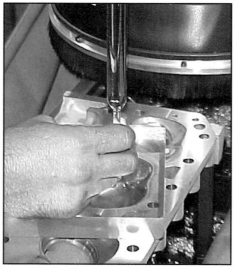

Check volume of the largest combustion chamber. This will tell you exactly how much volume is lost for each 0.001-in. removed from head.

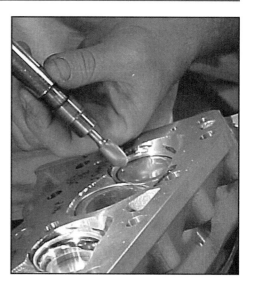

Oval burr is used to knock off sharp edges from periphery of combustion chambers.

in. To verify chamber volume change, we made a light cut, or 0.005 in. Using the ratio of 1.00cc volume change for 0.0065 in. milled off, volume change should drop 0.77cc for a 0.005-in. cut. Mathematically, this is found by using this ratio, or 1cc/0.0065 in. x 0.005 in. = 0.77cc.

Making the 0.05-in. cut allowed us to accomplish two things: to check surface roughness and confirm the change in combustion chamber volume. After making adjustments, we had another 0.044 in. to remove. In such cases, play it safe. Don't remove all the stock. Instead, take another 0.005-in. cut and recheck volume and surface roughness. After this, triple-check volume and finish. Make the final cut only after you've checked your numbers and are satisfied you'll end up with the desired chamber volume and surface finish.

After milling a head, chamfer all edges, particularly around the combustion chambers. Using your die grinder and burr, put a small chamfer around each combustion chamber. Go lightly here. Don't remove too much material, but just *break* the ragged edges that could cause preignition and the resulting detonation. Chamfer all bolt holes and other sharp edges, too.

Equalize Chamber Volumes—If you found that combustion-chamber volumes are not the same, enlarge small chambers to match largest one. Because you've equalized valve heights, the problem is with shape of the small chambers. Double-check to make sure, though. Open up low-volume chambers to match large chamber. You'll need pattern-making material, a small ball-peen hammer, layout dye, a scribe, two old valves and a die grinder with paper rolls.

Use 6-in. square or larger piece of cardboard such as used to package rings or bearings for making a pattern of the largest combustion chamber. You'll need two points to position pattern to chamber so it can be positioned accurately to the other chambers. These can be the valve guides or two head-bolt

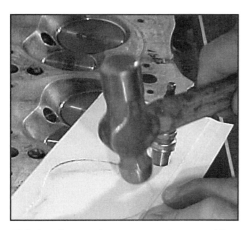

Old ring box makes great pattern-making material. With it held in position over largest combustion chamber—dowel and old sparkplug used here—cut out pattern. Lightly tap with the peen end of hammer around periphery of combustion chamber.

Finished pattern.

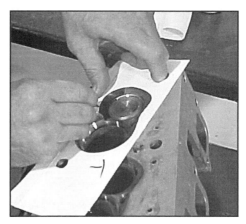

After bluing small combustion chambers, position pattern with reference holes over first chamber. Lightly scribe line on head where flat surface of head projects from under pattern.

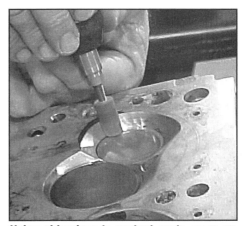

Using old valves to protect seats, open up chamber to scribe line. Paper roll is less aggressive than burr.

Using new valves for that chamber, recheck combustion-chamber volume. Make corrections if necessary.

holes. In the example we use bolts holes. They are farther apart, thus position pattern more accurately to the combustion chambers.

Position cardboard over largest combustion chamber and two bolt holes. Using peen end of hammer, lightly tap out holes in pattern over bolt holes. Find something to fit into the bolt holes such as a tapered punch or bolt that will hold pattern in place while you tap out outline of the combustion chamber. Slowly work around combustion chamber with hammer until piece of cardboard matching shape of combustion chamber falls out. Using a piece of sandpaper, smooth the edge of the pattern. You now have a pattern that matches the largest combustion chamber.

Using layout dye, coat periphery of small combustion chamber or chambers—there may be more than one. Lay pattern over that combustion chamber and secure it in position using the two holes. Using your scribe, mark around pattern to transfer shape of large

chamber. Remove pattern and install two old valves. These will protect the seats against damage while you're reworking the chamber.

Using a burr or paper roll, open up chamber to the scribe line while maintaining basic shape of chamber. Repeat this process on other small chambers, and then recheck volume of each with mated valves. If they are not the same, they should be very close. If they are still too small, you may have to remove material from inside the chamber to achieve the desired volume.

Pushrod Clearance

Although pushrod clearance is checked during preassembly, check pushrods and clearance holes in heads for signs of interference when refreshing an engine. Pushrods that seem to clear at preassembly may touch as they bow out from high loads from the dynamics of the valvetrain when at high rpm. Such was the case with example in the photos. Rub marks on pushrods and clearance holes indicate interference. Although not a major problem, rubbing action of the pushrods creates some drag. Simply open up holes with a die grinder and burr where you find such marks.

Rub mark (arrow) on pushrod is sure sign it touched clearance hole in head.

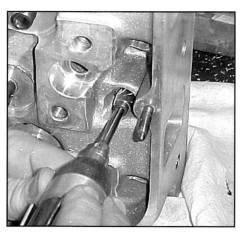

Use carbide burr to clearance areas touched by pushrods.

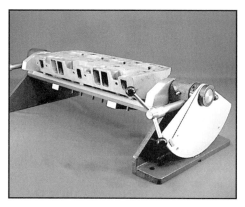

Angle scale on BHJ fixture makes setup for milling heads and manifolds quicker and easier.

Angle Milling

Be aware that angle milling cylinder heads can lead to complicated and time consuming work. Besides, it is not be allowed in many racing classes. And there are too many hard-core performance cylinder head choices in the aftermarket that allow you to accomplish the same thing and at lower cost. However, because power is the name of the game, do just about anything for a little more. With that said, the good news is you can order angle-milled heads from most high-performance cylinder head manufacturers. This is much less expensive than setting up to do it yourself. But whichever way you go, check the rulebook first and talk with the manufacturer's rep before you make the decision.

What does angle milling do in the first place? Although it reduces cylinder-head clearance volume slightly less than flat milling, or typically 0.0065 in./cc for angle milling versus 0.0055 in./cc for flat milling for a specific head, angle milling does reduce clearance volume, thus increasing com-pression. But raising compression is not the primary objective, we want to increase intake flow. By removing more material from exhaust side of the head, say 0.040 in. from the exhaust side and 0.010 in. from the intake side, the head is tilted down at the exhaust side. The effects are raised intake ports and valves that are stood up, albeit slightly. Be aware that angle milling changes two important relation-ships; matting surfaces between heads and intake manifold, and valve angles to pistons.

After angle milling a head, you'll need to remachine the dowel holes, head bolt and intake manifold bolt holes. This includes spot-facing the head bolt holes at the new angle. This will keep the bolts or studs from binding due to the offset loading under the nut or bolt head. Similarly, the valve-to-piston relationship will be changed. Consequently, valve reliefs in the pistons may need to be machined deeper and at the new angle to provide sufficient piston-to-valve clearances. And at preassembly, pushrod-to-head clearance should be checked, too. Additionally, a gap is opened up at the intake manifold, requiring spacing, playing with gaskets or machine work at the manifold gasket surface to compensate for the angle mismatch.

VALVES

As part of a head assembly, arguably the most abused and critical components in an engine are the valves. Consider that at 9,000 rpm, each valve must open and close 75 times a second. This and the fact that the exhaust valve must operate at temperatures up to 1,600°F in extreme situations illustrates what this small, but critical component must endure. And we've all seen damage from a valve that fails and drops into a cylinder at high rpm. So choose valves wisely.

Valve failure can be very ugly.

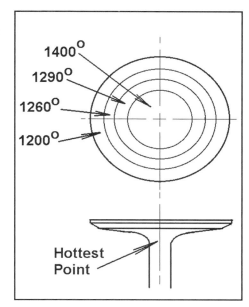
Typical exhaust valve temperatures. The valve is hottest at the stem and coolest at the face due to cooling from heat transfer to the seat. The temperature skyrockets at the face when a leaks occurs.

Although relatively simple at first glance, intake and exhaust valves are very complex in design and function. This complexity becomes real when choosing valves. Putting rules aside, you must address features such as head diameter, head shape, stem diameter, length, material, lock types, coatings and finish. It's fortunate that, in addition to catalogs, valve suppliers have very competent tech support personnel that can help you through this maze of choices. And don't forget cost. This should be a consideration unless you are part of a well-healed race team. For example, a coated titanium valve may be the best choice due to strength, durability and low weight. But titanium valves come at a premium. Next on the list are hollow-stem stainless steel valves. The least costly and sophisticated valve is the two-piece OEM steel valve. Use this one only if required by the rules. Then there are inconel valves used in extreme temperature situations.

Choosing Valves

It was once common practice to reshape a new valve, but high-end racing valves can now be installed out of the box. They typically require little or no modifications to improve performance as shown through flow testing. When choosing a valve, performance factors to consider are flow, wear, strength, heat transfer and weight. Flow is directly related to size and shape of the valve from the bottom of the guide to its head. Wear, strength, heat transfer and weight are directly related to material, shape and coating. Then there are the basics: head diameter, face angle, stem diameter and stem length.

Valve Head—Taking basics first, valve diameter has its limitations. Unless you're working with a hemi or angle-valve head that moves the valve away from the cylinder wall as it opens, the biggest intake valve you can install is usually not best for flow. This is due to *shrouding* at the cylinder wall. You may have confirmed this on a flow bench. Rules may limit valve size, too. At the face, an angle of 45° is usually best, but a 30° valve may flow better. Stem diameter also has an effect on flow, as does anything in the bowl area of a port. Smallest is best in this respect.

Other than basic shape, the profile of a valve will optimize flow into or out of a port. Just mentioned was a smaller stem size. This could be in the form of a larger stem that's undercut/necked-down. Anything that increases area in the valve pocket across the backside of valve usually improves flow. Additionally, sharp corners should be minimized or reduced to optimize flow. The easiest way to do this with an intake valve is typically with a 30°/15° backcut behind a 45°/30° face or simply blending the face to the backside of the valve with a smooth radius. Again, the best way to confirm this is best done by flow-bench, dyno- and, ultimately, track testing. At the outside edge of the face, some gain can be made by creating a *clip angle*, or chamfer, to knock off the sharp edge at the margin. This usually improves flow out of an intake port, but restricts reverse flow—*reversion*—at lower rpm. But for an engine that operates in a narrow, high-rpm range, it is usually best to radius this edge because reversion is not a factor. Again, testing is the only way this can be confirmed.

Valves are sometimes referred to by angle, say 12°, 15° or 30°, which describes the angle between the backside of the valve and the plane of the valve head. Where the flatter 12° intake valve performs better in most heads where intake flow is across the valve head, a higher-angle

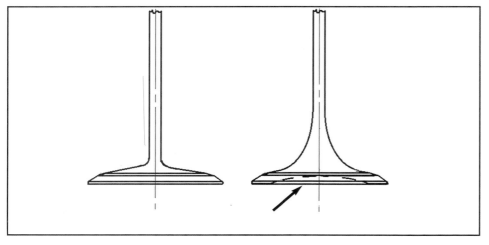

Flat valve and tulip valve illustrate extreme valve head shapes. As port angle is raised relative to center of valve guide, increased valve head angle usually improves flow. Note dish (arrow) of tulip valve.

Slight necking of valve stem reduces weight and improves flow.

valve, or *tulip valve*, typically shows superior flow with a port that directs flow more to the backside of the valve head. Such is the case with a hemi head. So as a port is raised so airflow is directed more to the backside of the valve, the tulip intake-valve shape will likely flow best. The same principle applies to exhaust valves even though flow is in the reverse direction.

Other factors to consider are *dish* (illustrated above) and finish. Although dishing has no effect on flow or strength, it is used to lighten higher-angle valves. Because the dished portion of the valve head is on the combustion-chamber side of the valve, it affects clearance volume and, thus, compression. So if a valve has more dish, compression will be slightly lower, .

As for finish, two types are available for racing valves; swirl polished and polished. Although flow is not affected much one way or the other, the advantage of a highly polished surface is it has less tendency to crack and ultimately break. In addition, the highly polished surface is less apt to accumulate deposits.

Valve Stem Considerations

Diameter—Common stem diameters are 7mm (0.2756 in.), 5/16 in. (0.3125 in.), 11/32 in. (0.3438 in.) and 3/8 in. (0.3750 in.). Less common are 0.3080-in., 0.3095-in, and 0.313-in. stems. The question is why use a 7mm stem? Increased flow and reduced weight is the answer, but at the cost of wear and strength. A 7mm compared to a 3/8-in. stem is less resistant to flow. The smaller stem also reduces valvetrain inertia, thus allowing higher rpm. However, the 3/8-in. stem, with its higher stem-to-guide bearing area wears less and is stronger. So engines where frequent valve replacement is expected, the advantage of a smaller stem wins outs over durability. Even though power rules, you must consider strength. A small-stem valve with a stiff spring that gives as much as 250 lbs. on the seat must be reckoned with. A highly stressed stem will eventually break and result in catastrophic engine failure. This became clear to me why this happens when viewing a high-speed video of a valve wagging in the wind like a dog's tail when off the seat at high rpm.

Wear—If you are expecting your engine to go a full season before it's refreshed, wear must be considered. Maintaining minimum stem-to-guide clearance is critical to ensure the valves close squarely on their seats. This is to ensure the valve doesn't bounce around on the seat when closing. So wear in this area should be kept to a minimum, but with minimum sacrifice in power. Again, don't ignore strength. A valve head that breaks off ends up with ugly results. Considering this, the 5/16-in. stem is a happy medium. Going further, a necked-down 11/32-in. stem achieves both goals; improved flow with reduced wear.

Length—Finally, there is stem length to consider. Although a longer stem is not desirable due to increased weight, it may be

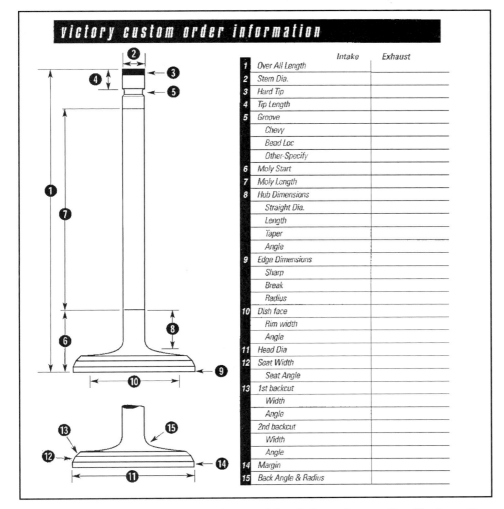

victory custom order information

		Intake	Exhaust
1	Over All Length		
2	Stem Dia.		
3	Hard Tip		
4	Tip Length		
5	Groove		
	Chevy		
	Bead Loc		
	Other-Specify		
6	Moly Start		
7	Moly Length		
8	Hub Dimensions		
	Straight Dia.		
	Length		
	Taper		
	Angle		
9	Edge Dimensions		
	Sharp		
	Break		
	Radius		
10	Dish face		
	Rim width		
	Angle		
11	Head Dia		
12	Seat Width		
	Seat Angle		
13	1st backcut		
	Width		
	Angle		
	2nd backcut		
	Width		
	Angle		
14	Margin		
15	Back Angle & Radius		

Victory references drawings for making special-ordering valves easier. Chart courtesy Victory.

necessary to accommodate a stiffer spring. As discussed in Chapter 6, spring rate is increased by increasing wire diameter and adding a second or even third spring inside the main spring. However, there is a limited amount of room both inside and outside of a spring. So as wire diameter is increased to increase spring rate, installed height of the spring must also be increased to prevent coil bind at open height. Therefore, stem length must be increased to accommodate the taller spring.

Speaking of weight, consider hollow-stem valves for your application. A stem contributes a large percentage of weight to a valve, particularly an intake, so removing material from its center will reduce overall valve weight without much reduction in strength. This should be done by gun drilling and polishing to minimize stress risers. Going further, filling the hollow stem of an exhaust valve with sodium greatly assists in cooling. For a racing valve, this sodium should be of the higher-temperature variety to ensure it stays in liquid form at higher temperatures. Otherwise, the sodium will flash to gas and

not provide the needed heat transfer.

At the top of the stem is the lock groove/s. For racing use, the single radial-groove is best, however square single grooves and double grooves are used. Be aware that grooves are for positioning keys to the valve in the retainer. It is the wedging action of the keys, or keepers, that secure retainer to the valve.

Valve Material

The most common base materials used in racing engines for valves are stainless steel and titanium. At the less expensive end is a combination of carbon-steel alloy intake valves and carbon-steel/stainless-steel exhaust valves such as those used in OEM engines. At the high end is high-nickel exhaust valves for very high-heat applications. Common to all valves regardless of base material is they are *alloyed*, or mixed with elements to obtain specific properties such as strength, hardness and heat transfer. This is to tailor them for various applications. A valve may consist of two materials. As an example, OEM exhaust valves typically have a forged stainless-steel head that is friction welded to a carbon-steel stem. For high-performance use, hard discs are welded to or pressed on the tips to provide the needed wear resistance resulting from high inertia loads, spring pressure and cylinder pressure. Separate hard tips, or lash caps, may be used in place of integral tips.

Various types of alloys and materials used for racing valves have been in use in other applications for years. Most were developed for use in jet engines, diesel engines and aerospace technology. This trend will continue along with advances in technology, so to say one material or alloy is best now will likely be replaced by improved materials in the future.

Carbon Steel—Carbon-steel performance valves are alloyed with elements such as manganese and chromium to improve corrosion resistance, high-temperature strength and overall durability. Although such a valve should perform with reasonable success in some racing applications, consider stainless or titanium valves for your application unless restricted by rules.

Stainless Steel—Stainless-steel valves are the most common types used in racing. Your challenge is to decide which stainless valve to use.

A trade name, stainless steel was originally developed in 1916 by an English metallurgist for cutlery to resist atmospheric corrosion, acids and scaling at high temperatures. It contained no more than 0.70% carbon and 9–16% chromium. As stainless steel was developed, it was found that nickel improved resistance to abrasion and gave a higher *elastic limit*, or stretch before it broke. Similarly, chromium increased hardness, toughness and stiffness. These are critical qualities, particularly for exhaust valves. But because these early stainless-steel alloys were difficult to machine and form, sulphur or selenium were added to improve machineability and formability. The problem was such alloys had a detrimental affect on strength, elongation, hardness and abrasion resistance. But as developments were made over the years in alloying, forming and

machining processes gave the performance properties needed in industrial and defense applications that made stainless steel desirable for use in high-performance valves.

Common stainless-steel valves are 21-2N and 21-4N. The first number refers to the percentage of chromium and the second to the percentage of nickel, or 21% chromium and 2 or 4% nickel, respectively. These alloys were originally developed for two-piece OEM exhaust valves. The 21-4N alloy is preferred for street performance stainless-steel intake and one-piece exhaust valves. For higher-end racing applications, the percentage of nickel is increased to improve strength, heat transfer and ductility. The exact percentage of alloys used by valve manufacturers is not publicized. Rather, valve manufacturers use terms in their catalogs such as "super-duper alloy" to label their valves along with recommended applications. This practice allows a manufacturer to list and recommend valves without revealing the makeup of the alloy. It also makes it convenient to choose valves for your particular application.

Inconel—The International Nickel Corporation (INCO) developed the nickel alloy *Inconel* for extreme-temperature applications. The typical composition of Inconel is 76% nickel, 0.2% copper, 7.5% iron, 15.5% chromium and 2.5% titanium with small amounts of aluminum, silicon, manganese, carbon and sulphur thrown in to enhance certain properties. It has a much higher heat resistance than all other valve materials, or up to 2,000°F

with a strength of over 100,000 psi. Such properties are particularly critical for exhaust valves where temperatures are extremely high as with high-compression, turbocharged or supercharged engines.

You don't need to consider this material unless you're building an engine that will see very high combustion chamber temperatures as just mentioned. Inconel exhaust valves should also be considered if your high-compression engine will be used in long-distance races at continuous wide-open throttle at a leaned-out air/fuel mixture.

Titanium—Here's a material that was used almost exclusively in the aircraft industry because of its low weight-to-strength ratio. Not a ferrous-based material, titanium is approximately 44% lighter than stainless steel and alloy steels. Additionally, it can be made equal in yield and ultimate tensile strengths and with a high corrosion resistance and tolerance to high temperatures. With the addition of iron and chromium, so called ferrochromium, or manganese alloys, tensile strengths exceeding 100,000 psi can be achieved.

A downside to titanium other than cost is low abrasion resistance. This problem, however, has been solved through the use of coatings, particularly on the valve stem. Further, to reduce the tendency of titanium to become brittle with use, alpha-beta Ti 6246 and Ti 6242 alloys are used. A major advantage of these alloys is they can be strengthened by heat-treating and aging, which is done after forging or welding. The primary use of Ti 6246 and Ti 6242 alloys is for jet engine compressor and

Rough-machined titanium stem and guide before they are joined.

With head in mandrel at left and stem in mandrel at right, they are friction-welded by forcing the two pieces together under pressure at high speed.

turbine blades, but it is used extensively for racing valves.

Ceramics—When ceramic valves are mentioned, the reference is to ceramic coatings and not the base material of the valve. Although ceramic, silicon nitride (Si_3Ni_4) valves have been used in selected race engines, they are extremely expensive—or much more than titanium valves due to high production costs. But with the great advantages of lightweight, anti-corrosion qualities and resistance to high heat, ceramic valves are sure to become available for automotive racing engines. Advances in technology and production techniques will eventually make the cost of ceramic valves competitive with stainless steel and titanium valves. As for now, ceramics will be confined to coatings.

Coatings

Engine parts can be coated with one or more materials to perform single or multiple functions. The simplest example of a coating is paint. It used to be common practice with race engine builders to coat the interior of blocks with materials such as General Electric's Gyptal. Arguably, this was to allow

oil to flow more freely back to the oil sump and seal debris such as casting sand so it wouldn't contaminate the oil. But this coating also carried with it the problem of separating from the surface to which was applied. The same was true with thick ceramic thermal barriers applied to pistons and combustion chambers. It did a great job of keeping heat in the combustion chamber, but when it flaked off, the abrasive ceramic particles caused damage similar to sand getting into the intake system. So obtaining good adhesion through preparation and other factors has always been a challenge when applying coatings of any kind.

Today's modern thin coatings reduce friction, transfer heat, protect machined surfaces in the event of low or no oil pressure, shed oil or act as thermal barriers. To understand the composition of these coatings and exactly how they are applied, a degree in metallurgy would be helpful. For the latest information on coatings and suppliers that offer such services, consultant literature offered by the Performance Racing Industry.

Their annual *Buyers Guide*, which has a comprehensive list of suppliers and manufacturers, is great for finding businesses that cater to the racing community. Better yet, attend their annual trade show to get first-hand information.

Thermal Barrier—Thermal barrier coating is one of the most important developments in engine performance to come along in the late 1900s. Such a barrier protects components against burning and other damaging metallurgical changes that result from high heat generated in a racing engine. Applied in critical areas, thermal barriers also allow tighter clearances by reducing the expansion of parts as they are heated. Thermal barriers also increase power by reducing underhood temperatures and the loss of heat or retaining it where useful. Heat from combustion should be retained in the combustion chamber and exhaust system as long as possible for maximum power to be realized rather than rejecting it to the coolant, oil, fuel or atmosphere.

The most effective thermal barrier is ceramic, or silicon combined with elements such as boron, chromium, nickel, zirconium and aluminum. Used in cylinder heads, it can be applied to valve heads, exhaust valve faces, combustion chambers and intake and exhaust-port runners. For example, 0.001–0.002-in. thick thermal barriers are applied to these and the surfaces of other engine components. Ceramic-coated valve heads and combustion chamber surfaces keep heat in the combustion chambers where it can contribute to producing power. Thin ceramic coatings lower operating temperature range of the valves. On the exhaust side, this reduces valve fatigue. On the intake side, it lowers the temperature of the intake air charge as it flows past the cooler intake valve enroute to the combustion chamber, thus providing for a denser mixture.

Heat in a valve not removed through the valve seat or the air/fuel charge travels up the stem, through oil at the clearance between the stem and guide. Heat transferred to the guide or seat is transferred to the coolant or oil and atmosphere via the radiator or cooler, respectively. A portion of the heat on the exhaust side is transferred to the valve springs through the spring seats, causing fatigue and gradual loss of spring tension. Oil directed at the springs from a spray bar helps prevent this annealing effect.

Thermal barrier coatings can also be applied to the underside of intake manifolds and exhaust headers. This will block heat from getting into the intake and getting out of the exhaust systems. This provides for a denser air/fuel charge and a higher-velocity exhaust-gas flow for increased scavenging. Underhood temperatures are also reduced, all beneficial for increased power.

Wear & Friction Reduction—
Wear and friction are like partners in crime—reduced friction reduces wear. A reduction in friction also reduces heat. Unlike ceramics used as a thermal barrier, you have more choices in thin coatings for reducing wear or friction. Such coatings are

particularly important if you will be using aggressive oiling techniques such as tightening clearance, limiting top-end oiling or using a low-viscosity oil.

Components that benefit from a wear- or friction-reducing coatings include valves, bearings, oil pumps, pistons and piston pins. And some materials benefit more from coatings than others do. Titanium is one. This is due to the tendency of titanium to gall. Consequently, titanium valve stems must be coated. However, coating valve faces and hard tips can also be beneficial regardless of the material.

Coatings for valve stems other than hard chrome include thin dry-film PTFE/moly, DLC (diamond-like coating) and boron nitride. Of these thin dry-film coatings, PTFE/moly is the most economical. In case you were wondering, PTFE, or polytetra-flouroethylene, is commonly know as Teflon. Calico applies a 0.0004–0.0005-in. to valve stems and a similar coating to main and connecting rod bearings. Acting as a lubricant, this coating reduces wear at startup. More importantly, it can save bearings or a crankshaft in the event of low or total loss of oil pressure. Calico stocks pre-coated bearings, which is more convenient than purchasing them and coating them later.

Shown above is hot moly plasma spray being applied to the stem of a titanium valve. To prepare the stem for coating buildup, Xceldyne turns down the stem 0.007-in. undersize to allow a 0.0035-in. thick moly coating after grinding. This type of coating can also be applied to tips, precluding the need

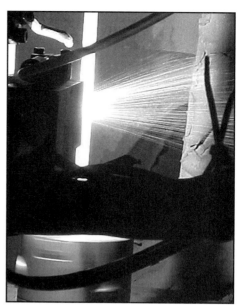

Following preliminary machining, Exceldyne coats titanium valve stem by plasma-spraying moly to provide abrasion resistance.

for separate hard tips or lash caps.

Some piston manufacturers supply pistons with a PTFE coating on skirts, however pistons can also be coated by a specialist such as Calico. They apply their CT-3 dry-film coating on piston skirts. Sacrificial coating—yes, it wears off—allows tighter clearances while preventing scuffing.

DLC, or diamond-like coating, is a silicon-carbide, tungsten-carbide, or other carbon compound. DLC is the most durable and expensive thin coating available. This is largely due to the method of applying the carbon compound. Rather than using conventional spraying techniques, DLC is applied using a PVD (plasma vapor deposition) process. Simply put, PVD involves spraying the component in a vacuum chamber with the compound in a plasma state, a very expensive process.

When introduced for use in racing by Anatech under the trade name Casidiam, DLC coated wrist pins proved to be very successful. A hard coating over 60 Rc and a friction coefficient as low as 0.1, DLC coated wrist pins can be run in unbushed connecting rods without galling. Among other components, DLC coatings are beneficial to prevent wear and galling when applied to valve stem tips and valve faces. Because a DLC coating can be so thin—it will add as little as 0.00008 in. (2 microns) to the surface—a small part such as a valve stem doesn't have to be sized to allow for coating buildup.

A final coating is used for shedding oil much like water off a duck's back from rotating and reciprocating components. Two major components benefiting most from this coating include crankshaft counterweights and connecting rods. The reduction in the clinging affect of oil when PTFE based coating reduces drag and extra weight which translates into a quicker accelerating engine and more horsepower. When applied to other components such as windage trays, valve covers, oil pans and scrapers, oil-shedding coatings also assist the flow of oil back to the sump and, consequently, reduced windage.

VALVE REFINISHING

When refreshing a racing engine, grinding valves is not usually part of the process. This is simply because valves should not be reused unless you are refreshing an engine that has relatively low time. If you are dealing with such a case, exercise caution. A used valve that looks good may not be. As with any metal, particularly that of a valve, it

fatigues from cycling between heating and cooling, loading and unloading. The result of this if allowed to continue is an over-fatigued valve that ultimately fails.

As for new valves, it was common practice to grind them. However, valves supplied by manufacturers such as Del West, Ferrea, Xceldyne and others can be installed out of the box. However, if you want to perform a secret "tweak," make sure know what you're doing before making a cut. You may do more damage than making an improvement.

Valve Restoration

More than refinishing the valve face, valve grinding involves total inspection and reconditioning. Start with a thorough cleaning with a wire brush on the bench grinder and parts washer. Inspect each valve from end to end. Obvious flaws you find at this point allow you to make a decision as to whether or not a valve can be reconditioned or should be replaced.

Areas of a valve to check are the tip, lock groove, stem and face. If there's any perceptible stem or lock-groove wear, toss the valve. As for the tip and face, you can resurface them unless the tip is chipped or the face is burned or badly pitted. If valve tips or face are coated, grinding will remove it. You'll either have to run the valves without the benefit of the coating or have them recoated.

Use a good inspection light or Lupe to inspect the lock groove. There should be no signs of wear or deformation here except for a light burr. Make sure each stem is straight. Do this with a valve set up

Cleaning backside of valve with wire wheel.

on a dedicated stem-checking tool or between two V-blocks. With a dial indicator that reads in tenths and the plunger set square to and in the center of the stem, rotate the valve. If the dial moves even slightly, replace the valve.

If you grind the valves, start by lightly resurfacing the tips. This ensures the valves will center in the grinder during refacing and material removed from the tips compensates for material removed from the faces. Be aware that when installed, all valves should be at the same height. Remove equal amounts from each tip based on what you remove from the faces. There's about a 1.4:1 ratio of tip-height change for a 45° face and a 1.2:1 ratio for a 30° face. In other words, for every 0.001 in removed from the face of a 45° valve, 0.0014 in. should be removed from the tip to maintain tip height and 0.0012 in. for a 30° face. Keep your notebook handy for making notes.

After grinding, lightly chamfer the tips—just enough to break the ragged edge. The chamfer should be no larger than 1/32 in.

For grinding the face of titanium

or stellite valves, use a dedicated grinding wheel rather than a general-purpose wheel. Grinding wheels are identified by color. For example, a specific valve grinder may use a green wheel for titanium and gray, white or ruby wheel for stellite. General purpose wheels can be orange, blue, pink, white or gray. This can be confusing. If you are in doubt about which wheel to use for your machine to grind a particular valve, check with your tool supplier.

With the wheel issue settled, set the machine to the correct face angle, or the usual 45° or 30°. Dress wheel with a diamond tool so it will provide an accurate and smooth, straight finish. I don't recommend grinding valves with an *interference angle*, or 1° less than the seat angle. This is typically done when building street engines on a high-volume basis, but an

accurate valve job will provide a good seal between the valve face and seat with no interference angle.

Grind valve by moving it across the full face of the stone with clean coolant directed at the valve face. This will cool the valve and flush away metal and abrasive particles to assist in producing a smooth and accurate finish. Speaking of coolant, use a good brand such as Posi-Flow 2000. Take a light cut, then let the wheel *spark out* to give the valve face a smooth finish. Remove the same, but minimal amount from each valve face. After finishing with grinding the faces, consult your notes and make adjustments at the tip to maintain tip height based on what you removed from faces. In either case, limit the material you remove from the valve faces, as this will reduce margin thickness.

Use quality coolant such as Mondelo's Posi-Flow 2000 for grinding valves. Coolant works well with titanium, stainless-steel, and stellite valves.

After tipping, grind valve face with strong flow of coolant on valve head.

With valve chucked in lathe, edge of lock groove is lightly chamfered with honing stone.

CAMSHAFT & VALVETRAIN 6

In simplistic terms, the sole purpose of a camshaft and valvetrain is to open and close the valves so that the maximum air/fuel-charge volume will enter the cylinders and will be totally expelled when burned in the most efficient manner possible. This is easier said than done. Many factors must be dealt with, one of which is rpm range needed to produce maximum power. If the range is narrow, the job is easier. It becomes more difficult when building an engine for a wide rpm range because it involves giving up a little horsepower. It's all about compromises. But there's one thing for sure: It not wise to build an engine that won't produce the torque necessary at the bottom end to pull into the upper end to take advantage of "big" horsepower. If a car, boat or truck is lazy off the line or out of a turn, it is usually too late to take advantage of power at the upper end.

A LITTLE THEORY
The Four Strokes

As discussed in Chapter 1, power depends on the volumetric efficiency of an engine. Obviously, the more efficient an engine is during the four strokes, particularly the intake stroke, the more power it will produce. An engine that doesn't have an electronically controlled camshaft with variable

Dodge engine being dynoed at Labonte Racing with Frank Leisson at console. Other than the track, dyno testing is best way to determine if camshaft is right for the engine.

timing and lift can maximize power output only in a very narrow rpm range. Also, always be aware that a change to one stroke affects the other strokes. Knowing this, let's review how intake- and exhaust-valve openings, closings and lift affect engine performance during the 720° of crankshaft rotation.

Intake Stroke—Officially, the intake stroke starts at top dead center (TDC) and ends at bottom dead center (BDC). But because of a thing called gas dynamics, the intake stroke must begin earlier. The intake valve begins to open before TDC. At this point the piston is near maximum deceleration as it approaches TDC at the end of the exhaust stroke.

Looking at valve timing of a normally aspirated engine that produces maximum power in the 7,500–9,500 rpm range, the intake valve begins to open 42 crankshaft

113

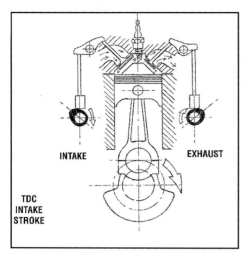

Exhaust valve begins to close as piston approaches TDC while intake valve begins to open. Amount both valves are open is overlap expressed in crankshaft degrees.

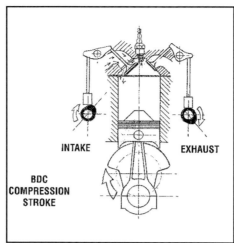

As the piston comes up from BDC, the intake valve closes to seal the cylinder so the air/fuel charge can be compressed. Late valve closing will allow more filling, but will result in reverse flow at lower engine speeds.

degrees before TDC as the piston comes up on the exhaust stroke. The intake valve remains open for the 180° between TDC and BDC, plus another 77° after bottom dead center (BDC), which is well into the official compression stroke. Total time—duration—in terms of crankshaft degrees the intake valve is open 42° + 180° + 77° = 299°. Going back to when the intake valve is opening and the piston is coming up to complete the exhaust stroke, the exhaust valve is in the process of closing. In this instance it closes at 42° after TDC, meaning both intake and exhaust valve openings *overlap* by 84° of crankshaft rotation.

With help from exhaust-header collector inertia, energy builds up in the exhaust gasses at high rpm as they rush out past the exhaust valve. At this point the piston is slowing to a stop at TDC. An effect called *overlap breathing*, or *scavenging*, takes place at the exhaust header collector and also occurs across the intake valve. The

low pressure at the intake valve produced by exhaust gas flow helps to draw in the fresh air/fuel charge. Ideally, during this overlap period, the exhaust valve closes just as the tail end of the exhaust gasses depart the combustion chamber, but before any fresh air/fuel charge can escape.

As the piston accelerates down the bore on the intake stroke, the exhaust valve has closed and the intake valve continues to open to maximum as cylinder pressure continues to drop. Piston velocity reaches maximum near 70° after TDC. Maximum valve lift should occur about another 40° later, or 110° after TDC. As was the case with exhaust flow, considerable energy has built up in the intake charge. It's now time to take advantage of this inertia to continue filling the cylinder as the piston slows to a stop and reverses direction as the crankshaft throw swings through bottom dead center (BDC). During this piston "dwell time," the intake valve remains

open another 77°. The intent is to allow cylinder filling to continue into the compression side before the piston reaches maximum acceleration. Closing the valve at the precise time and no later prevents *reverse pumping*, or reverse flow into the intake port.

Compression Stroke—The piston accelerates up the sealed cylinder just as the intake valve closes, allowing the fresh air/fuel charge to be compressed. Before the piston reaches TDC, the ignition system ignites the air/fuel charge, making the actual compression stroke the shortest of the four. This ensures complete burning in about 3/1,000 second after ignition.

Power Stroke—Ignition is timed to start the air/fuel charge burning before TDC so maximum cylinder pressure occurs at about 15° after TDC into the power stroke. The challenge is to take advantage of this pressure to produce power as long as possible, but use it before it's entirely gone to help reduce pumping losses. This is done by opening the exhaust valve early, or 77° before BDC, allowing residual pressure to *blow down* the cylinder and accelerate the exhaust gasses past the exhaust valve before the piston starts back up to complete exhaust gas removal.

Exhaust Stroke—With the exhaust valve opening at 77° before BDC, blown-down pressure, which is considerably higher than atmospheric pressure, accelerates exhaust gasses past the exhaust valve while the piston is moving down, but at a much slower rate. The piston reaches BDC shortly afterwards and reverses direction to

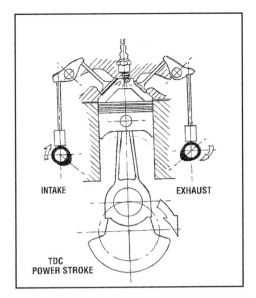

Exhaust valve opens before BDC on the power stroke to blow down the cylinder in preparation of the exhaust stroke.

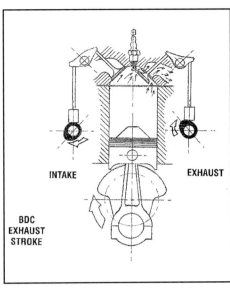

The piston takes over the job of pushing out the exhaust gasses as it comes up on the exhaust stroke to complete the fourth and final stroke.

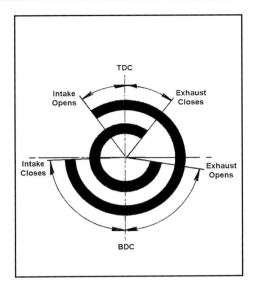

This chart, typical of those found on cam cards, shows valve openings and closings in relation to one another during 720° of crankshaft rotation.

increase velocity and inertia of exhaust gasses as the piston moves up toward TDC. At this point cylinder pressure is reduced to slightly more than atmospheric when the piston starts back up, meaning it has less pressure to resist.

Maximum exhaust valve lift occurs as the piston nears the maximum rate of acceleration. As the piston slows as it approaches TDC, the intake valve opens just before finishing the fourth stroke in the overlap phase. The exhaust valve closes before the piston reaches maximum rate of acceleration on the intake side. This minimizes the escape of a portion of the air/fuel charge past the exhaust valve. It also keeps the trailing end of the exhaust gasses from being drawn back into the cylinder to dilute the air/fuel charge as pressure in the cylinder changes from above atmospheric to below atmospheric.

Of the six valve events just described, some are more critical than others. In order of importance, they are:

1. Intake closing.
2. Intake opening (could be reversed with exhaust opening depending on conditions).
3. Exhaust closing (could be reversed with intake opening depending on conditions).
4. Exhaust opening.
5. Maximum intake valve lift.
6. Maximum exhaust valve lift.

Changing Valve Events

With a good understanding of what goes on with the four strokes of an engine and what the valves are doing in relation to piston position, it's important be aware of what happens with engine performance when valve events are changed.

Intake Valve Opening—Early intake opening is half of the overlap story. The piston would be farther away from reaching TDC on the exhaust stroke, which will cause engine to be rough and balky at low engine speeds because of exhaust gas dilution of the air/fuel mixture.

As engine speed increases, flow efficiency to and from the cylinder improves. Velocity and the resulting inertia of the mixture at higher rpm overcomes most exhaust gas dilution to improve power output. But earlier intake valve opening may hurt power at low- and mid-range engine speeds while improving it at higher rpm.

Exhaust Valve Opening— Opening the exhaust valve earlier has little effect on engine performance at high rpm because most useful cylinder pressure is used up between 80° and 90° before BDC of the power stroke. But a too-early exhaust valve opening can reduce power output at lower engine speeds. The bottom line: exhaust valve opening has the least effect on engine performance than other valve events.

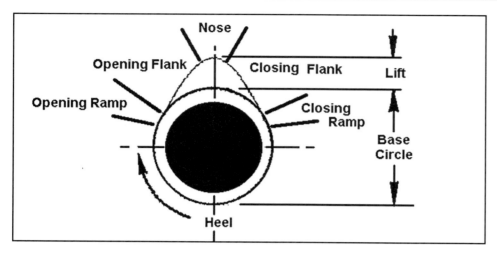

Basic features of camshaft lobes. Lobe lift is typically given in inches, with duration and overlap in degrees of crankshaft rotation, or twice camshaft rotation. As lift is increased, duration and overlap are usually increased. Other terms defining a cam lobe are base circle, opening and closing ramps and the heel and toe, or nose.

Exhaust Valve Closing—The other end of the valve overlap period is exhaust valve closing. Late exhaust valve closing—piston farther down on the intake stroke—contributes immensely to evil low-rpm performance. The air/fuel mixture keeps going through the combustion chamber and continues past the exhaust where it does nothing useful except help cool the closing exhaust valve. But as rpm increases, late exhaust-valve closing allows a higher percentage of the exhaust gasses to exit the cylinder as increased inertia keeps things moving. This results in higher cylinder pressure and power output even though some "bleed-off" of the air/fuel charge may occur.

Intake Valve Closing—In order of occurrence, the exhaust valve was opened, the intake valve was opened and the exhaust valve was closed. Although intake valve closing is the last valve event to occur, it is the one that can make or break engine performance. *Where the intake valve closes in relation to piston*

position has more effect on engine performance than the previous three opening and closing points combined. When optimized, late intake valve closing can capture within the cylinder a larger air/fuel-charge volume before pressure reversal caused by the rising piston forces it back past the closing intake valve. Just where the most desirable intake valve closing point is for a particular application is difficult to determine. Later intake valve closing is necessary at high rpm can be self-defeating due to increased reverse pumping as engine speed drops.

Extremely late valve closing makes the effect of reverse pumping worse. It can get so bad that mid-range response will be so poor that the engine won't be able to pull itself into a favorable power-producing speed range. A balancing act goes on at this point in an effort to avoid a "peaky" engine—one that operates best at a high, but narrow rpm range. An engine that has the intake closing point delayed too long will have a driver that is accustomed to the competition

going by when coming out of corners or off the line. By the time the engine is making "good power" it's time to get off the throttle and on the brakes.

Earlier intake valve closing is what gives an engine power at the broadest speed range. It also improves part-throttle response because of minimal reverse pumping, allowing more of the air/fuel charge to be trapped in the cylinder and put to work. Again, you must deal with compromises when it comes to valve timing. It's a trade-off between what you want versus what you can get. "Over-camming" an engine is the easiest trap to fall into. The result is a lazy, soggy-performing engine at the bottom end. Dyno and track testing proves this out.

When choosing a camshaft, listen closely to recommendations made by cam manufacturers' tech representatives. What competitors use is a closely held secret, so don't expect manufacturers' reps to give away secrets. Regardless, listen to what they say, then push the envelope *a little* and test your choices on the dyno and track.

CAMSHAFT

Given a set of lifters, pushrods, rocker arms and valve springs, the camshaft is what makes the valve do what it's supposed to. So you'll need to know and understand technical terms that describe a camshaft when checking or ordering. Of these terms, the most familiar are *lobe lift, duration,* and *overlap.*

Base Circle

Centered on the axis of the

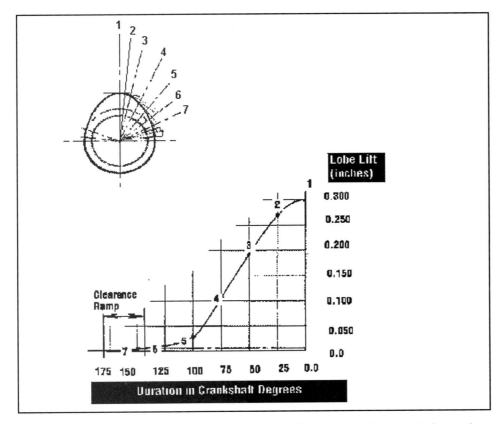

Opening profile of a low-lift cam graphed in 25° increments of crankshaft rotation. Closing profile is the same with a symmetrical lobe, but different with an asymmetrical profile.

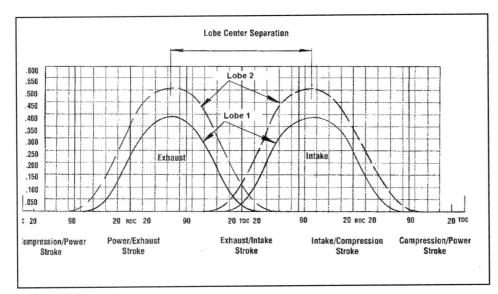

Lobe profile graph illustrates effect lift and duration have on overlap. Lobe 1 has considerably less overlap than Lobe 2.

camshaft, the *base circle* is the foundation of a cam lobe. When the lifter, or follower or tappet, is on the base circle, the valve is closed. The valve is fully opened when the lifter is on the *nose*. The

difference between the base-circle radius and distance from the center of the camshaft to the nose is *lobe lift*. As a lobe rotates, it raises and lowers the lifter the distance the nose is above the base circle.

How much the valve opens is lobe lift multiplied by *rocker-arm ratio*. To open and close a valve as gently and quickly as possible, *opening* and *closing flanks* are ground into the lobe profile. For solid-lifter cams, *clearance ramps* are added between the base circle and opening and closing flanks to take up lash between the rocker arm and valve-stem tip before rapid valve acceleration or deceleration occurs. Because a hydraulic cam operates with a zero lash valvetrain, clearance ramps are not needed.

Duration

Duration is lobe lift in crankshaft degrees between opening and closing points based on a predetermined lift, or baseline. There are two published durations for a camshaft. The first is for advertising and the other for checking accuracy. For example, a cam may have 281° duration at 0.020-in. lift, but 253° at 0.050-in. lift. The first is for advertising; the second for accuracy when degreeing the cam.

Lobe Center

Lobe center is at the highest point of lift of lobe given in crankshaft degrees. Maximum lift will occur approximately 110° after TDC for the intake lobe.

Profile graphically describes the shape of a cam lobe encompassing all features just detailed. Lobe profile may be a mirror image on

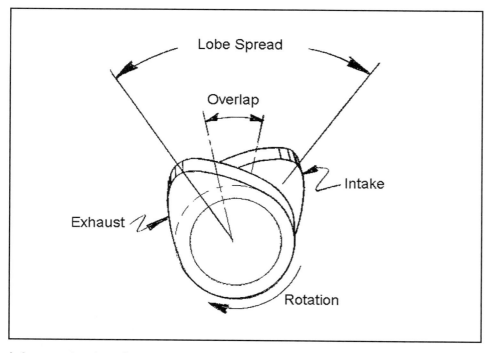

Lobe spread and overlap are expressed in crankshaft degrees.

opening and closing sides of the lobe centerline, making it a *symmetrical* profile. However, it may be desirable that it has different opening and closing profiles, or an *asymmetrical* profile. Further, because exhaust and intake functions are different, lobe profiles for intake and exhaust sides may be different. Such a camshaft is termed a *dual-pattern* camshaft.

Lobe Separation Angle

Lobe separation angle, or spread, and overlap describe the relationship between intake and exhaust lobes. It is the angular separation in crankshaft degrees between intake and exhaust *lobe centers* as illustrated. Also illustrated is *overlap*, or degrees of crankshaft rotation both valves are open.

Typically, duration increases as lobe lift is increased. This is due to the limitation of how fast a valvetrain can be accelerated or decelerated due to loading on the flanks and valve impact with the seat. As for overlap, it increases with duration providing lobe separation is not changed. Increasing lobe separation reduces overlap and vice versa providing lobe profiles are not changed.

Flat Tappet vs. Roller

Compared to a flat-tappet cam, a roller cam runs with less friction, which reduces power loss and wear, and with higher lobe lifts. Roller followers can tolerate virtually any lift the valvetrain can tolerate. As for a flat-tappet cam, lobe lift is limited by tappet diameter. So for maximum lobe lift, 0.875-in. diameter lifters are used to prevent edge contact with the lobe. To maximize lift at the valve, high-ratio rocker arms are required, but using such rocker arms come at a price. As discussed later, valvetrain

instability and higher lifter-to-lobe pressure are the main disadvantages.

Camshafts designed for flat tappets and roller lifters are distinctly different in shape and material. Viewed head-on, lobes for roller lifters are square to the cam centerline whereas flat-tappet cam lobes are tapered, or lower at one side by approximately 0.001 in. Also, flat tappets—lifters—are not really flat, but crowned described by a spherical radius of about 60 in. The combination of lobe taper and lifter crown ensures minimum lifter-to-lobe contact that is off-center with the lifter. It also prevents edge contact with the lobe, which would quickly destroy the lobe and lifter. The off-center contact with the lifter rotates the lifter in the bore constantly moving the contact point with the lobe to increase lobe and lifter durability.

Flat tappet and roller cam profiles are distinctly different due to how the lifter contacts the lobe. Viewed in profile, a flat tappet contacts the lobe nearly across its full surface and almost in the same plane. Except when on the nose and base circle, this is not so with a roller lifter. Lobe-to-roller lifter contact is offset to the lobe centerline on the opening and closing ramps, meaning the lifter would not be raised as much in its bore if used with the profile of a flat-tappet cam. Consequently, roller cam lobe flanks must be "fattened" to provide valve events similar to that of an equivalent flat-tappet cam. More so, the roller cam has a major advantage because there is no need to consider edge contact with the lifter as with a flat-tappet cam. Consequently, opening and closing

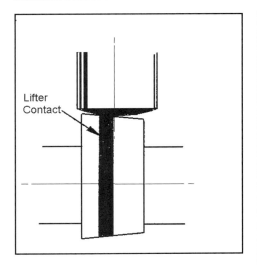

Lobe taper and lifter-foot crown combine to rotate lifter and provide minimum lifter-to-lobe contact.

Jesel Dog Bone guide plates attach to block and straddles flats milled on two sides of lifters.

flanks of a roller cam can be much more aggressive, which allows more aggressive valve openings and closings.

The material used for flat-tappet and roller cams is different. Except for NASCAR Cup engines, cast iron is used for flat-tappet cams and steel for roller cams. The sliding contact flat tappets have with the lobes requires the use of

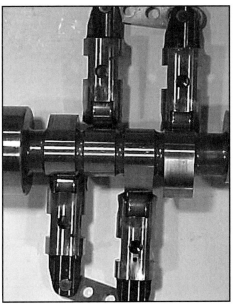

Classic tie bars, or blades, hold paired lifters in line with cam lobes. Lifter bosses may have to be ground to clear tie bars as shown, page 145.

cast iron. The graphite in the cast iron and its porosity, which allows it to absorb oil, provides lubrication to reduce wear and friction. Additionally, cast-iron cam lobe surfaces are parkerized or nitrided to enhance oil absorption and improve lubricity, particularly for the critical break-in period.

Cup Camshafts

Cup camshafts are a breed of their own. Since rules require flat-tappet cams be used, engine builders do whatever is possible to make them perform similarly to a roller cam. First, camshafts are manufactured from hard steel, i.e., tool steel with hardened lobe surfaces. To get maximum duration, 0.903-in. diameter lifters are used. A slight rake on the lobes accommodate lifters with a 40-in. foot radius, giving a 1.600— 1.800-in. drop from the center of the foot to the outer edge.

Additionally, the enclosed cam tunnel is flooded with oil, ensuring lifter and lobe contact surfaces receive maximum lubrication.

To simplify manufacturing, steel is used for roller cams. It doesn't need the lubricating qualities of cast iron. Machining can start with a billet, not a casting. Another major advantage is the lobes and lifters don't need to be drenched in oil. Therefore, pumping losses can be reduced. Less oil is needed up top, so less returns to the sump.

One requirement needed for roller lifters not needed nor desired for flat tappets is a way keep them from rotating in the lifter bore. This is so they remain square and straight in relation to lobe rotation. In chassis terms, lifter camber and toe relative to the lobe must be zero. Squaring is taken care of with true lifter bores, but lifters that would otherwise be free to turn in their bores must remain in a straight-ahead position so the rollers don't skid on the cam lobes. This is done with tie bars, guide plates or keyed lifter-bore bushings.

Final thought as to flat-tappet versus roller-cam use: Don't use a flat-tappet cam unless you are required to do so by racing rules. There are just too many advantages to using a roller cam, particularly for racing. First, a roller cam doesn't require breaking it. On the other hand, a flat-tappet cam requires special treatment during break-in. Unlike a flat-tappet street cam that can be broken in less that 30 minutes at fast idle, a racing cam with stiff valve springs must be broken in with either light valve springs or low-ratio rocker arms. The superior durability, lubricating

Tray is handy for keeping lifters in order as they are removed.

Wear is rapid on both lifter and lobe. Note pitting and concave shape of lifter foot matched with "flat" lobe.

Note pitted lobe surface. Cam should not be reused.

Used roller cam lobes should look like this—with a slight burnish on the surface caused by contact with the roller.

indicated by rutted wear surface on flank (arrow).

Bearing journals on roller cam are microfinished to provide smooth surface required for running in needle bearings.

and low-friction qualities of a roller cam makes it a no-brainer decision unless rules demand the use of a flat-tappet cam.

Camshaft & Follower Inspection

Whether new or used, inspect the camshaft. Granted, lobe, bearing-journal and distributor-drive gear condition should not be an issue with a new cam. However, this is not so with lobe profile and timing. These should always be suspect, thus part of your inspection process. But don't

assume any part you'll be putting in your engine is without fault, new or used.

Inspect the Lobes—This is particularly important with a flat-tappet racing cam. If a lobe starts to wear, it does so with the lifter at a very rapid rate. See the photo above. In the first place, I don't recommend you reuse a flat-tappet cam, certainly not the lifters. But if you insist, keep used tappets in order to inspect them and the lobes with which they were mated. If the cam checks out OK, reinstall it with new lifters.

Roller-cam lobes are not totally immune from damage. Pitting is the most common problem. But if a roller were turned sideways on a lobe, the lobe and follower would be destroyed. But unlike flat-tappet cams, a roller cam and followers are more likely to be reusable. Regardless, closely inspect the roller cam and lifters.

Bearing Journals—When using needle bearings, bearing-journal roughness should not exceed 0.4 microinches on the Ra scale. In addition to roughness, check that journals are free of scratches, nicks

Pushrod guide plate is used to stabilize stud-mounted rocker arm.

Standard racing setup, 1.60:1 T&D aluminum rocker arms installed in pairs on single shaft secured with bolts at each end. Note they are marked for #2 cylinder.

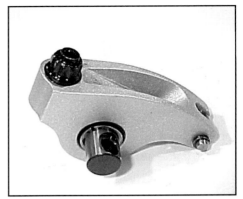

This is a single shaft-mounted Jesel rocker arm for a Mopar Cup engine. This setup is used for heads with valves staggered at different angles.

or dents. Holes are permissible, though, edges should be blended into journal surface.

Degreeing the Cam

Degreeing the cam accomplishes two important goals: it verifies that the cam is ground to the correct specifications and it can be timed correctly. For this critical inspection step, refer to Chapter 8.

ROCKER ARMS

A highly loaded rocking beam, the standard high-performance rocker arm is manufactured from a high-strength aluminum or stainless-steel alloy. Typically, it has a shaft-mounted needle-bearing trunnion, a roller tip and a provision at the pushrod end for making valve lash adjustments with a cup- or ball-type adjuster. Gone for hard-core racing is stamped-steel or cast rockers with ball pivots—too much friction and too little strength. Pushrods are guided by either the rocker arms on shafts or guide plates. Guide plates are used when shaft is secured by a rocker-arm stud and nut at center of trunnion. Guide plates are not required with shaft-mounted rocker arms.

Rocker Arm Ratio

Used to multiply camshaft lobe lift at valve, rocker arm ratio depends on two dimensions in relation to the rocker arm pivot, or pushrod-to-pivot and valve tip-to-pivot. Using one as a standard, if the distance from the pushrod contact to pivot is 1.00 and the distance from pivot to the contact point with the valve is 1.50., the rocker arm ratio is 1.50:1. Common rocker arm ratios are 1.5:1, 1.6:1, 1.65:1, 1.70:1 and 1.75:1. A 1.3:1 ratio rocker arm is also available for breaking in high-performance, flat-tappet cams.

Rocker arm ratio is a movement and force ratio. As an example, if the pushrod end of the rocker arm moves 0.100 in. in either direction, the valve end moves in the opposite direction 0.150 in. for a 1.50:1 rocker arm. For a 1.6:1 rocker arm, movement at the valve is 0.160 in. for 0.100-in. movement at the pushrod and so on. But higher movement at the valve is not a "something-for-nothing"

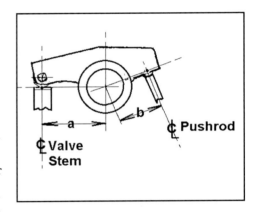

Rocker arm ratio is determined by the distance from the contact point with the valve to the pivot compared to the distance from the pivot to the pushrod end center. Ratio is expressed as a/b = rocker arm ratio.

proposition.

Just as rocker-arm ratio is an indicator of relative movement at both ends, it is also an indicator of relative forces. Forces are reversed with movement. For example, a 1.5:1 ratio rocker arm with a force of 100 lb at the valve end results in a 150-lb force at the pushrod. This increases with rocker-arm ratio, or 160 lb for a 1.6:1 rocker arm and 170 lb for a 1.7:1 rocker arm. These forces result in higher loads at the pushrods, lifters and cam

Failure wasn't too far away. Magnifying glass wasn't needed to see crack (arrow) at pushrod end.

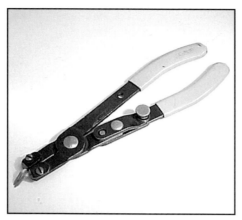

Reversible internal/external retaining-ring pliers fitted with bent tips.

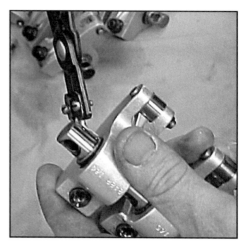

Remove retaining ring, then slide rocker arm off shaft.

Inspect needle bearings. Lighted magnifying glass is used to inspect bearing.

lobes which increases valvetrain deflections, wear, friction and power loss. The hope is additional power losses will be overcome by an increase in power. So stay with 1.50:1 or 1.60:1 for more than 7,000 rpm. Ratios exceeding 1.65:1 should be considered aggressive because they flex more and contribute to valvetrain instability as proven out by testing. But—there is always a but. A major advantage of using high-ratio rocker arms is the valve springs are more effective at returning the pushrods and lifters to the closed positions. This is a major advantage when using high-lifts at high rpm. See sidebar on testing valvetrains, page 123.

Inspect Rocker Arms

Begin rocker arm inspection by removing the retaining ring at one end of the shaft. You'll need retaining ring pliers with fine tips for this job. Once you've removed the retaining ring, slide out the shaft. Clean disassembled rocker arm and shaft in parts washer.

Besides checking rocker arms for cracks, inspect needle bearings, roller tip and pushrod seat. Always expect to find the unexpected. Also check shaft bearing surface for wear. A magnifying glass and light will help reveal faults you may otherwise not detect. Look closely at the needle bearings. If a cage is used, make sure it is not broken. Look also for broken needles. If you find any problem, push out the old bearing and install new one. If there's a problem with the bearing, chances are the shaft will also be damaged, so check it closely, too. Make sure roller at tip rotates smoothly and is not flat spotted. At the other end, check cup or ball pushrod seat for scoring. Replace any damaged parts. If all is OK, reassemble rocker arms with clean assembly lube and set them aside for installation time.

PUSHRODS

A pushrod is a simple column with pivoted ends. It's the middleman between the cam and rocker arm. Not only must pushrods support loads from spring pressure multiplied by rocker arm ratio and valvetrain inertia, they

must support loads imposed by mysterious valvetrain harmonics, such as spring surge. When overloaded, a pushrod will bow much like a pole vaulter's pole, which amplifies already high loads and introduces instability into the valvetrain. Consequently, a pushrod must be sufficiently strong, light and *in tune* with the valvetrain.

The two main features of a pushrod are strength and weight for a given diameter, wall thickness and length. Hardened balls are at

VALVETRAIN TESTING

Speed, or rpm, of a pushrod engine is limited by the valvetrain. However this speed envelope has been pushed to limits we couldn't have imagined a few years ago. As discussed in previous chapters, the use of lightweight, high-strength materials has contributed to allowing large-bore engines to touch 10,000 rpm intermittently and operate at 9,500 rpm continuously. In addition to materials, another factor allowing engines to survive at such high speeds are modern testing and monitoring methods.

Ultimate engine testing is done as it always has been, or on the track or dyno. This is very expensive if not impossible to test individual engine components or systems using a track or dyno because it must be done with a complete engine. Add to this the cost and time required for dyno or track testing, crew and car costs, the whole process becomes cost prohibitive for even the most well-financed race team. Fortunately, equipment such as the Spintron is available for making it possible to isolate parts or systems for testing and monitoring such as valvetrains. A Spintron can be programmed for either short tests, preprogrammed durability tests or simulated racing situations such as an entire 500-mile race.

A Spintron appears to be a dyno in reverse. It was originally developed for driving a partial engine to test valvetrains rather than sacrificing a complete engine to perform the test. To simulate a valvetrain in whole or in part for testing, a straight shaft that simulates the crankshaft at the front and rear. For tracing valve movement, the Spintron Laser Valve Tracking System (LVTS) is used. A hole is cut through side of the block and through the cylinder to allow access for a laser transducer. A plate seals the bottom of the cylinder, and the entire interior surfaces of the cylinder, combustion chamber and valves are coated white for maximum reflectivity. Heads are installed with valves. Also installed is the camshaft, timing set and valvetrain for one or all cylinders. A laser transducer is inserted into the cylinder through the access hole and positioned so the laser beam will be square to the valve head. Beam reflection is received by the transducer to indicate valve positions at speeds from 500–20,000 rpm.

The operator controls the Spintron at the console while the computer monitors and gathers data supplied by the valve-position sensor. Other engine functions are also monitored, either by the computer or separate gauges. An

CVProducts' Spintron setup in soundproof room for testing Mopar valve-rain components. Similar to dyno testing, CVProducts leases Spintron time to individuals for testing their parts or systems.

Laser transducer is installed through hole cut in side of block. Note shaft through cylinder bores installed in place of crankshaft for driving timing set and sealing oiling system.

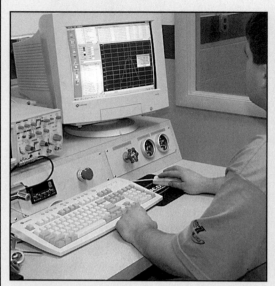

Operator controls and monitors Spintron from console similar to that of a dynamometer.

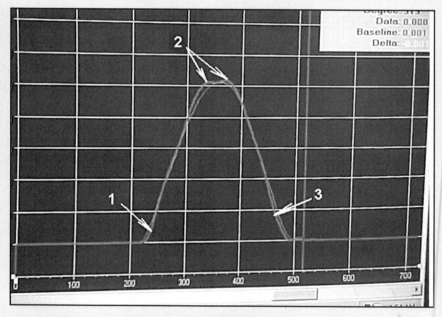

Scan of valve movement at 6,000 rpm overlaid on baseline scan indicates unstable valvetrain. 1. Valvetrain deflections or harmonics causes valve to loft as it approaches nose of cam. 2. Valve returns to baseline scan, but lofts as it approaches nose of cam, probably due to spring surge. 3. Movement is relatively stable on closing flank. 4. Valve bounces off seat.

initial trace made of stable valve lift at 2,000 or 3,000 rpm becomes the baseline scan. Observing traces made at higher, different engine speeds overlaid on the baseline trace can be startling as well as revealing. Variations from the baseline trace indicate everything from pushrod bending, rocker arm deflection and spring surge to valve bounce off the seat. Mysterious valvetrain failures that were previously difficult or impossible to identify can be isolated using these traces. In addition to valve traces, the Spintron can also be used to test valvetrain durability by running an entire race programmed into the computer.

Major valvetrain failures have occurred in engines that lived at 8,500–9,500-rpm for 500 miles on big tracks, but failed on shorter tracks at lower rpm. The problem was a valvetrain that was stable at higher engine speeds, but was unstable at a lower rpm due to undesirable harmonics and resulting higher loads. Typical failure was a valve spring abrading its way through the titanium spring retainer, causing the valve to drop. Unlike stock car engines that operate more at sustained engine speeds, drag engines aren't plagued with such valvetrain failures to the same extent. This is because they go through any undesirable harmonics at a quicker rate.

Scan at 9,000 rpm. 1. Trace under baseline reveals pushrod or rocker arm may be from bending at beginning of opening flank. 2. Double hump at nose indicates lofting at end of opening flank, then again after crossing nose. 3. Trace falls under baseline at closing flank possibly due to pushrod bending.

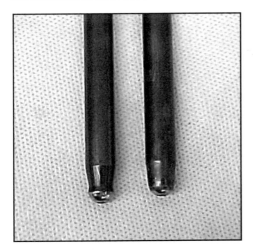

Pushrod end at left is undercut for extra clearance at the rocker arm.

Highly developed valve spring assembly for NASCAR applications. Spring assembly consists of highly polished inner and outer springs with flat-wound damper in between.

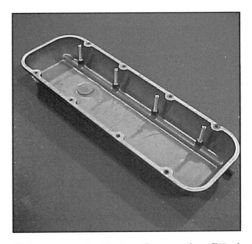

Valve cover for Dodge Cup engine fitted with oil-spray nozzles for cooling valve springs. Fitting at end of valve cover is for connecting oil-supply line.

each end or a ball at one end and cup, or socket, at the other. The most common diameters are 5/16 in. and 3/8 in. For some applications some pushrods are available up to as large as a 7/16-in. (0.4375 in.) diameter with increments of 1/32 in. in between. Wall thicknesses are 0.060 in., 0.065 in. and 0.080 in.

Material, Size & Ends

Other than the all-important length—determined during preassembly—concentrate on pushrod material, heat treatment, finish, diameter, wall thickness and end types for now. All have an effect on strength or weight. For material, use hardened 4130 chrome-moly steel with a hardness of 60 R_c on the Rockwell C scale. As for diameter, 3/8-in. with a 0.065-in. wall thickness will do for most applications, but 0.080-in. wall should be used with high-lift flat-tappet cams and 1.65:1 or 1.70:1 rocker arms. Lighter weight pushrods with tapered tubing are also available.

Keep in mind when using guide plates that pushrod diameter must match guide-plate-slot width. Also, large pushrods may need more clearance at the cylinder heads, especially next to the intake runners. Check clearance during preassembly. It be surprising that 5/16-in. pushrods sometimes require more clearance than 3/8-in. pushrods. This is due to excessive flexing of the smaller pushrod.

Ball ends are used at lifters and cups or balls at the rocker arms. This requires adjusters at rocker arms be compatible with those at pushrod ends. Also consider top-end oiling. Some are drilled and others are not. For example, if spray bars are used up top, drilled adjusters are not required. Work with valvetrain tech personnel on your engine requirements.

STUD GIRDLES

Stud-mounted rocker arms need extra support for studs from stud girdles. Girdles distribute load from one rocker arm stud to the adjacent studs to limit deflections.

Compatible adjusting nuts with set screw at center are needed for mounting girdles. Taller valve covers provide additional room for girdle assemblies.

VALVE SPRINGS

Teamed with valves, one of the most highly worked components in an engine is the valve spring. A valve spring must cycle between installed height—valve closed—to open height and back every 720° of crankshaft rotation. That doesn't sound like any big deal until you consider how many times a second this occurs. At 6,000 rpm a valve spring will cycle 50 times a second or 75 times per second at 9,000 rpm. To find the rate of valve opening and closing, divide engine rpm by 120.

While allowing a valve to open and close, the spring must have sufficient force to keep all slack out of the valvetrain. It must do this while closing the valve firmly on its seat, pushing the lifter onto the cam lobe and holding it there until it's time to open the valve again at all speeds within the range of the

Three-piece valve spring; an inner spring, outer spring, and damper between the two.

flow to the top end. An example is the high heat generated by one set of valve springs when tested on a Spintron. Oil temperature quickly reaches 200°F! So manufacturers of high-performance valve springs have many challenges to ensure their springs survive in a racing environment.

Valve Spring Terms

The typical racing valve spring consists of two constant-pitch helical springs that are squared and ground at the ends. Three springs are used when extreme lift and loads are required. A flat-wound helical damper is sometimes used between the inner and outer springs. Besides material, each spring will have a specific wire diameter (d), number of active coils (n), spring diameter (D) and free height (H) as shown in the photo above right. These dimensions determine the force required to compress a spring a given distance. This *rate*, or stiffness, of a spring is typically expressed in pounds per inch (lb/in.).

As wire size **d** expressed in inches is increased, spring rate increases. As coil diameter **D** expressed in inches and number of active coils **n** is increased, spring rate decreases. A challenge spring manufacturers face is as wire size d is increased to increase spring rate, so is the effect of the spring index **C**. Spring index is a ratio of spring diameter to wire diameter, or $C = D/d$. Spring index has an inverse effect on spring stress.

As wire diameter is increased, internal spring stresses automatically increase if spring diameter is not increased to com-

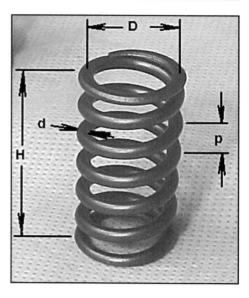

Basic dimensions of a helical valve spring. These and the number of active coils determine spring rate. Spring has 5-3/4 active coils and 6-1/4 total coils.

pensate. As a spring is stiffened—the rate is increased—by increasing wire size, the spring diameter must also be increased to prevent excessive stresses and premature spring failure. This is why larger diameters are used with higher-rate springs.

Other factors affecting spring forces are the number of active coils, free height, installed height and open height. But there are limits on how large a single spring can be made to achieve the desired installed and open forces. As a result two springs—three in extreme cases—must be nested to do the job. The spring must apply forces needed to ensure the valvetrain operates in such a manner that the valve follows a prescribed path during opening and closing without lofting and bouncing at all engine speeds, but doesn't overload the cam so excessive wear and power loss results. In addition, a spring must be designed and developed to limit

engine. Moving a valve and lifter to the closed positions, must be done against the inertia of the rocker arm, pushrod, lifter, retainer, valve and, yes, the spring itself. Then there is the mysterious spring surge that must be dealt with. See next page for more information.

Another example of what a valve spring must endure is heat, not so much from the exhaust valve, but heat generated due to *hysteresis*, or internal friction, as the spring is cycled. This is akin to bending a section of wire back and forth in an effort to break it. The same thing happens to a valve spring if it's overheated and cycled beyond its limits. Thus the reason for using oil spray for cooling. Although not a factor with drag racing engines, cooling by oil spray is a must for endurance engines, particularly those that turn high rpm, with high-lift valves and have limited oil surge caused by the *natural frequency* of the spring and valvetrain as a package.

Spring Surge—Spring surge is a phenomenon manufacturers of camshafts and valvetrains have a difficult time dealing with, particularly with high-lift, high-speed applications. It is directly related to natural frequency in cycles per second. It is that frequency that causes a spring to dance much like the tire of a car bouncing at 55 mph or so when out of balance. A guitar string or surging ocean tide are other examples. Surge is a situation where all coils don't share the same deflection equally when loaded. Rather, the coil closest the spring retainer will deflect first, then transmit this deflection to the next coil and so on. This sets up a progression of deflections, or wave of compressed coils along the spring to the spring base where it is reflected back to the deflected end. The result of severe spring surge—*resonance*—is excessive loads and stresses from very large deflections of the coils that show up as power loss from valve bounce to component failure in the valvetrain.

Rather than making valve springs the culprit, the total natural frequency of the valvetrain must be considered. This begins at the camshaft, but includes everything between the followers and valves. Spring surge can be minimized by using a damper, but the total natural frequency of the valvetrain must also be considered as a total package. The best way to ensure your engine will have a stable valvetrain is to work with a manufacturer to supply a valvetrain

package matched to the camshaft.

Manufacturers develop their systems using equipment such as the Spintron. They also have experience gained from many engine builders that allow them to determine what works and what does not during R&D work.

Note: It's not unusual for a valvetrain to perform as it should, then become unstable when original parts are replaced with those from another manufacturer that are perfectly adequate with their system. So it is not only important that a camshaft and valvetrain provides the valve opening events you want, it is critical the valvetrain is in proper tune.

Spring Material & Finish

The most common valve spring material is a chromium-silicon steel alloy because of its resistance to relaxing when subjected to high operating temperature, although titanium may be used if rules allow. Aside from material, what makes one spring better than another starts with the quality of wire used to manufacture it. Quality is further ensured by the accuracy of a winding spring, heat treating, grinding the ends, shot-peening and final inspection. In addition, the spring may be heat set, or compressed, brought up to an elevated temperature and held at that point for a prescribed amount of time. This procedure reduces the effect of spring relaxation—*modulus of elasticity*—during engine operation provided the spring is not overstressed during its expected service life.

Spring Inspection

There are two primary spring

Check inner and outer springs for installed and open forces. Digital display provides force and dial indicator height. Organize springs with recorded results.

forces with which you must deal. They occur when the valve is open and when closed. As an example, such specifications will be given as 250 lb @ 2.020 in. installed; 675 lb @ 1.270 in. open. This reflects a spring used with a valve lift of 0.750 in. and a rate of 567 lb/in. where *spring rate* is the differences in forces divided by differences in spring heights, or (675 lb – 250 lb) ÷ (2.020 in. – 1.270 in.). Also given is inside and outside dimensions of the springs, or ID and OD. Other specifications sometimes given are height at *coil bind* and height at maximum valve lift. Coil bind is the height a spring can be compressed to where each coil touches the adjacent coils. A valve spring should never see this condition in operation. To prevent coil bind, there should be at least 0.0015-in. minimum clearance between each coil when the spring is compressed to maximum valve lift. This applies to both inner and outer springs. Specifically, spring height at maximum lift should allow at least 0.060-in. more travel before coil-bind height is reached.

For checking new or used springs, the two main specifications to concentrate on are force, commonly called *pressure*, at open height and force at installed height. Springs should be within +/- 10%, but I prefer a +/-5% tolerance. So a spring with a specification of 675 lb at open height is acceptable within a range of 608–742 lb or 641–709 lb using the tighter +/-5% tolerance. Shimming or taller spring retainers can be used to correct. You'll also use spring ID and spring OD combined with other specifications to prepare the cylinder heads. Each spring should fit snugly in the cylinder head spring pocket to prevent it from dancing around and causing excessive wear. This may require machining or the use of spring cups or locators, as is required with aluminum heads.

The squared ends of all valve springs should be chamfered to prevent sharp edges from damaging the retainers or spring seats. Using a bench grinder, knock off the hard edges of both inner and outer springs with a 1/16-in. x 45° chamfer. Take care not to touch any other part of the spring with the grinder to avoid creating a stress riser.

Ordering Valve Springs

Work closely with the camshaft manufacturer on choosing valve springs. Typically, springs come as a package with the camshaft. But work with him on ordering springs separately. Considering the critical nature of this component, supply the manufacturer with all the details you can put together about your engine and the intended application. Supply information that includes the rpm range the engine will operate at and duration of the typical race down to the installed height of the spring. You may not be able to provide information about some things, but you'll get it from him. As with most dealings having to do with engine building, this will be a back-and-forth relationship.

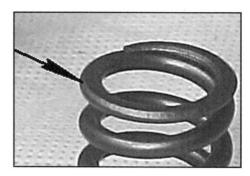

All valve springs should be chamfered as shown (arrow).

Rev Kit

A rev kit supplements the valve springs in keeping the lifters against the cam lobes by adding springs between the bottom sides of the heads and tops of the lifters. They are useful with extremely high valve lifts and high-rpm operation. Just as rocker arm ratio multiplies lobe lift at the valves, it multiplies valve spring load in the same manner at the lifters to keep them against the cam lobes. So follow the old rule, "Parts left out don't break." Also, parts left out have zero weight and don't cost anything. So unless you absolutely need a rev kit, don't use one. Work with your cam and valvetrain supplier on this one.

THE LUBRICATION SYSTEM

7

An engine must be provided with an uninterrupted supply of clean oil that is free of air bubbles. This is the primary job of the lubrication system. Cooling and sealing are secondary functions. Doing this with minimal power loss requires optimum clearances, an efficient pump, oil viscosity that matches clearances, low crankcase pressure and minimal drag on bottom-end components through shielding and rerouting oil.

Oil is stored in a reservoir until it can be picked up and pumped back into the engine. In a wet sump system this reservoir is the engine sump, or oil pan. For a dry sump system—so called because the sump is pumped dry—oil is pumped from the sump to a remote reservoir. Wet or dry sump, oil is picked up from the reservoir and pumped under pressure to the filter and cooler, if used, then into the engine. Oil galleries in the engine then route oil to the cam bearings, main bearing journals, crankshaft, rod journals, and lifters. Oil is then sent under pressure, by spray or drip lubrication to the rockers arms, valve guides, valve springs, oil pump/distributor gear and timing set. At the bottom end, oil is also delivered to the rings, pistons, and piston pins. Oil drains back to the sump where the lubrication cycle continues. One variation with some wet sump and

Dry sump lubrication system plumbed for dyno-testing engine.

most dry sump systems is oil from the lifter valley is pumped to the oil reservoir rather than by draining.

The most complex details of any lubrication system, wet or dry sump, are how oil is picked up in the sump, filtered, cooled, routed after passing through the engine and where it is stored. If an engine is installed where room is unlimited and there are minimal g-forces to contend with, a wet sump system can be equipped to work as well as a dry sump system. However, with an engine that must

fit in the tight confines of a chassis, mounted low for maximizing vehicle performance, and will undergo high g-forces from cornering, braking and accelerating, a dry sump system has definite advantages.

While lubricating and cooling, oil is whipped around with extreme turbulence, or windage, in the crankcase, causing aeration and loss power. Major improvements can be made by making internal engine modifications and choosing or modifying system components. This is best done by maximizing oiling system efficiency and reducing windage without compromising lubrication and cooling. While doing this, remember that all areas of an engine get an adequate supply of oil, so err on the safe side. However, engines have been sacrificed in an effort to maximize power through the use of reduced clearances, coatings, and lower viscosity oils.

WET SUMP SYSTEMS

Wet sump systems are relatively lightweight, inexpensive and simple. The sump, or oil pan, in the basic wet sump system catches and stores the oil draining from above after it's been pumped through the engine. This makes it the reservoir, storing the oil until it is picked up again by the pump. Such a system is reliable enough except when one must perform under racing conditions. Then extensive modifications are required before a wet sump oiling system will be reliable enough to prevent engine damage or total failure.

Sump

When placed in a racing environment, the single biggest problem a wet sump system has is oil handling. First, an oil pump pickup must remain immersed in oil to prevent oil starvation. Air doesn't lubricate very well. When starved of oil, it only takes an instant for an engine under load at high rpm to score a journal or seize a bearing. And keeping the pickup immersed in oil must be done in a sump that is usually packaged between the bottom of the engine, chassis components and, in most cases, the ground.

TRIBOLOGY

Studies by fluid engineers at universities in cooperation with bearing manufacturers using the science of tribology have revealed some interesting things. For one, as oil is circulated through an engine, air is *entrained*. This produces aerated, or bubbles in the oil called aeration. Interestingly, the viscosity of aerated oil is higher than "pure oil." Aerated oil has a number of undesirable features such as faulty hydraulic tappet operation, although not a problem with most racing engines using solid lifters, there are other serious affects. Oil aeration and the resulting cavitation include bearing erosion, friction losses, oil-film thickness and heat transfer. These result in power loss or bearing damage. So make a special effort to eliminate oil aeration using the methods discussed in this chapter.

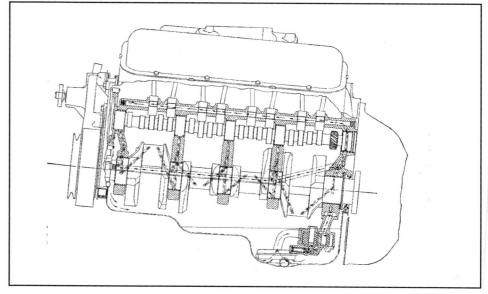

Illustration of stock big-block Chevy shows simplicity of the basic wet sump lubrication system.

To prevent oil starvation, a compartment with baffles and a series of trap doors surrounding the pickup is used to maintain a constant supply of oil at the pickup. The sump is bulged at one or both sides to increase oil volume. This is to provide additional oil to the outboard side of the sump during cornering and compensate for oil used. How this is accomplished depends on the type of racing; accelerating and braking coupled with left turns only for stock-car racing, right and left turns for road racing or only accelerating and braking for drag racing. Trap door/s and runners direct oil flow into the pickup compartment and trap it there during braking, turning, accelerating or a combination of these.

Windage Tray and Scraper

Attached to the bottom end or combined with the oil pan, whether a wet- or dry-sump system, is a windage tray and possibly a separate scrapper. Windage, or air turbulence, inside

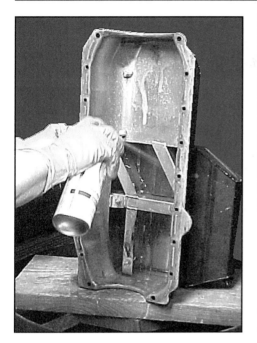

Sump extended to right of stock car oil pan uses baffles and trap doors to maintain oil level at pickup during braking, accelerating and turning left.

Louvers in the windage tray are oriented to scrape off oil clinging to spinning crank and rod assembly. Hole in windage tray provides clearance for pump and pickup.

Oil scraper and baffle are attached to main cap bolts on record-setting Bonneville Salt Flats engine. Note orientation of scraper to crankshaft.

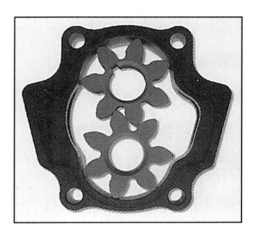

Straight-cut gears, or spur gears, are used in most GM engines and dry-sump systems. Drive gear is keyed to driveshaft and idler gear rotates on fixed shaft. Photo courtesy Aivaid.

the crankcase is caused by the reciprocating action of the piston-and-rod assemblies combined with the rotating crank-and-rod assembly. A windage tray provides a horizontal partition in the crankcase between the crankshaft and oil sump. Scrapers, screens or louvers are positioned to reduce drag on the crankshaft and oil aeration, or mixing of air and oil, by stripping oil from the spinning bottom-end assembly and isolating the area below the crankshaft from turbulence above.

Oil Pump

The abundance of components and accessories available for wet sump lubrication systems include blue-;printed or reworked internal pumps, external pumps, an array of oil pans, windage trays, remote filters, inline filters, coolers and lines.

Mounted in the crankcase to the block, OEM wet sump oil pumps are traditionally driven at 50% engine speed by the camshaft through a common gear and shaft arrangement with the distributor. However, setups are available that allow you to mount a pump externally so it can be driven by a crankshaft belt. This makes it easy to service the pump, change the pump drive ratio, add a vacuum pump and use more than one scavenging stage. A two-stage pump has two pumps driven by a common shaft. A separate pickup or suction port is used with each stage.

Regardless of mounting, all oil pumps are *positive displacement*. The volume of oil taken in equals the volume pumped out. Such pumps are classified by type of gears used. Traditionally used in OEM and racing applications are spur-gear or gerotor pumps. All one-stage pumps, where a stage consists of a suction side and pressure side, GM typically used spur-gear pumps whereas Ford and Chrysler used the gerotor type pump. Gear-type pumps use one gear to drive another. In gerotor pumps, a gear drives a rotor. Lobe-type rotors of the Roots-type are used in some dry sump systems.

For each rotation of the driving gear or lobe, the driven gear or lobe of a gear- or lobe-type pump turn once. The rotor of geroter pump turns slower, or typically at 80% of drive-gear speed. When it comes to efficiency, gerotor and Roots pumps are superior whereas the gear pump is more tolerant of debris. When using a gerotor or Roots pump, it's good practice to install a low-restriction filter/s in the scavenge lines, or before the pump.

Pump Volume—Oil pump volume is typically increased by

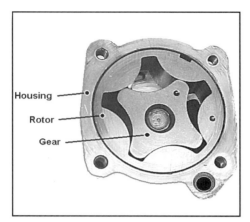

Efficient gerotor pump uses four-tooth gear to drive rotor.

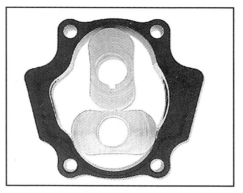

Roots-type oil pumps are very good at creating a vacuum as high as 20 in.Hg in dry sump crankcases. Straight lobes or those with a helix are available, with the latter being the most efficient. Photo courtesy Aivaid.

Use a small die grinder to chamfer and deburr edges inside the pump housing.

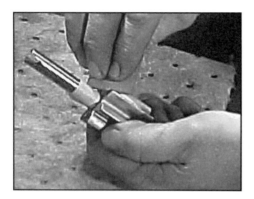

After chamfering with a die grinder, gear tooth edges are smoothed with sandpaper. Note masking tape used to protect pump shaft.

Gerotor gear-to-rotor clearances are checked. Typical clearance for gear-to-rotor and rotor-to-housing is 0.006 in. Cover-to-rotor and -gear clearance is tighter at 0.002 in.

Chevrolet pump ready for assembly; gears, housing and cover are deburred, checked for clearances and cleaned.

lengthening the housing and gears. More oil is then pumped for each revolution. Larger diameter gears can also be used to increase pump volume. Doing this is practical where a big-block pump will replace a small-block pump as with the SBC and BBC. Changing pump volume on an externally mounted pump is done by simply changing the pump's drive ratio. Turning a pump faster will increase volume and vice versa, however this must be done with care, because oil cavitation can result.

More or bigger is not always better. Increasing pump volume or pressure by more than what is

needed to maintain pressure of about 60 psi, or 80 psi max, at racing speeds plus a slight excess in volume for safety wastes power. A self regulating pump—one that pumps enough volume needed to maintain pressure—would be ideal, but these vane-type, variable-displacement pumps used on automatic transmissions have yet to be developed for engines. So for a pump to sustain pressure at a given flow rate, the oil pump must bypass excess oil back to the oil pan, thus wasting precious horsepower. The more oil it bypasses, the more it wastes. Therefore, only slightly more

volume should be pumped than what is needed to maintain oil pressure. And excess pressure can damage the bearings. So match the pump to the oil requirements of your engine.

When using an external pump, choose and install it according to the manufacturer's recommendations. You'll have choices of pump sizing, mounting requirements, drive ratio, filter location, oil-cooler options, hose sizes and provisions for connecting scavenge hose to oil pickup. As discussed, pump size should be sized to meet engine requirements. You may accomplish this using drive ratio

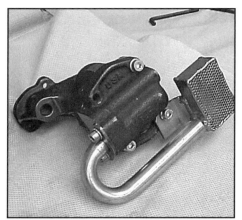

Two bolts at flange and one through the tab ensure the pickup stays in place. The coarse screen prevents large particles from entering the pump.

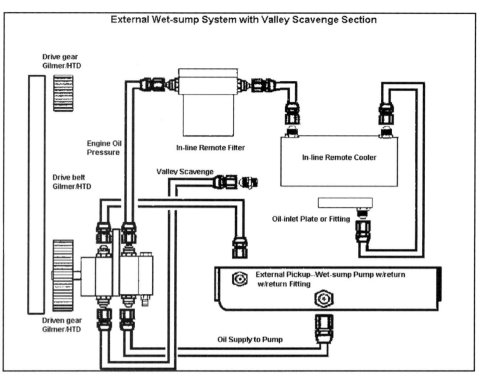

A wet sump system with an externally mounted pump. The system shown provides for lifter valley scavenging with return to sump. Oil is routed on the pressure side from the filter to the cooler then the engine. Drawing courtesy Aiviad

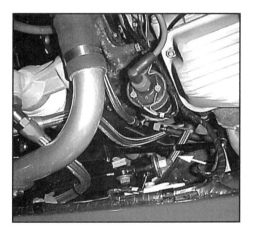

Remote filter on competition Cobra uses −12 lines. Bottom line to filter is from engine; line at top is too cooler; line below at right (arrow) is from cooler to engine. Note 45° and 90° fittings at filter mount.

with an external pump—faster increases volume and vice versa.

Oil Cooler and Filter

You have several options when choosing coolers and filters. Although oil coolers are always remotely mounted, the filter needn't be. If the block has provisions for mounting a filter and you're using wet-sump system with an internal pump, there is no good reason to use a remote filter if access to it will be unrestricted in

Adapter for remote filter and cooler installs in place of filter. It provides −12 AN fittings for installing lines to filter and from cooler, if used.

the original location. Remotely mounting the filter will increase the potential for leaks, introduce a slight pressure drop, and add weight, complexity, and cost, considering the addition of lines, fittings and connections. If you are installing a remote filter, you'll need an adapter at the block, a

remote filter mount, and lines. Use −10 or −12 AN lines into and out of the filter.

To use a cooler and retain the original filter location, install a sandwich adapter between the filter and block. The adapter has two threaded holes for plumbing in and out cooler lines. Check clearances before you decide to use a sandwich adapter because it will space the filter about 1 1/2-in. away from original mount. Whatever the filter location, always plumb filter so it comes before the cooler on the pressure side, or after pump. See drawing.

Oil Accumulator

If allowed by the rules, a device that could prevent engine damage from oil starvation is the Accusump. An accumulator that stores two or three quarts of oil under pressure in a 4 1/4-in.

High pressure, 3-quart Accusump recommended for racing applications. Air pressure separated by floating piston forces pressurized oil into engine at instant pressure drops below preset value. Photo courtesy Canton Racing Products.

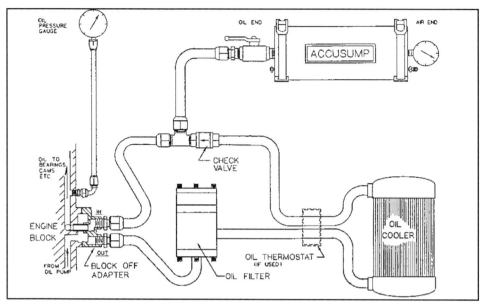

Accusump plumbed into external circuit with filter and cooler.

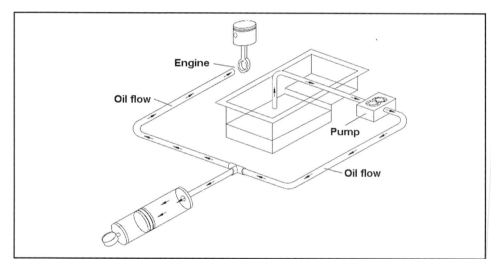

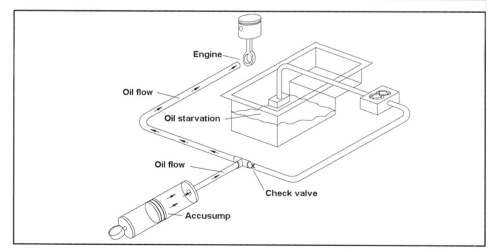

Circuit in middle drawing shows normal operation of Accusump system. Flow to accumulator stops when unit is fully charged. Circuit at bottom shows flow of oil from accumulator to engine when oil pressure drops below preset value.

aluminum tube, the Accusump supplies pressurized oil to the engine oil system when pressure drops to or below a preset value. This gives the oil system time to recover. The accumulator is then recharged by the engine oiling system. It can also be used to prevent dry start by prelubing the engine at startup.

The Accusump is tee'd into the engine oiling system between the pump and engine. A directly or remotely operated manual valve or fast-acting electrical pressure control—EPC—valve can be installed between the accumulator and tee at the engine oiling system. At shutdown, the EPC valve closes to maintain accumulator pressure.

Vacuum Pump

Reducing pressure—creating a vacuum—in a crankcase increases power output. This and removing air and vapors from the crankcase reduces windage. The lowest-cost method of doing this with a wet sump system is to plumb in an evacuation system between the crankcase at each valve cover and exhaust collector. To install such a system, weld in nipples that project

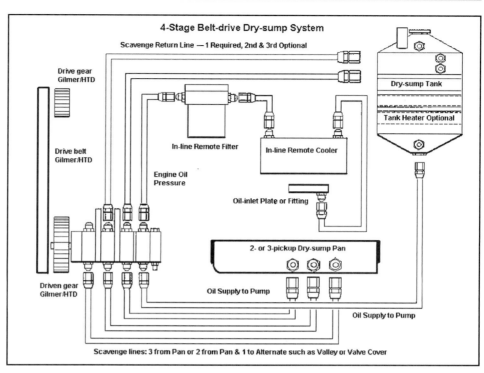

4-Stage Belt-drive Dry-sump System

Scavenge Return Line — 1 Required, 2nd & 3rd Optional

Drive gear Gilmer/HTD

Drive belt Gilmer/HTD

Engine Oil Pressure

Driven gear Gilmer/HTD

In-line Remote Filter

In-line Remote Cooler

Dry-sump Tank

Tank Heater Optional

Oil-inlet Plate or Fitting

2- or 3-pickup Dry-sump Pan

Oil Supply to Pump

Oil Supply to Pump

Scavenge lines: 3 from Pan or 2 from Pan & 1 to Alternate such as Valley or Valve Cover

A four-stage dry sump system. Remote breather or catch can—not shown—is plumbed into top of oil tank. Cooler can be installed in scavenge line, but manifold must be used to bring lines together into one line. Coarse filter/s in suction side of scavenge lines will protect pump from damage. Drawing courtesy Aiviad.

back into the exhaust collectors at a 45° angle so exhaust pulses will "pull" a vacuum on the line to the crankcase, much like fuel flow through the discharge nozzle of a carburetor. A smog-pump check valve at each header protects the crankcase in the event of an exhaust-system backfire. Air/oil separators at the valve covers prevent excess oil loss.

Pan evacuation can be accomplished more effectively with a belt-driven vacuum pump. Smog pumps were initially used, but purpose-built vacuum pumps that operate at engine speeds, or up to 9,000 rpm, can create vacuums of over 14 in.Hg in crankcase. Significant power gains can be realized with such setups because they reduce windage and allow the use of low-tension oil rings. This reduces the biggest cause of parasitic friction in an engine.

A crankcase evacuation system must have baffling at the suction side of the system to separate oil vapor from being pulled from the crankcase. Install breather tank at outlet side of the pump to catch any oil that finds its way into the evacuation system. Also be aware that the oil pump must work against crankcase vacuum. Cavitation, or aeration of the oil, can cause a drop in oil pressure. Work with your oil pump supplier to determine what will work with your engine.

DRY SUMP SYSTEMS

If the rules allow for one, and you have the budget, you should take advantage of a dry sump lubrication system to reduce sump depth, evacuate the crankcase and

reduce the chance of oil starvation. Even the best wet sump system cannot perform with complete reliability under the severest racing conditions.

Dry sump systems are used almost exclusively on race cars. The notable exception is the LS-7 Chevrolet that uses two gerotor pumps driven directly by the crankshaft. Mounted in tandem behind the damper on the crankshaft snout, one is the scavenge stage and the other the pressure stage. For racing setups, external belt-driven or cam-driven pumps are used depending on system requirements.

For a typical dry sump racing setup, the oil circuit starts with multiple pickups on the suction side that draws oil from a low-profile sump and lifter valley, passes it through low-restriction in-

line filter/s to a multiple-stage pump, then possibly to a manifold that joins the lines on the outlet side of the pump. Oil is then fed to the top of an oil tank, or reservoir, where air and vapors are separated from the oil as it drains to the bottom of the tank. From the bottom, oil is drawn into the pressure stage of the pump, pressurized and passed through a filter, a cooler in most cases, then on to the engine.

The Sump

Use a minimum of two pickups mounted solidly in the sump, no closer than 1/4 in. from the bottom to ensure most oil returning to the sump will be picked up, but not restricted. Although not as critical as with a wet sump pan, choose a sump with pickup placement that favors where

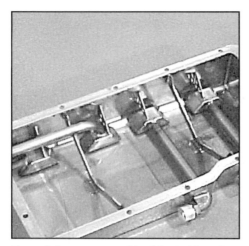

Four pickups are used in this NASCAR Cup pan. Sumps have been divided into four sealed compartments in attempt to reduce aeration further.

Waterman mechanical fuel pump mounted on fuel tank is driven by cable (arrow) from back of oil pump. Setup satisfies NASCAR rule mandating an engine-driven fuel pump.

Sectioned Dailey Engineering pump for display. From left to right, gear pressure stage, straight-lobe Roots scavenging stage, and vane-type air/oil separator.

Gilmer belt-driven pump mounted on right side of Busch Ford engine. Orientation of inlet and outlet ports must be specified.

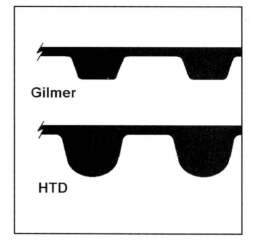

Profiles of Gilmer and HTD belts. HTD cogs provide deeper engagement for higher drive loads.

oil will likely to be most of the time. For drag racing, oil will be at the rear of sump except during braking. For oval track racing pickups should be at the right side. Oil will be in various locations when road racing, offshore boat and offroad racing, so pickups should be centered in the sump.

Sumps were typically fabricated from sheet steel or cast from aluminum. Although fabricated steel pans are the most popular, you now have the option of using fabricated-aluminum or CNC machined billet aluminum pans. Some aluminum pans such as those from Dailey Engineering have provisions for mounting pumps directly to the sump. This eliminates plumbing between the pump and sump, reducing complexity, potential leak points, pressure drop, and weight.

The Pump

Choosing a dry sump pump involves deciding on the number of stages, types of gears or rotors, drive ratio and belt type. Other considerations are materials used for gears/rotors and housings. Aluminum with coating as an option is typically used for housings and gears/rotors, but cast-iron housings are offered by some manufacturers for the pressure section. Related accessories include an air/oil separator and cable-drive adaptor for driving a mechanical fuel pump at tank. Decisions can be overwhelming, but manufacturer tech support people will help with what you need for your application.

Using more than one scavenging stage is not only for picking up oil from different locations, such as the lifter valley and multiple points in the oil pan, but to add pumping volume. A major percentage of the volume removed from the crankcase is air, which creates a vacuum. So adding stages—up to six—is usually beneficial. But keep in mind that as air is removed, it is mixed with oil. Therefore, you must provide for removing air and vapors from the oil. This can start with a pump driven air/oil separator, so there's less to deal with at the tank. As oil

Six-stage dry sump pump driven by HTD belt.

Pump mounted directly to billet-aluminum oil pan eliminates need for hoses between engine and sump. Photo courtesy Dailey Engineering.

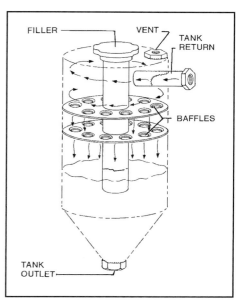

Typical oil tank construction, air and vapors vent out the top of the tank. Oil flows to the bottom where it can be pumped back into the engine. Drawing courtesy Ron Fournier.

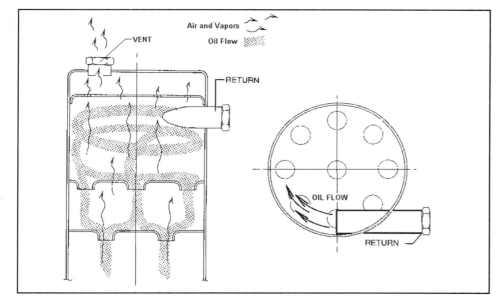

Oil is directed through the return into the tank so it enters the tank wall in a tangential manner. The swirling action created removes air and vapors from the oil and vents them out top. The heavier oil flows to the bottom of the tank. Drawing courtesy Ron Fournier.

creases or drive ratio decreases—pump speed gets closer to engine speed—drive-belt load increases. The solution to reducing the chance of belt failure is to use a HTD (high torque drive) belt.

Oil Tank

The oil tank, or reservoir, does more than just store oil before it is pumped back into the engine. Internal baffling must be designed to separate air and vapors from the oil. That done, air and vapors vent at or near the top of the tank while oil drains to the bottom where it is picked up by the pump. As shown by the accompanying drawing, the oil return fitting is placed so oil enters tangentially to the circular tank surface, creating a swirling action that helps remove air and vapors from the oil. As oil flows over and through the baffles, remaining air and vapor separate so that they can be vented at the top.

flows into the tank, air and vapors must be separated and vented to a remote tank.

Other pump options include mountings, or blade orientation for left- or right-side mounting if pump is belt-driven. This, orientation, and number of inlet and outlet ports must be also specified. Also, if pump will be cam- or accessory-driven,

allowances must be made for driving it. For example, if the pump is to be cam-driven, it must be mounted to a dedicated front cover that centers the pump on the nose of the cam. And since it displaces the water pump, it must be relocated.

Tooth-belt driven pumps traditionally used Gilmer belts. However, as pump capacity in-

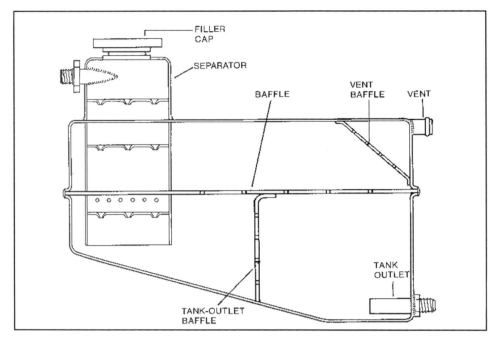

Short rectangular tank is fitted with round air/oil separator. Further separation is done as the oil flows down the ramp and through the baffle. Vented baffle prevents oil from escaping out vent. Drawing courtesy Ron Fournier.

Oil tank in NASCAR modified mounts securely to tabs welded to the roll cage behind the driver.

Oil tank for road-race car is mounted at the extreme right, rear corner for weight distribution, requiring very long hoses. Breather is mounted to rear bulkhead at right.

Choose the tallest tank of the desired volume that will fit in a safe and secure location. A taller tank is more efficient at air/oil separation. If a short, odd-shaped tank must be fabricated so it will fit in a tight area, additional baffling is needed to ensure air/oil separation and venting as shown in accompanying drawing. As for volume, big blocks require more volume than small blocks. But the overriding factor when determining tank volume is the time and length of the race. For example, short-track cars can use small tanks whereas endurance racing cars require larger tanks. Specifically, drag cars can use a 1-1/2-gallon tank whereas a stock car set up for 500-mile events require 4- or 5-gallon tank. The same goes for long distance road-race or off-road vehicles. A sprint or midget car will be in the middle at about 2.5 gallons. Regardless of tank volume and location, mount it securely.

Breather or Catch Can

Vented vapors and air contain some oil in the form of a mist. Even though it may not be required by the rules, provide a breather or catch can to prevent oil from being vented to the air. In the case of a dry sump system, if the breather is not integral with the tank, mount it so the tank-to-breather line runs up and forward to the breather. Oil that falls out of suspension will then drain back to the oil tank. Likewise for a wet sump system. The line should run down from the breather to the air/oil separator.

Filters and Screens

Filters and screens, or strainers, have one purpose; to keep debris out of the lubrication system. This not only means the engine proper, but the pump, lines and cooler. Filtering must be done with the least amount of restriction to limit

pressure drop, particularly on the suction side.

The first the line of defense in the lubrication system is the pickup screen, or strainer. It should cause minimal flow restriction, but block large particles from entering the pump. Even though small particles can pass through the screen, they shouldn't be large enough to lock the pump. To further protect the pump, low-restriction inline filters can be installed in the suction lines of a dry sump system or wet sump setup with an external pump. Such

Pickup with small-area and coarse strainer prevents large particles from entering pump with minimum restriction. Tab bolted to pump supports pickup.

Inline filter for pressure side includes -6 AN fitting for connecting line valve-spring oiler or turbocharger oiler. Photo courtesy Peterson.

Oberg take-apart filter (arrow) installed in scavenge line between pump and tank for dyno testing engine makes checking for contamination quick and easy.

FILTERS: AREA & MICRON RATING

Oil filters are specified by micron rating and area. One micron measures 0.000039 in. Filter micron rating specifies the largest particle the filter will pass. Particles larger than the micron rating of a filter will be trapped. Typical metal-screen type inline filters range from 100 microns to 45 microns. A 100-micron filter will trap particles larger than 100 microns x 0.000039 in. = 0.0039 in., whereas a 45-micron filter will trap particles larger than 45 microns x 0.000039 in. = 0.0018 in. Therefore, a 45-micron filter will trap particles less than half the size of a 100-micron filter. Pleated-paper spin-on racing filters trap very small particles, or those larger than 25 microns (0.0010 in.).

Given filtering ability, filter area determines the amount of contaminates a filter can trap before it clogs. As area increases, the tendency of a filter to clog is reduced. Just think of the paint it takes to cover a given area. More paint is required to cover a larger area. Increasing filter area also reduces pressure loss. As an example, a new pleated-paper spin-on filter will cause as little as a 2 1/2 psi loss. As a filter traps more contaminates, pressure loss increases. To prevent total oil pressure loss, many filters have a built-in bypass. These include most spin-on filters and many inline filters. When a filter bypass opens, unfiltered oil enters the engine, allowing it to survive longer than it would without oil pressure.

Using a high or low micron rating filter depends on where it will be placed in the circuit. The finest filter—low micron rating—should be installed in the high pressure side of the circuit. This would be at the oil pump output. To minimize restriction, only the coarsest—high micron—filters should be used in suctions lines, or those from the sump to the pump.

filters are particularly useful with gerotor or Roots pumps as these pumps have closer tolerances.

Oil Cooler

Use an oil cooler that will maintain average oil temperature within a 185–250°F range. Running oil temperatures above 185°F ensures contaminants such as moisture will boil off and no more than 250°F will prevent oil oxidation. A cooler that maintains oil temperature in this range depends on the duration of the typical race. Therefore, a cooler is not needed for drag racing, but a high-capacity cooler is required for endurance racing. A thermostat can be place in line to allow oil to bypass the cooler when oil temperature is below a preset value.

If the cooler has been run previously, make absolutely sure it is clean. Have it ultrasonically cleaned. In the case of a cooler that was used with an engine that failed, don't use it. There have been too many engines damaged or destroyed from debris that worked loose from a "clean" cooler. The cost of replacing a cooler is a lot

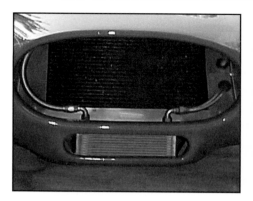

The front of the car is the best location for an oil cooler, but it is more vulnerable to damage.

A high-capacity oil cooler for endurance racing.

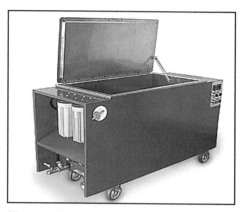

Ultrasonic cleaning is the best way to remove debris from the cooler. Flush and blow out the cooler and all oil lines and fittings. Photo courtesy Omega.

less than replacing or rebuilding an engine.

Install the cooler in the pressure side of the circuit between the filter and the engine to protect the cooler from contamination. Install the cooler in a high-pressure area and duct it to a low-pressure area so air flow will be the highest. To protect the cooler from damage, install the cooler as far back from the front as possible, then install ducting from the front. Seal duct work so air flows through and not around cooler.

Oil Heater

Available in different wattages, 100V immersion or blanket oil heaters are used to preheat the engine oil. Preheated oil is beneficial, particularly if it's a drag engine that must run at full load immediately after startup. However, all engines will benefit at startup, notably those with tight clearances.

Basically large-diameter threaded rod, immersion-type heaters require a threaded bung in the oil tank. If the tank is not so equipped, cut a hole at the appropriate location and weld-in the bung. Blanket heaters attach with an adhesive directly to the exterior surface of an oil tank or pan.

OIL LINES & FITTINGS

While flowing hot oil at high or low pressure with minimum resistance, oil hoses must resist vibration, abrasion, flexing or high heat while sealing oil and presenting minimum resistance to flow. This is accomplished with the use of aircraft-quality AN (Army-Navy) oil lines and fittings.

Size lines and fittings so they aren't too large, but will provide minimal flow resistance. Refer to the recommendations below as a guide for sizing hoses and fittings:

Wet Sump Hose

Suction (in) Pressure (out)
Remote filter and cooler w/internal pump: AN –10 or –12*
Remote filter and cooler w/external pump: AN –12 or –16*, –10 or –12*
Vacuum Pump: AN –12

Dry Sump Hose

Pressure: AN –10, –12 or –16*
Scavenge: AN –12, –16 after

Immersion oil preheater with threaded bung and extension cord. Photo courtesy Steffs.

manifold; -12 before manifold
Breather: AN -12

Flow resistance—pressure drop—increases with hose length.

A long hose such as one between a pump and the tank that is at extreme ends of the car should be increased at least one size. Also, when making 45° or 90° turns, particularly in a suction side, make them as gradual as possible.

Hose features to consider are covering type, basic construction, lining and internal support. Don't even think about using heater hose

AN SIZES			
AN Size	Tube OD (inches)	Thread Size (inches-threads/in.)	Hose ID (inches)
-4	1/4	7/16-20	7/32
-6	3/8	9/16-18	11/32
-8	1/2	3/4-16	7/16
-10	5/8	7/8-14	9/16
-12	3/4	1 1/16-12	11/16
-16	1	1 5/16-12	7/8
-20	1 1/4	1 5/8-12	1 1/8

Developed for aircraft, AN (Army-Navy) sizes describe the outside diameter of rigid tubing in 1/16-in. increments, or so-called "dash" (-) sizes. As an example, a -8 AN tube OD is 8/16 in. Therefore, the inside diameter of a hose or tube is smaller than tube or hose OD. Referencing the above chart, the ID is smaller than the OD by 5/16 in. (0.03125 in.) for -4 and -6 tubes; 1/16 in. (0.0625 in.) for -8, -10 and -12 tubes; and 1/8 in. (0.125 in.) for -16 and -20 tubes.

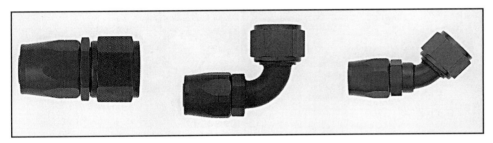

Straight, 45,° and 90° swivel fittings are a few of many AN-style fittings from which to choose.

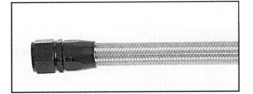

The choice for most racing applications has been stainless-steel braided, Teflon-lined hose (top). Kevlar or nylon braided hoses are not as pretty, but much lighter.

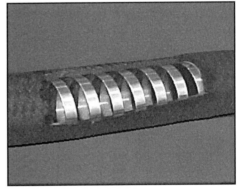

Flat-wound spring inserted into hose prevents collapse when subjected to low-pressure as on suction side of scavenging circuit.

Tightening swivel fitting at pump with -12 wrench.

in an oiling system. Hose material must resist high-temperature oil at pressures up to 100 psi and as low as 25 in.Hg. For the ID, an elastomeric lining is preferred. As for hose exterior, it must be tough. Although stainless braided hose is strong, pretty and highly resistant to abrasion, it is heavy. Consider, then, Kevlar or nylon braided hoses that are flame retardant. Such hoses are significantly lighter. Opposite of pressure, scavenge hoses on the suction side have internal support to prevent collapse. This is done by inserting an internal flat-wound spring into the hose. If unsupported, a scavenging hose may collapse and cause oil starvation.

Spring Oilers

Even though rocker arms with needle-bearing trunions need some oil, valve springs need much more. This is not so much for lubrication, but for cooling. Rapid cycling of valve springs as the valves open and close creates considerable heat. This is due to hysteresis—internal friction between spring material molecules—and friction between inner and outer springs and damper. Heat generated is significant for engines turned at a steady 7,500 to 10,000 rpm. If heat is not controlled, particularly for engines running duration events, spring

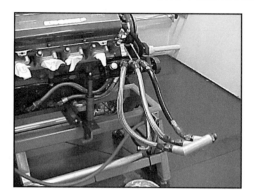

Scavenging outlet hoses joined with three-into-one 12-12-12-16 manifold.

Five-stage Aviaid pump has manifold directly attached to outlet ports on scavenging side. Photo courtesy Aviaid.

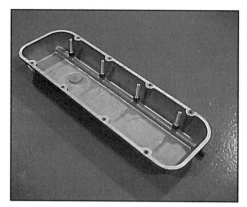

Dodge valve cover for NASCAR cup engine with cast and drilled oil passages. Nozzles are aimed at valve springs.

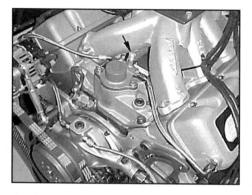

Spring oilers on NASCAR Chevy are connected with AN -6 line. Oil supply line connects to capped T-fitting (arrow).

Oil supply source for a spring oiler can come from the engine oil gallery (arrow) or inline filter.

Enclosed cam tunnel in Dodge NASCAR block prevents oil at top end from draining onto spinning crankshaft-and-rod assembly. Tapped into oil galleries at each side of the block, banjo fittings with squirt nozzles at bottom of each bore direct oil to undersides of pistons.

fatigue and eventual failure will occur. To prevent this, springs can be cooled with a steady stream from spring oilers built into the valve covers.

BLOCK MODIFICATIONS TO IMPROVE LUBRICATION

For efficient oiling, start by checking that all oil passages are unrestricted. Deburr sharp edges and make sure intersecting passages do so in a smooth manner. If one is offset from the other, open it up. Chamfer sharp edges, such as those at the main bearing bores. Smooth the interior of the block and remove any flashing or core sand. Do not paint the block's interior. It is best when the block is ground smooth and cleaned. Once you've

done basic block preparation, make modifications to the lubrication system that will increase or reduce oil to critical areas and improve oil return to the sump.

Oil Restriction

While ensuring that all friction points will be lubricated and cooled, the challenge is to restrict oil to areas that may cause parasitic power loss. Two areas to deal with are valvetrain lubrication and how oil drains or is removed from the top end.

An enclosed cam tunnel prevents oil in the top end from draining onto the crankshaft. If you don't have such a block, you can replace sleeve bearings with needle

bearings. Although needle bearings won't reduce friction, oil supply to this area can be reduced substantially. Likewise for roller lifters and rocker arms. Less oil to the top end means less oil that must drain back to the sump or be recovered by pumping.

To prevent the top end from filling up with oil and problems related to draining or recovering it, the solution starts with restricting oil flow to the top. Using needle bearings and roller followers that require less oil is one step in this direction. Follow up by restricting oil to the top end by installing

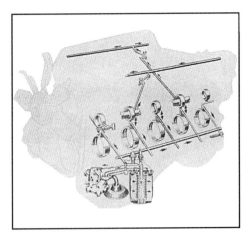

One of the first race-oriented OEM engines was Ford's cross-bolted 427 side oiler. The main oil gallery running along the left side of the block ensures main and rod bearings receive oil directly. Oil galleries for lifters were not needed as only solid lifters were used. Drawing courtesy Ford.

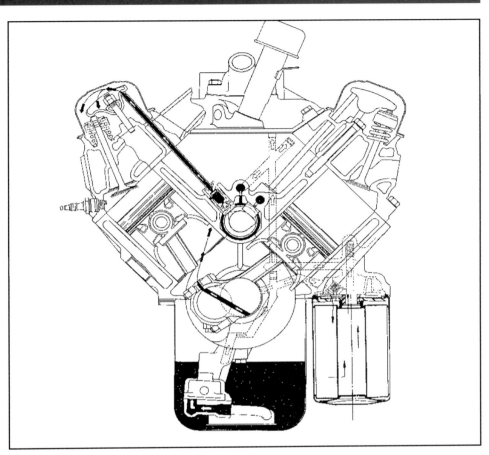

Traditional factory setup is illustrated by small-block Chevy oiling system. After passing through the filter, oil is directed to the rear cam bearing and oil passages that intersect lifter bores. Oil is channeled from the rear cam bearing to the main bearings and rocker arms through pushrods by way of the lifters. Drawing courtesy Chevrolet.

restrictors or metered plugs in the oil galleries that intersect lifter bores. Some restrictors install in place of the rear plugs; others install in front of the plugs. The second method requires tapping the oil galleries ahead of the original plug threads for the restrictors.

This may not be a factor with blocks built strictly for racing. They may not have lifter oil galleries. Rather, oil is routed directly to main bearings, then fed up to the cam bearings. To restrict oil to the cam bearings with such a setup, tap passages and install restrictors as shown. Order restrictors based on how your engine is equipped. Determining the correct oil restriction to the head is tricky; too much oil wastes horsepower, but run too little oil and you stand a chance of ruining valve springs early. Here's where the spring oilers make up the deficit.

Restrictors for Chevy block install in oil galleries in place of plugs. Oil for mains passes through the groove behind the rear cam bearing and around the reduced section of restrictors. Oil that is restricted from entering lifter oil galleries by O-rings is metered through holes (arrows).

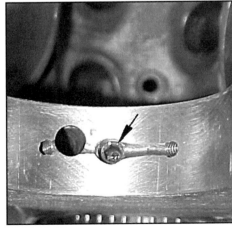

Large hole in upper half of main bearing bore feeds oil to main bearing. Drilled plug (arrow) meters oil to camshaft needle bearing. Smaller holes at far right and left are fitted with plugs that meter oil to piston squirt nozzles.

Plugs for metering oil to lifter galleries in Ford block installs ahead of plugs. Hole meters oil sent to lifters.

Wire through metering plug and squirt nozzle shows how oil is directed at the bottom of the piston.

Spray bar is set up to oil cam lobes and lifters. Hose connects spray bar to oil gallery.

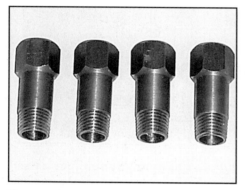

Vent-tube kit for lifter valley. Photo Courtesy Stefs.

Install vent tubes—stand pipes—in lifter valley to block oil from draining onto cam and crankshaft.

Install screens in front drains to block debris.

Sealing, Isolating and Evacuating the Top End

Oil in the top end must drain or be evacuated from the lifter valley. Debris must be blocked while oil is routed around the crankshaft. Do this by rerouting or restricting and straining oil with a combination of screens, dams and plumbing. Kits and components are available for making the job easier. You may have to fabricate others.

Secure the screens with high-strength epoxy. J-B Weld works well for small jobs, but for those requiring a lot of epoxy, a putty-like marine product such as Splash Zone Z-Spar A-788 works well. Check for this product at your local marine supply store. It comes as a kit in quart and gallon sizes with primer and catalyst. Wear rubber gloves when using this stuff.

For preventing debris from getting to the bottom end, fit screens at the front, rear or bottom of the lifter valley. Secure screens with epoxy. For those in the end that are used for venting only, prevent oil spillover by sealing off bottom portion of the screens with epoxy. To prevent oil from draining on the cam while allowing the bottom end to vent, install standpipes, or vent tubes, in the lifter valley. Drill and tap drain holes to match thread size of the standpipes. A 1/4-in. NPT thread is typically used.

To remove oil from the lifter valley with a wet vac or dry sump system, build dams to block oil from draining. This will allow the bottom end to vent. Do this by sealing the bottom half of the screens with epoxy or placing dams around vent holes as shown. Fabricate dams from 0.060-in. sheet metal—steel for cast-iron blocks and aluminum for aluminum blocks.

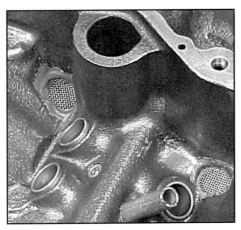

Screens for wet sump system cover drains at back of block.

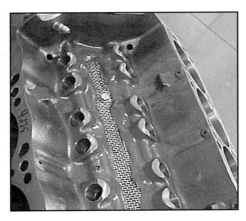

Full-length screen keeps debris off cam and lifters. Note lifter bosses ground to provide clearance for roller-lifter tie bars.

For wet vac or dry sump systems, seal bottom half of screens to prevent oil from draining to sump.

Suction line is plumbed into lifter valley at right and routed to left side where it exits top of bellhousing flange.

For scavenging, drill and tap hole at lowest point in lifter valley. Hole is tapped so it will accept 1/2-in. NPT fitting.

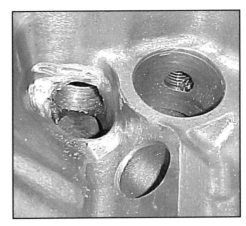

Note how hole intersects existing drain hole.

For scavenging, drill and tap hole in the back of the block at a low point in the valley so it will accept an AN fitting. The line from the scavenging stage of the pump will connect to the fitting. As shown in the photo at right, a 90° AN –12 fitting was modified to accept a pipe nipple. A 4 x 1/2-in pipe nipple was then inserted through the drilled hole in the bellhousing flange. To finish off, a 1/2-in. NPT to AN -10 fitting was threaded onto the end of the nipple. When using Teflon tape to seal pipe threads, start wrapping the tape two threads back from the end. Errant pieces have been known to break

Cutting AN -12 end off 90° 1/2 in. NPT to -12 fitting. Cutoff end was then smoothed and chamfered before tapping.

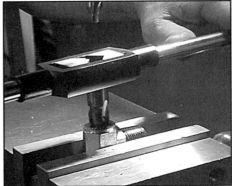

Cutoff end is threaded with 1/2-in. NPT tap.

loose and block oil passages. So use liquid sealer on threads, not Telfon tape. Line from pump is connected

to nipple to complete the scavenging circuit. Make sure when installing such a setup that the

Modified 90° fitting is installed with sealer in block so it's aimed at hole drilled in bellhousing flange. A 4-in. long 1/4-in. pipe nipple is threaded into fitting.

A 1/2-in. NPT to -10 fitting is then fitted to pipe nipple to complete block side of lifter valley scavenging circuit.

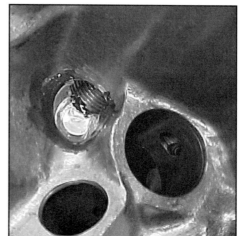

Plug drain hole with epoxy...

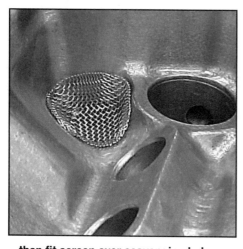

...then fit screen over scavenging hole.

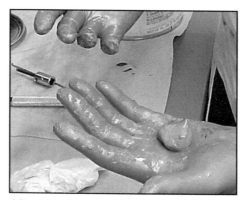

After screens or dams are fitted, clean area, then mix epoxy. Latex gloves protect hands while mixing putty-like epoxy.

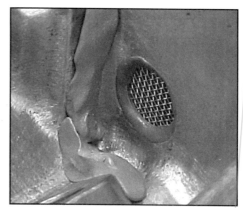

Apply line of epoxy that matches contact area with dam.

flywheel will clear all plumbing.

Clean surfaces where dams or screens will be placed in block. Do this with solvent that accompanied kit, brake clean, carburetor cleaner or PVC pipe cleaner. Fit dams or screens by trimming with aviation snips, then indicate their positions by marking on them with a felt marker. Mix epoxy, roll it like modeling clay, then apply in a line to block where dam or screen will make contact. With a finger, smooth epoxy on both sides of dam.

A final word about the lubrication system: Make absolutely sure all oiling system components are as clean as possible before installing them. If you don't, the time, effort and money you put into preparing your engine may be wasted. With that admonition, double-check that you have disassembled and cleaned the oil tank, flushed out all the lines and the cooler, and cleaned or replaced the filters. The extra effort will be worth it!! Any debris in the system will be removed that would otherwise be pumped into the engine, possibly damaging or destroying the oil pump or your new engine!

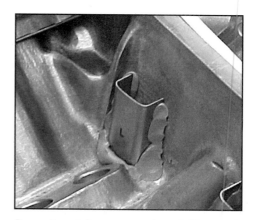

Press dam into epoxy and work it smooth with a finger. Note L for left marked on dam.

PREASSEMBLY

8

This engine building step distinguishes an engine builder from an engine assembler. Because of the critical nature of this step, I treat preassembly separately. For example you must make sure the main bearings will provide the correct oil clearance or there is sufficient valve-to-piston clearance. This can mean the difference between a durable engine and one that will self-destruct the first time out of the trailer. Less involved procedures such as degreeing a cam or fitting an intake manifold to the heads can make the difference between an engine that is competitive or has mediocre performance. So, be very attentive when performing each preassembly procedure. Problems dealt with now won't bite you later.

A preassembly procedure frequently requires partial assembly of a part or component. It may also mean some machining or fabrication. Degreeing a camshaft is a perfect example; the cam bearings, crankshaft and timing set must first be installed. Revising an oil pump pickup to provide sufficient clearance to the bottom of the oil pan is another. So, refer to the appropriate chapters for installation, assembly or fabrication details when the need arises.

Before you get started, make sure the parts and area you'll be working in are at room temper-

A comprehensive preassembly will ensure that insufficient clearances will be corrected before final assembly. Critical valve-to-piston clearance is being checked.

ature, or about 74°F. Parts varying much from this temperature will show incorrect measurements.

MAIN BEARINGS

You should have already checked or align-bored the main bearings to ensure they are correct. Check bearing inserts. Measure the thickness of an insert at the center. You'll need a micrometer with a ball adapter to get a true reading. Compare the reading to the main

bearing journal diameter you recorded in your notes. This will indicate if the bearings will provide the correct main journal oil clearance.

Wipe bearing inserts clean with a paper shop towel soaked with lacquer thinner or brake cleaner. Do the same with the bearing housings in the cap/block and cap/block parting lines. Any debris in any of these locations will cause measurement inaccuracies. After

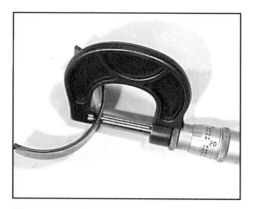

Measure main bearing insert at thickest point. Bearing-housing ID less twice insert thickness is bearing-bore ID. Ball at anvil eliminates inaccurate reading that would result from bearing curvature.

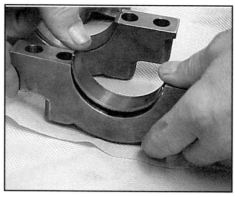

After cleaning inserts, main-bore housings and parting lines, install bearing inserts in block and caps.

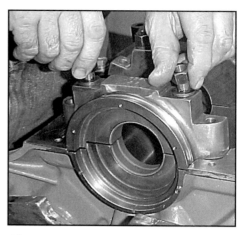

After lubricating threads and bolt/nut or washer bearing surfaces, install caps.

installing bearing inserts in the block and caps, fit caps into block registers, making sure cap numbers match positions and they are oriented correctly.

Lubricate bolt/stud threads and underside of bolt heads/nuts or washers. Thread lubricants choices include Loctite #51609 anti-seize or a molydenum-based paste mixed with motor oil. Install bolts/nuts and torque to specifications and, if specified, in order. Torque bolts/nuts first to specifications in stages. For example, if specified torque is 100 ft-lb, torque them all to 33 ft-lb, then 67 ft-lb and finish with 100 ft-lb. Next, loosen bolts/nuts slightly, then retorque to specification.

Using bore gauge zeroed to a specified bearing diameter, check diameter of each bearing. Position bore gauge plunger 90° to the parting line. Swing it about 30° degrees to both sides to check roundness. Record results in your notes. Compare bearing diameter to published specifications. Refer to your notes for crankshaft main-bearing journal diameter. Subtract journal diameter from bearing diameter to find oil clearance. This

Tap caps into registers with light mallet, then install bolts/nuts and torque them to spec. Cross bolts such as with this Dodge block are torqued last.

can vary from 0.0005 in. to 0.003 in. The oil clearance you use depends on oil viscosity. Oil clearance should be about 0.0026 in. However, if a low-viscosity oil such as 0-20W is used to reduce pumping losses, clearance should be on the tight side, or about 0.0018 in. But don't be surprised with low oil pressures at speed. Ten psi is typical on the high banks. Likewise, zero oil pressure has been observed in the lights with drag cars. In both cases, coated bearings have allowed crankshafts and bearings to survive.

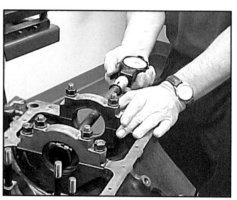

Measure bearing diameter 90° to the parting line and a few degrees to each side. Record results and compare to specifications and main journal diameter.

INSTALL CRANKSHAFT

If bearings check out OK, remove caps and install the crankshaft. Keep bearings in caps. Install the rear main seal in block and cap if seal runs on rear-main journal. If you are using a full-circle seal on the flywheel flange, install seal after crank and rear-main cap are in place. With the two-piece seal, stagger ends so they project about 3/8-in. up from the cap and block parting line. Coat bearing inserts and seals with an assembly lube such as GM's EOS, Ford's Oil Conditioner or Torco's MPZ.

If you need to make modifications

Double-check that the crankshaft is clean before laying it in the block. If not, give it a good scrubbing.

Lower the crankshaft squarely onto the main bearings. Note hoses fitted to end main cap studs to avoid damaging bearing journals.

Mount dial indicator so plunger is square to sprocket or crankshaft snout.

Pry crankshaft back in block, zero indicator and pry crank forward to determine endplay.

for piston deck clearances, valves connecting rod or crankshaft, the crankshaft may have to come out again for balancing. Otherwise, consider this final crankshaft installation. Soap it down, scrub the crankshaft from one end to the other, rinse and dry it. If block is fitted with main-cap studs, avoid damaging the main-bearing journals while installing the crankshaft by slipping short sections of heater hose over inboard studs at the front and rear mains. While supporting crankshaft at snout and rear throw or flywheel flange, lower it straight down into block and squarely onto bearings.

Check Endplay

Do your initial crankshaft endplay check before installing the main caps. This will avoid the need to remove the caps if an adjustment must be made. Also, this will allow you to confirm the thrust flanges are aligned when the caps are installed and torqued.

Mount dial indicator to front of block and position plunger square against nose of crank or timing sprocket. Using a small pry bar or large screwdriver, force crankshaft to back of block. While holding it there, zero dial indicator. Now, pry crankshaft forward and read the indicator. End play should be 0.003–0.005 in., although it can go as high as 0.007 in. for oval track racing. End thrust and resulting wear from a heavy clutch during shifting will not be a factor. Limit end thrust for road racing to 0.005-in.

If endplay is too low, remove the crankshaft and bearing insert with thrust flanges. Flanges can be thinned to get more endplay. Do this by sanding one flange on a precision-flat surface such as a granite block. Using 400 wet-or-dry sandpaper flooded with honing coolant or solvent, lap the thrust flanges by holding the upper and lower inserts together with the flanges flat against the sandpaper. This will help ensure you remove even amounts from the flanges. Measure flange thickness with 0–1 mikes to start and remeasure frequently. When you remove an amount that matches the additional endplay needed, clean inserts, reinstall upper one, lubricate it and install crankshaft. Recheck the endplay.

It is highly unlikely that you will have the unfortunate situation of too much endplay, but if you do, look for a mistake. You've already declared the crankshaft fit, but remeasure the distances between the thrust faces. Compare the results to crankshaft specifications. If they are incorrect, the problem is with the crankshaft. If the crankshaft is correct, it's with the bearings. Either way, get on the telephone and sort out things.

Torque main cap bolts/nuts to complete crankshaft installation.

Guiding cam into bearings is made easier with long bolt threaded into nose of cam.

This crankshaft sprocket has nine cam-timing positions; zero and four advance/retard positions in 2° increments. Sprocket is in 2° advanced position. Many have three; zero and 4° advanced and retarded.

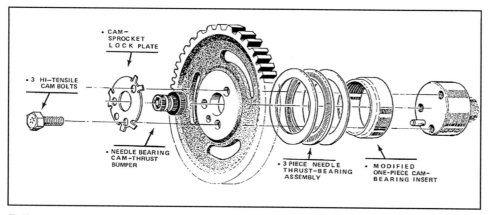

Roller cams require endplay control. Shown is Iskenderian's Anti Cam-Walk Kit for the small-block Chevy with Torrington needle bearings behind the sprocket and button at nose. Drawing courtesy Isky Racing Cams.

Final Crankshaft Installation

Providing crankshaft endplay is within limits, install the crankshaft using the procedure described in Final Assembly, pages 170 and 171. Make a quick recheck of endplay. If endplay is good and remains the same, the thrust flanges are aligned. Spin crankshaft to check that it turns freely. It may seem a little tight due to drag from the main seal, but this will quickly loosen up. Finish torquing the main cap bolts/nuts, spinning crankshaft each time you secure a main cap.

DEGREE THE CAMSHAFT

Just as with the crankshaft, if all is OK with the camshaft, you shouldn't have to remove it after checking. Start by lubricating the bearing journals and, if it's a flat-tappet cam, the lobes. The cam manufacturer will have provided his special high-pressure lubricant to protect the lubes for initial startup and lobe break-in. If not, molybdenum-disulfide grease will do the job. To make the job of guiding the camshaft through the bearings easier, thread a special handle or long bolt into the cam nose.

Install timing set by first installing the key, then slide the

sprocket onto the crankshaft and over the key. If fit is tight, tap the key into the keyway with a soft mallet. Align sprocket to straight up—zero—position for now. Although you can compensate for crankshaft sprocket position when degreeing the cam, positioning it at zero position for now will keep the math simple. You can advance, retard or leave the sprocket in the straight up position later.

If thrust plate and/or Torrington bearings are used, position to the nose of the cam with the appropriate hardware. Secure the thrust plate with bolts. Lay the timing chain over the cam sprocket, then engage it to the crankshaft sprocket so the timing marks are in alignment. Rotate the cam so it aligns with the sprocket, then attach the sprocket to the cam with bolt/s. You may have to adjust the cam position more than once.

Finding TDC

True TDC must be found before the camshaft can be degreed. This ensures there will be an accurate baseline for checking—degree-

With cam rotated so the dowel aligns with the cam sprocket, fit the sprocket to the cam.

Once in position, bolt the sprocket to the cam.

Positive stop fabricated from length of 1 1/4 x 1 1/4 x 1/8-in. angle. Sleeves over studs with nuts secure stop firmly to deck.

After bringing piston up light against stop to get first degree-wheel reading, turn crank counterclockwise against stop to get second reading.

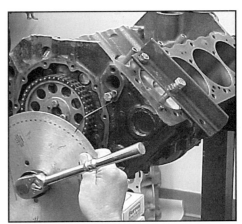

Adjust degree wheel by half the amount of first and second reading and recheck.

ing—the camshaft so it will be in phase with the crankshaft. Because there's very little piston movement, or "dwell time" during the few degrees of crankshaft rotation before and after TDC, two points of piston movement and relative crankshaft position at 30° or more degrees farther down on both sides of TDC must first be found. Finding TDC is simply a matter of placing the degree wheel at the center of these two positions.

Install the rod-and-piston assembly for cylinder #1 with an old set of rings installed to stabilize the piston. Two methods can be used to find TDC. The first uses a positive stop and the other a dial indicator. You'll also need a piston stop or dial indicator with stand, degree wheel and a pointer.

Oil the piston, bore and rod bearings, and then install the piston-and-rod assembly in cylinder #1. Snug the rod bolts. They don't have to be torqued.

With the piston down in the bore, bolt the piston stop to the deck. Bolt the degree wheel to the crankshaft snout and the pointer to the front face of the block. Fabricate the pointer from heavy wire, such as a welding rod. Grind one end to a point and shape the other end so it can be bolted to the front of the block. Position and bend pointer so it's close to the degree wheel. The closer the pointer is to the wheel, the more accurate your reading. Bring the piston up to TDC, or as close as you can estimate, then rotate the degree wheel so it indicates zero at TDC. Secure the degree wheel.

Positive Stop Method—Rotate crankshaft so piston is at least 2-in. down the bore, then install the positive stop. Turn the crankshaft clockwise until the piston comes in light contact with the stop, and then adjust the degree wheel so it's a few degrees BTDC, say 30° BTDC. Turn the crankshaft counterclockwise, again bringing the piston up into light contact with the stop. Check degree-wheel reading. This is not likely to happen, but if it reads 30° ATDC, consider yourself lucky. You've found TDC on the first try. But if you're like the rest of us, the degree wheel will read more or less than 30°, say 36°. In this case add the

151

two different readings and divide by two, or (30° + 36°) = 66°/2 = 33°. The difference is 3° from each side, or 30° plus 3° or 36° minus 3°.

Rotate degree wheel 3° toward the side with the highest reading, which will make the reading 33° ATDC. Recheck by backing up the crankshaft until the piston contacts the positive stop on the BTDC side. If it reads 33° BTDC, you've got it. Otherwise make checks and adjustments until you've found TDC, then secure the degree wheel. You can now degree the cam.

Dial Indicator Method—The other method of finding the two crankshaft positions on both sides of TDC requires a dial indicator. Start by bringing piston to the top of the bore. Mount the indicator stand to the block deck. Position the dial indicator plunger square to and at the center of the piston so the indicator has approximately 0.400-in. preload. Rotate the crankshaft back-and-forth while observing indicator travel. The needle will swing one direction, stop and swing in the reverse direction. This reversal occurs at TDC. Bring piston up to where this occurs. Zero the indicator. The piston will be close to TDC, but not exactly at it.

Turn the crankshaft in the clockwise direction with the piston coming up until indicator reading is between 0.250–0.750-in., say 0.500 in. Note degree wheel reading. Continue turning the crank clockwise. The indicator reading will reduce and slow as it approaches TDC, then reverse direction. When indicator reading is the same on the other side of TDC, or 0.500 in. in this case,

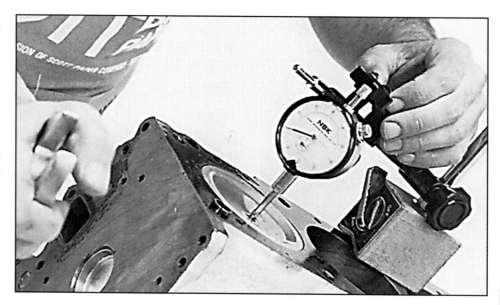

Check that the indicator plunger is compressed about 0.500 in. at TDC before finding BTDC and ATDC crank positions. Turn crankshaft clockwise when using indicator method of finding TDC.

stop. Note again the degree wheel reading. If it's the same, fine. But chances are it will be a few degrees off. As with the positive-stop method, add the two readings, divide the sum by two and subtract it from the initial smaller reading. Likewise, adjust the degree wheel by this amount and repeat the dial indicator procedure until the degree wheel reads the same on both sides of indicated TDC. Secure the degree wheel.

Check Camshaft

After lubricating with light oil such as CRC or WD-40, install the lifter on the intake lobe for cylinder #1. Look at the valve reliefs in the piston if you're in doubt which one is the intake lifter bore. If it's a roller cam, you'll have to install the lifter guide, which means you need to install a lifter in the adjacent bore. Rotate the crankshaft a few times to make sure the lifter moves freely. Position the

crankshaft until the lifter is on the lobe base circle—it will be at its lowest position in the lifter bore. As shown at right, install a dial indicator so the plunger is in line with the lifter bore and entered in the lifter.

Refer to the specification card that accompanied the camshaft. Note and use checking lift specified for degreeing your camshaft. In this example checking lift is 0.050 in. Referring to the cam card pictured nearby, rotate the crankshaft in the clockwise direction while observing the dial indicator. When the indicator reading is 0.050 in., stop. Read and record the degree wheel reading. Using the example specifications, the degree wheel should read 19° BTDC. Continue rotating the crankshaft clockwise. The indicator reading will increase, stop and then begin to decrease. When the indicator reading reaches 0.050 in., stop rotating crankshaft. The

Set-up the dial indicator so the plunger is in line with the lifter bore. The plunger extension makes it easier to read the indicator.

Roller tappets need to be installed in pairs when guide bar is used.

Always rotate crankshaft in clockwise direction when degreeing a cam. Reference both dial indicator and degree wheel to verify degree-wheel reading and relative lift.

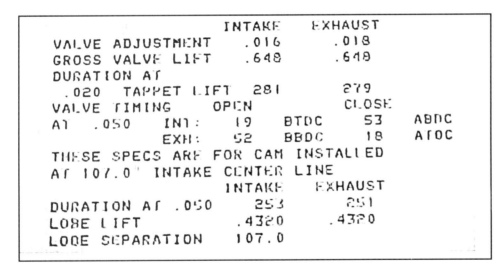

	INTAKE	EXHAUST	
VALVE ADJUSTMENT	.016	.018	
GROSS VALVE LIFT	.648	.648	
DURATION AT			
.020 TAPPET LIFT	281	279	
VALVE TIMING	OPEN	CLOSE	
AT .050 INT:	19 BTDC	53	ABDC
EXH:	52 BBDC	18	ATDC
THESE SPECS ARE FOR CAM INSTALLED			
AT 107.0 INTAKE CENTER LINE			
	INTAKE	EXHAUST	
DURATION AT .050	253	251	
LOBE LIFT	.4320	.4320	
LOBE SEPARATION	107.0		

As indicated by COMP Cams cam card, specifications are checked at 0.050-in. lift. A slightly different checking lift may be used depending on cam manufacturer.

degree wheel should agree with the cam card, or 53° ABDC in this case. This makes total duration 19° + 180° + 53° = 252° @ 0.050-in. lift. Being that this is a symmetrical lobe, the centerline will then be 1/2 this amount, or 126°. Subtract 19° from this figure to find lobe centerline in relation to TDC, or 126° − 19° = 107° ATDC. Rotate the crank until the degree wheel reads 107° and read the indicator to find the lift at the lobe centerline. Lift should be 0.4320 in. according to the cam card.

The degree wheel opening and closing points would have been different if you had advanced or retarded the cam. As an example, advancing the cam 4° would cause opening and closing points to be earlier, or 23° BTDC and 49° ABDC, respectively. Likewise, the lobe centerline would have moved to 103° ATDC. Had the cam been retarded 4°, events would have moved in the reverse direction, or 15°, 57° and 111°, respectively.

While set up, check the exhaust lobe. However, if you're the obsessive-compulsive type, you'll also what to check all cam lobes. To do this you will need to find TDC for each cylinder, then check the intake and exhaust lobes for each cylinder. Doing this is not too much of a stretch considering the consequences, but checking cylinder #1 lobes should suffice considering the high quality of performance camshafts being produced.

Referencing cam card, exhaust-lobe duration at 0.050-in. lift is

Rocker arm stands were clearanced by milling areas (arrows) where they interfered with the head bolts.

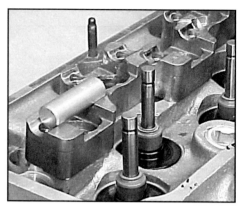

Lay a dowel on the rocker arm stand to begin checking geometry of shaft-mounted rocker arm.

52° + 180° + 18° = 250°. Lobe centerline is then 250°/2 − 18° = 107°, which is the same as intake duration. Note that lobe separation is found by adding the centerline positions of the two cam lobes, or 214° in crankshaft degrees. But because lobe separation is expressed in camshaft degrees, lobe separation in crankshaft degrees must be converted to camshaft degrees by dividing by two, making lobe separation 107°—a *split overlap* condition.

Degreeing a dual-pattern cam is no different than that for a single-pattern cam as just described. Use the cam card as reference for determining whether events agree with those specified by the manufacturer. Regardless of the cam you are checking, always record numbers for later reference, such as for when you make changes on the dyno or are building your next engine.

ROCKER ARM GEOMETRY

Rocker arm geometry is a combination of the ratio of the rocker arm and how it moves across the tip of the valve. A simple concept, it is something you need

to understand. This will allow you to set up the rocker arms so valve lift is maximized and valve stem and guide wear is minimized.

Rocker arm geometry begins with the relationship of the rocker arm to the center of the valve, which is a line drawn through the rocker arm pivot and contact point with the valve stem tip. Rocker arm manufacturers approach this differently. Most use the traditional method, which has a line that intersects the center of the rocker arm pivot and contact point at the valve tip square to the center of the valve at half lift. This is to minimize travel of the rocker arm as it arcs across the tip of the valve.

Another approach, called the *low trunnion setup*, reduces lateral arc travel from mid-opening to full valve opening. The purpose for this is to reduce lateral valve stem loading in the guide at higher spring forces to reduce friction and resulting wear. The rocker arm with this setup should be as close to square as possible with the centerline of the valve stem during full rocker arm travel. Sweep, or side-to-side movement of the rocker arm tip across the valve tip

will be minimized and remain near the center of the valve tip. Setting up rocker arms in this manner will also achieve maximum valve lift with a given cam and rocker arm ratio. Otherwise, the foreshortening effect of the arc described by this radius as the rocker arm swings reduces valve lift and increases side loading.

Don't ignore what happens to the pushrod end of the rocker arm. Just as the valve end of a rocker arm, the pushrod end swings through an arc, albeit shorter. This foreshortens the distance between the rocker arm pivot and pushrod end, which counteracts the foreshortening effect at the valve and maintains the ratio of the rocker arm. But how a manufacturer sets up the relationship between the two ends of a rocker arm and pivot has an effect on how his rocker arms should be installed. That's why there may be a slight difference between the instructions of one manufacturer versus another for establishing correct rocker arm geometry. Therefore, it is crucial to follow the setup instructions supplied with the rocker arms.

Regardless of manufacturer, correct rocker arm geometry depends on the vertical position of the rocker arm pivot relative to the tip of the valve and the pushrod. For shaft-type rocker arms, rocker arm geometry is determined by rocker arm stand height. Pushrod length is then determined by the distance between the rocker arm and the lifter. For stud-mounted rocker arms, pushrod length determines rocker arm geometry, requiring that heads be installed on the engine for checking.

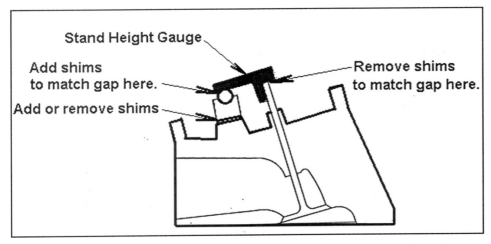

T&D rocker arm geometry checking gauge. Gap between the valve stem tip and gauge represents the shims to be removed. The gap between the dowel and gauge represents thickness of shims to be added.

Jesel checking gauge fits over valve stem. Amount stem is below gauge surface represents thickness of shims to remove from under the stand. Distance tip is above the gauge surface represents the thickness of shims to add.

Change the rocker arm stand shim thickness and recheck rocker arm geometry.

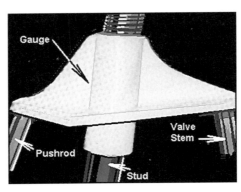

Manley rocker arm geometry checking gauge is fitted over the rocker arm stud and the long tip is held flush against the valve stem tip. Correct length pushrod fits under short end of the gauge.

Caution: If the rocker arm stands bridge any head bolts, check for interference between bolt heads and stands. If bolt heads project above the rocker arm and mounting surface, the stand will crack as it's tightened down. With the head installed, slide a straightedge across the stand mounting surface at each bolt head. If it hits the head, there is a problem. Provide clearance by either grinding the tops of the bolt heads a slight amount or clearancing areas of the rocker arm stand with an end mill.

Check Geometry

To make life easier, manufacturers supply specific instructions and setup gauges to check and adjust the geometry of shaft-mounted rocker arms by shimming under the rocker arm stand. With rocker arm stand in place on head and valve in guide, lay dowel in rocker-arm stand. Using gauge supplied by rocker arm manufacturer, fit it to the valve stem and dowel as shown. If the geometry is right, the gauge will be flush with valve stem tip or

dowel. However, the amount the gauge is not flush represents the thickness of the shim needed to make the rocker arm geometry correct. Check the gap with feeler gauges to determine the shim thickness. Add or remove the appropriate shims between the rocker arm stand and head, then recheck the geometry. Keep the shims with the stands.

Checking the geometry of the stud-mounted rocker arms requires the heads to be installed with the gaskets on the engine. Geometry is adjusted by using different length pushrods. A gauge can be used in place of the rocker arm over the rocker arm stud. With the lifter on the base circle, the long end of the gauge is placed against the valve tip so a pushrod can be found that fits against the short end. An adjustable pushrod is handy when doing this procedure.

To double-check rocker arm geometry, blue the valve tip, install a rocker arm and rotate the crankshaft a few times. Remove the

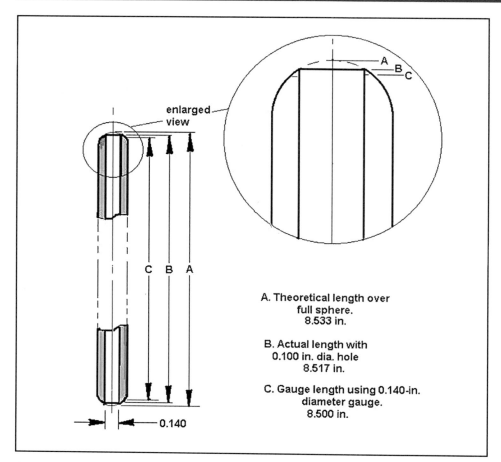

A. Theoretical length over full sphere.
8.533 in.

B. Actual length with 0.100 in. dia. hole
8.517 in.

C. Gauge length using 0.140-in. diameter gauge.
8.500 in.

Illustrated are three ways of measuring pushrod lengths: A. gross length; B. actual length; and C. gauge length. Check with manufacturer to see how they specify pushrod length.

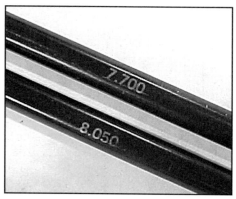

Lengths printed on pushrods come in handy.

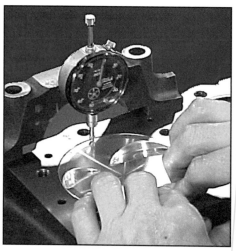

With the dial indicator at the inside edge of the piston, rock the outboard side down by pushing on it to get minimum deck clearance.

rocker arm and check the wipe pattern on the valve tip. Although manufacturers may specify a slightly different pattern, if it is narrow and centered on the tip, geometry is good. However, if the pattern is wide and on the exhaust side of the valve tip, the rocker arm pivot is low and the pushrod is short. If the pattern is wide and on the intake side, the pivot is high and the pushrod is long.

DECK CLEARANCE

Piston deck clearance should be nearly zero, even negative, on many high-compression race engines to maximize quench for increased combustion efficiency.

Regardless, you're in the danger zone if you use less than 0.040-in. piston-to-head clearance with steel or titanium rods and 0.060 in. with aluminum rods. If it's maximum quench you're shooting for, make sure you know the compressed head gasket thickness. Ranging from 0.027 in. to 0.120 in. with 0.039—0.041 in. being the most common, compressed gasket thickness is usually supplied by the gasket manufacturer.

Check deck clearance by first installing the piston-and-rod assembly. Bring the piston up to TDC and check the distance from the block deck to the flat surface at the outboard edge of the piston.

Zero depth gauge on the block, then move the gauge over to the piston so the indicator plunger is against the inboard or outboard edge of piston. Push down on the piston on the opposite side of the indicator to rock it up and read the deck clearance.

Deck clearance should be less than needed if you purposely ordered slightly taller pistons. This should be the case if you planned on getting an exact deck clearance by milling the tops of the pistons. So, if you need to increase deck clearance, determine how much you need to remove from the

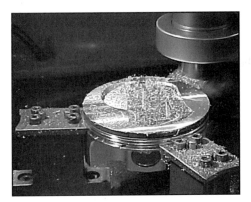

Secured in vise, piston compression height is reduced by cutting with an end mill.

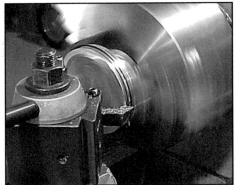

After milling tops, a 45° x 0.020-in. chamfer is put on the pistons.

Bounce springs are used in place of valve springs.

piston tops. For example, if deck clearance measures 0.020 in. and you want 0.039 in., remove 0.019 in. Remove the rod and piston from the block, then the piston from the rod. Secure it with a vise in your mill, then using an end-mill, remove the amount you determined will give the desired deck clearance. Recheck the deck clearances until you get it right. Surface all pistons, and then deburr them so a narrow chamfer is left, or about 0.020 in. as shown.

PISTON-TO-VALVE AND OTHER CLEARANCES

There should be a minimum of 0.100 in. *axial clearance* and 0.050 in. *radial clearance* between the pistons and valves. Add another 0.020 in. to the axial clearance if aluminum rods are used. Axial clearance is square to the valve head and radial clearance is the distance from the side, or margin, of the valve to the relief.

Although piston manufacturers do a good job of mating pistons to every conceivable head and valve combination, don't assume clearances will be adequate. There may even be interferences. This is not uncommon, particularly when

using custom pistons in a high-compression engine with one of the many heads that are available. Also check clearances to sparkplugs and combustion chambers, particularly if you're using domed pistons. Just as with deck clearance, there should be 0.040-in. minimum clearance with steel and titanium rods and 0.060-in. minimum with aluminum rods.

Piston-to-Valve Clearances

Use one of two methods for checking piston-to-valve clearances: The first is the old clay-mashing method. The second, and most preferred method, involves the use of a dial indicator and light springs in place of valve springs. Both methods require that you degree the camshaft as it will be run. To be on the safe side, also check clearances with the cam set at 4° before and after TDC. This will give you the flexibility of being able to change cam timing while dyno or track testing and not be concerned about piston-to-valve contact.

Clay Method—Temporarily install rod-and-piston assembly in cylinder #1. With the piston at TDC, lay a 1/8-in. thick strip of clay on the piston, particularly at

the valve reliefs. Also put some clay in a location that will be closest the sparkplug and across the dome, providing the piston has one. Keep the clay from sticking to the valves, sparkplug or combustion chamber by coating them with flour, cooking spray or a light oil. Although not necessary, I prefer using bounce springs in place of valve springs. Leave out the sparkplug. Install the lifters for cylinder #1, and then rotate the crankshaft to TDC on the power stroke. Both lifters will be at their lowest positions. Set the head on the engine with or without a gasket and secure lightly with some bolts or nuts. If you're not using a gasket, remember that there is less clearance by the thickness of the gasket, be it 0.020 in. or 0.040 in.

Install the pushrods and set valve lash to zero. Rotate the crankshaft, feeling for any resistance. Don't force the crankshaft. If there is resistance, remove the head and check for valve interference. But if the crank rotates freely after two complete revolutions, rotate it two more times. The crank position will now be back at TDC on the power stroke.

Remove the head and inspect the

clay. The valves will have made impressions in it. At the point of the deepest impression, cut the clay with a sharp knife. It is usually best to cut across the centers of the impressions made by the two valves and the sparkplug. The thickness of the clay where you sectioned it will reveal axial and radial piston-to-valve clearances. Measure it with a machinist's scale or the depth gauge end of dial calipers.

Minimums are 0.100–0.120 in. with aluminum rods to the bottom of the valve reliefs and 0.050 in. to the edge of reliefs. Check also the sparkplug area. The minimum here is 0.040/0.060 in. for steel or titanium/aluminum rods, respectively. If clearance is below the minimums, remove material in the affected area.

Dial Indicator Method—Install bounce springs in place of the valve springs for cylinder-# 1. They must be light enough that you can compress the springs with your fingers. Also install the two rocker arms. With the crankshaft positioned at TDC between the intake and exhaust strokes, install the cylinder head with or without a gasket. Whether you use a head gasket depends on how tight the clearances will be. If you think things will be close, use a head gasket. Otherwise, don't use a gasket. When using a gasket, install and torque the head bolts or nuts. Otherwise, you don't need to use bolts or nuts. Remember that when not using a gasket you need to allow for it when checking axial valve clearances by the thickness of the gasket.

With the head in place, install the pushrods and set the lash to zero. Mount the indicator base to

Note the steel plate bolted to the aluminum for attaching a magnetic indicator base. Adjust the indicator so the plunger is firmly against the spring retainer and in line with the valve stem.

the cylinder head and position the indicator so the plunger contacts the intake valve spring retainer and moves in line with the valve stem. Compress the indicator about 0.500 in. Zero the dial. To check actual clearance between the valve and piston, push on the rocker arm until the valve contacts the piston. The dial indicator reads exact piston-to-valve clearance. Do this in 2° increments on both sides of TDC while noting the indicator reading before and after the valve contacts the piston. Check both valves. If clearance is tighter than the minimums, work must be done to the pistons.

Take this opportunity to recheck valve retainer-to-guide clearance. Minimum clearance to the top of the guide is 0.100 in. or 0.060 in. to seal at full lift.

MACHINE VALVE POCKETS

If piston-to-valve clearance is insufficient, check first to see if valve pocket/s need to be enlarged. To do this, install head on block

Using degree wheel as reference, check piston-to-valve clearances 10° on both sides of TDC in 2° increments.

Push down on rocker arm to check clearance from point of valve opening in 2° increments from TDC.

with piston positioned at TDC. Install intake and exhaust valves and hold them in place with valve stem seals or by wrapping stems with rubber bands. Coat valve pocket areas with machinist's blue. Install the cylinder head on the block less gasket and bolts or nuts.

Push down and rotate valve against the piston.

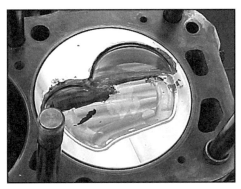

Bright line at the edge of the intake valve relief indicates interference.

Check thickness of the piston top to ensure there is sufficient thickness to go deeper with the valve relief.

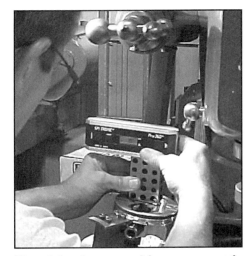

The piston is secured in a compound-angle rod vise, then the angles and centers of the valve reliefs are set.

A fly cutter is used to enlarge the valve relief.

Bluing highlights recut valve reliefs and ragged edges.

Push down firmly on the valve while rotating it against the piston. Do this to both valves. Remove the cylinder head and inspect the piston. Bluing will be wiped away to indicate where the valve contacted the piston.

If the relief centers need to be found, install the head without valves. Using a valve stem or round stock matching stem diameter sharpened to a point *on center*, insert into the guide and push while rotating it against the piston. A slight tap will center-punch the relief to provide a center for setting up to enlarge the relief/s or make it deeper.

Paper roll is used to deburr newly machined valve reliefs.

Using a piston vise, set up the piston in a mill and at an angle that corresponds to that of the valve. Center the head on the valve relief, then deepen or open up the valve relief/s as needed to clear the valve/s.

Flip over piston and chamfer skirts.

If you're uncertain, reinstall the piston on the rod and repeat piston-to-valve clearance check as you did before. Once you've finished with machining the valve relief/s, deburr the sharp edges. To do this, use a

	Top Ring Gap (in.)	2nd Ring Gap (in.)	Oil Ring Gap (in.)
Oval track	0.018–0.020	0.022–0.024	0.016–0.020
Super/turbocharged	0.024–0.028	0.024–0.026	0.016–0.020
Nitrous oxide (drag)	0.028–0.030	0.028–0.030	0.016–0.020

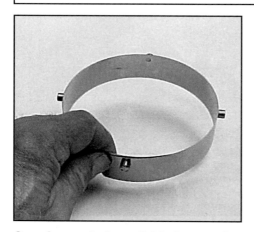

One of many tools available for squaring rings in bores. This one is from Goodson.

Doing it the old-fashioned way; squaring the ring in the bore with the top of a piston.

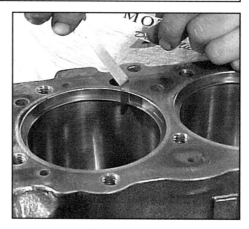

Ring end gap is checked after being squared in the bore.

paper roll in a die grinder to lightly chamfer the ragged edges. While you're at it, flip over the piston and deburr the skirt.

FITTING PISTON RINGS
Ring End Gap

How much gap a ring should have depends on bore diameter and heat that will be generated in the cylinder. Gapping according to bore size is straightforward—a simple calculation. Heat, on the other hand, depends on the type of operation and whether nitrous oxide, turbocharging, super-charging, gasoline or another kind of fuel is used, such as cooler-operating alcohol. As a general rule, though, gaps for ductile top rings vary from 0.0050 to 0.0070 in. per inch of bore, or 0.0050 in. for normally aspirated gasoline engines to 0.0070 in. for those using nitrous. Cast-iron 2nd-ring gaps are 0.0055 to 0.0073 in. per inch of

bore, which is nearly the same as for top rings. Minimum gap for oil ring rails is 0.0015 in. per inch of bore in all cases. As I said, these are general rules, so use what the ring manufacturer recommends.

Using general information, if you're gapping rings for a 4.000-in. bore in a naturally aspirated engine to be used for oval track, drag or road racing, ring end gaps will be 4.000 in. x 0.0050 in./in. bore size = 0.020 in. To be safe, give it another 0.001 in. of gap. Too much is better than too little gap. For typical end gaps, refer to the chart above.

Use rings for a bore that is 0.005-in. larger. This will provide extra material needed for file-fitting rings. Knowing that gap changes by a factor of 3.14 x bore size, a 0.005-in. smaller bore will reduce end gap by 0.016 in., which leaves plenty of material to remove. Start by making sure new rings are the

size you ordered. Having done that, begin checking end gaps. The ends of a ring for a 0.005-in. larger bore should just about butt when installed in the bore.

You'll need a ring organizer to hang each ring on it after gapping and deburring it. Start by fitting a top ring in each bore, then squaring each. Do this with a purpose-built tool or a piston, then go down the line checking end gaps with a feeler gauge. Working with one ring at a time, file one end.

If you're using a flat file, clamp it in a vise and hold the ring end square to the file and move it toward the file. This will remove metal from the outside edge to the inside, preventing facing material from chipping off or a burr from being formed at the outer corner of ring. Do the same with a ring filer. Position the ring so the file or stone rotates away from the outer edge. Pinch the ring together so the

With ring clamped in filer, it is moved in across the side of the rotating stone.

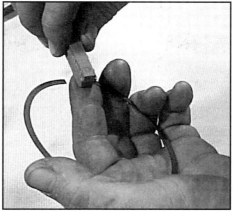
Using honing stone, very lightly chamfer corners of the ground end.

Rings organized according to the cylinder they were checked in. Note that the organizer is for a 6-cylinder engine. Cylinder #1 and #4 are also numbered for cylinder #7 and #8.

Remove material from side of ring by lapping it with 400 wet-or-dry sandpaper on precision granite stone. Doing this in parts washer washes away abrasive and metal particles.

ends butt. They should be square to one another or the outside corners should touch first. After filing or grinding the end, lightly chamfer it with a honing stone. Check end gap frequently. When you've finished with one ring, hang it up on the organizer and proceed with gapping the next.

Ring Side Clearance

As a precaution, check ring side clearance with a feeler gauge and the ring inserted into the piston groove. Clearance should be no less than 0.0010 in. and no more than

0.0020 in. Closer to 0.0010 in. is better, particularly with gas-ported pistons and thin rings.

You can't do much about changing side clearance when it is excessive other than replacing the pistons. For too little side clearance, lap each ring by holding down on it with even pressure and moving ring in a circular motion on 400 wet-or-dry sandpaper placed on granite stone while flooding it with coolant. A round aluminum block with a 0.020-in counterbore to set the ring in works well to ensure even pressure is exerted on ring so an equal amount of material is remove from side. Check ring thickness with 0–1-in. micrometers as you go.

Back Clearance

Check for sufficient ring back clearance. When pushed against the back wall of the groove, the face of ring should set back from the outer surface of the ring land at least 0.005 in. Check this with a wire gauge inserted between a straightedge, such as a machinist's scale, and the edge of the ring with it inserted into groove.

OIL PUMP PICKUP HEIGHT

There should be 1/4 to 3/8 in. between the bottom of the oil-pump pickup and the oil pan. This ensures oil will be picked up in driving situations the pan was designed for and not restrict oil flow into the pickup.

To determine the distance the oil pump pickup should be from the bottom of the pan rail, measure the oil pan depth, add compressed oil pan gasket thickness, and subtract the desired distance from the bottom of the pan to the bottom of pickup. Compressed oil pan gasket thickness is typically 3/32 in. (0.094 in.), but confirm specifications. As an example, if oil pan depth is 8.25 in. and gasket thickness is 0.094, then total distance from pan rail to bottom of pan is 8.25 in. + 0.094 in. = 8.34 in. (Let's ignore the extra 0.004 in.) For distance from the pan rail to bottom of the pickup, subtract the

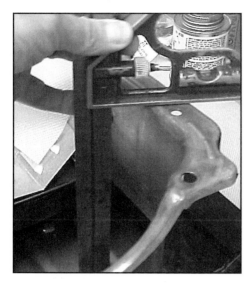

Measure the distance from the oil pan flange to the bottom of the pan in the area of the oil pump pickup. Add the oil pan gasket thickness.

A square set to the pan depth shows 1/4-in. gap. An additional 3/8 in. will allow for gasket thickness.

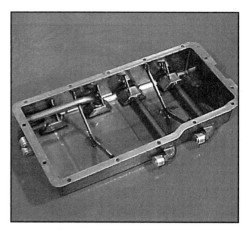

Multiple pickups in a dry sump system are fixed to the pan and not the pump.

Pickup location requires fabrication work—a little bending, cutting, drilling and welding.

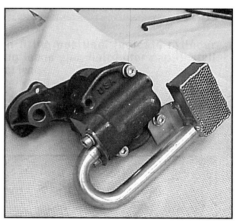

Bracket supports pickup at correct height and attitude.

gap you want between the pan and pickup, or 8.34 in. – 0.25 in. = 8.09 in. If you want more space, say 3/8 in., this distance will be 8.34 in. – 0.38 in. = 7.96 in.

Install the pickup and check the location by measuring the distance from the pan rail to the bottom of the pump pickup. A square and steel rule works well for making this measurement. If pickup height is where it should be to provide the necessary pan-to-pickup gap, you needn't go any further. However, if it's not, you'll have to purchase the pickup that is mated to the pan or do some fabrication. If you go the fabrication route, you'll need cutting, drilling, bending and welding equipment.

When setting up the pickup, make sure it is level or parallel with the bottom of the pan at the correct distance. Tack weld the pickup components, mount pickup loosely on the engine with the pump and check that the pickup is where you want it before you finish welding. When finished, the mounting flange must be flat and all joints 100% welded. This will ensure the pump will pick up only at the bottom of the pickup and not suck air, oil or anything else at any point between the pickup and the pump.

MATCH INTAKE MANIFOLD AND HEADS

To eliminate or reduce any restrictions, match the intake manifold runners to the ports in the heads. Also, trim the manifold gasket so it doesn't overhang into the airstream and act like a restrictor plate. Check your rulebook, first. It may be that you can't touch the runners or ports, or you may be able to modify only one. Other than a overhanging manifold gasket, the worst is runners that are smaller than the ports.

If you are restricted by the rules not to match the ports, the only thing you can do is make sure the gasket doesn't overhang into the airstream. Do this by following the process explained for port matching. This is because when the manifold and heads are matched, the gaskets will be used as templates.

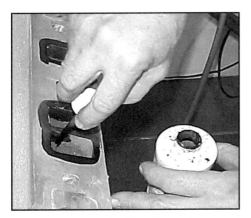

Apply machinist's blue in and around intake ports and manifold runners.

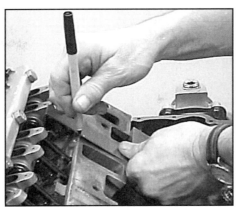

Using a straightedge, draw vertical lines from sides of ports and runners so they will be visible when the two are installed.

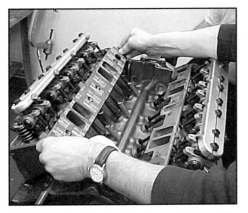

Fit the gasket to the head and align with the ports. Secure with manifold bolts with nuts and flat washers.

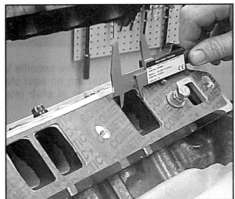

Measure the width of the ports to determine those requiring more or less material removal and shift the gasket accordingly. Note bolts with nuts and washers holding the gasket.

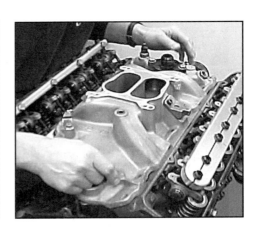

Lightly set the manifold on the head.

Match Gaskets

Providing heads have been resurfaced or don't need it, set them on the block with an old gasket. Secure them with at least two bolts. Lightly tighten them. Blue area in and around each intake port. Blue manifold, too. Using a small square and fine-tip felt marker, project a line alongside each port opening to the valve cover gasket surface of the head. Make similar marks on the upper surface of the intake manifold mounting flange.

Fit the intake gasket to the side of the head. Move it around to see how the holes align with those in the head. This is a balancing act.

Shift the gasket up or down and side to side so none or very little overhangs a port opening. Two manifold bolts fitted with a nut and flat washer can be used to hold the gasket in place while you're checking. When you find the best position for the gasket, mark its upper edges in a similar manner as you did the heads and manifold. Also, draw a witness mark across the head and gasket at each end. These will allow you to align the gaskets with the heads and manifold during final assembly.

If you used bolts and nuts to hold the gaskets in place, remove

them. Set the manifold in place and shift it back and forth, using witness marks on the heads, manifold and gaskets as a guide to find the best position for aligning everything. Hold the manifold and gaskets in place with a bolt at each corner of the manifold. To ensure everything will be in place for opening up the ports, runners and gaskets if needed, drill about a 3/32-in. hole deep enough that it goes 1/8 in. into head—no more. To determine drill depth, measure the distance from the gasket surface on the head to the surface of the manifold flange with depth gauge end of calipers and add 1/8 in. Wrap masking tape around drill bit this distance back from the end of

Move the manifold fore and aft to split the differences in witness marks on the heads and gaskets. Install and snug bolts at the corners of the manifold.

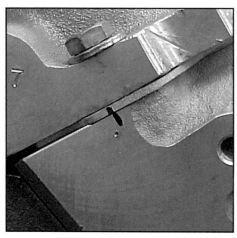

Draw a witness mark across the ends of manifold, gaskets and heads.

Drill holes through the manifold flanges, gaskets and into the head. Tape indicates when bit is at desired depth.

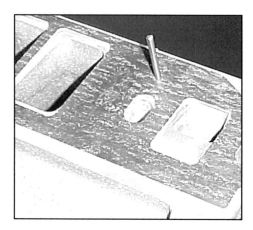

Gasket is positioned to the manifold with dowels.

Rules for racing class allows port work to extend into manifold no deeper than 1-in. for matching to ports to manifold. Rule-type depth gauge is used to indicate depth.

Use gasket as a template to scribe lines.

the drill point. Drill a hole at four corners as shown, then remove the manifold and heads.

Make four dowels from a 3/32-in. gas welding rod or use four 3/32-in. drill bits. For the dowels, cut and chamfer the ends of four, 2-in. long pieces of welding rod. Check that dowels or drill bits fit in the holes. Make a witness mark across each end of the gaskets, heads and manifold. That done, remove the manifold, gaskets and heads to see how the runners and ports line up.

Match Heads to Manifold

Position the gasket to the head or manifold with dowels and check the relationship to the ports or runners. Using the gasket as a template, scribe a line around the inside periphery of the opening. Do the same on both the heads and manifold. Also, if rules limit how far you can go into the head or manifold when matching the ports, indicate this distance with a depth gauge and a scribe. Using a die

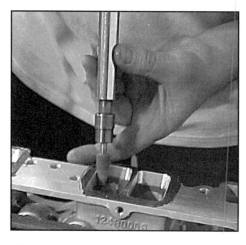

After using burr to rough out port, finish with paper roll. Keep close eye on scribe lines so limits are not exceeded.

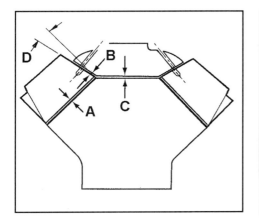

D (HEAD ANGLE IN DEGREES)	
5°	Amount removed at A x 1.1 = Amount to be removed at B
10°	Amount removed at A x 1.2 = Amount to be removed at B
15°	Amount removed at A x 1.4 = Amount to be removed at B
20°	Amount removed at A x 1.7 = Amount to be removed at B
25°	Amount removed at A x 2.0 = Amount to be removed at B
30°	Amount removed at A x 3.0 = Amount to be removed at B
35°	Amount removed at A x 4.0 = Amount to be removed at B
40°	Amount removed at A x 8.0 = Amount to be removed at B

Chart is for 90° blocks with heads using manifold surfaces at angles not square to deck surfaces. Remove material from side of manifold B based on material removed from head gasket surface A and angle of intake manifold gasket surface D to line that is square to deck surface. Amount removed from bottom of manifold C = A x 1.17.

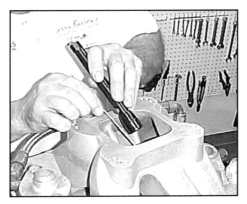

Checking port match with a flashlight and probe.

FelPro gauge checks angles of both cylinder-heads and manifold. Photo courtesy BHJ

grinder fitted with a stone, burr or paper roll, open up the port/runner to the scribe lines. Make this a smooth transition. However, if you find that the gasket overhangs the openings, reverse the procedure and open up the gasket. A paper roll works well for this.

After you've finished opening up the ports, runners or gaskets to the scribe lines, check that everything matches. Refit the heads to the block and secure each with two bolts. Set in place the gaskets and manifold. Using the witness marks or dowels, align the manifold and gaskets to the heads. Use a small flashlight and probe to check the manifold-to-head transition. Make probe from a section of welding

rod with about 1/8-in. of the end bent 90° to make a hook. Make it long enough so you can reach into the manifold and first inch or so of the head. Grind the end of a hook square so it will hang up on edges. Knock off the burrs, but don't chamfer it.

Using your flashlight, look into the manifold. Insert the probe into each runner and drag hooked end back-and-forth across the gasket. Check the full 360°. If the probe hangs up, make a note for later so you smooth the transition. If you detect a problem, repeat the matching process and recheck. Otherwise, remove the heads, manifold and gaskets and set them aside for final assembly.

INTAKE MANIFOLD

If you milled the heads, the mating face of the intake manifold may have to be refaced, but not in the traditional manner. Instead, only remove enough that will bring the floor of the intake runners down to the floor of the ports and no more. This may or may not fall within what would be removed using the traditional method. And by all means, avoid removing so much material that the floor of the intake runners end up below those of the heads. Rather, when the floors are both aligned, the intake ports and runners can be blended. This effectively raises the ports, albeit slightly.

With heads installed on the engine, use a height gauge to measure the vertical distance from the floor of the intake ports at the gasket face to the manifold gasket surface on the block. Set up the manifold to remove material from the sides of the manifold to match this distance or as referenced from the charts nearby. If using the charts, remove about one-half of the material indicated and recheck the manifold fit.

After fly-cutting the manifold

INTAKE MANIFOLD VS. CYLINDER HEAD MILLING REQUIREMENTS (90° AND 60° BLOCKS)

90° Block

Removed From Cylinder Heads	Removed From Manifold Bottom	*Removed From Manifold Sides
0.020	0.028	0.020
0.025	0.035	0.025
0.030	0.042	0.030
0.035	0.049	0.035
0.040	0.056	0.040
0.045	0.063	0.045
0.050	0.070	0.050
0.055	0.078	0.055
0.060	0.084	0.060

60° Block

0.020	0.023	0.011
0.025	0.029	0.014
0.030	0.034	0.017
0.035	0.040	0.020
0.040	0.046	0.023
0.045	0.052	0.026
0.050	0.058	0.029
0.055	0.064	0.032
0.060	0.069	0.035

*Double amount when milling one side of manifold only.

Chart for 60° and 90° blocks with heads using intake manifold surfaces that are 90° to head-gasket surface. As indicated, the amount removed from each side is a 1:1 ratio with a 90° block and about a 0.6:1 ratio with a 60° block.

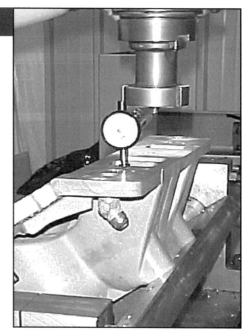

Set up manifold on fixture secured to milling machine bed at correct angle. Check with level gasket and indicator on gasket surface.

side/s, check the fit on the block with the heads. Use the port-matching procedure previously described to check runner and port alignment. If you removed more than 0.020 in., also check the bolt holes to ensure there is no interference, particularly with angle-milled heads. Finish up by deburring all machined surfaces.

After fly-cutting sides, revise setup to remove material from manifold bottom based on accompanying chart or formula.

Now that you've machined, cleaned, checked, rechecked and fitted all of the parts of your engine, it's time to do the final assembly. This doesn't mean that checking should stop. Surprises happen. Now is the time to find problems rather than after the engine is on the dyno or installed. Start by checking your parts inventory. It can be inconvenient to say the least to be nearing the end of assembling your engine and find you're missing something critical such as head gaskets. So make sure you have everything you need to assemble your engine. Include lubricants, sealers, cleaners and tools. Don't compromise on where you will be assembling the engine. It should be clean, dry, well lighted and at about 74°F.

INSTALL PLUGS
Core Plugs
Begin engine assembly by installing the core plugs, drain plugs and oil gallery plugs. If they aren't in place, install them now. Apply a light coat of sealer to the outer periphery of the core plug, then drive it into place with a large-diameter punch. Position the edge of the plug flange slightly below the bottom edge of the core hole chamfer.

To ensure plugs stay in place, do one or both of the following: Install three #2 round-head drive screws evenly spaced at the edge of each core plug. Drill holes square to the chamfer at edge of each core

Give the block a final scrubbing.

When installed, the drive screw heads overlap the core plug flange to ensure plugs stays in place.

Drive in core plug until edge of flange is about 1/16-in. below the bottom of the chamfer.

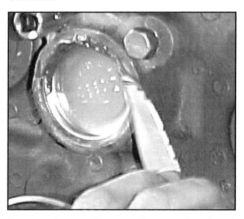

As was done with cam plug, apply a bead of epoxy around the core-plug flange. Epoxy is easily applied with the tip of a pocketknife or small screwdriver.

plug using a #44 drill. Place a piece of masking tape 5/16 in. back from drill point and drill hole to that depth. Drive screws into place so heads are hard against the edges of the core plugs. Or, you can apply a bead of epoxy around the edge of each core plug with or without the screws. Clean the chamfers and

core-plug edges with solvent, and then apply a smooth bead of epoxy such as J-B Weld or Z-Spar around the edges of the plugs.

Drain Plugs
Don't forget these little hex-head pipe plugs. There should be one at the bottom on each side of the

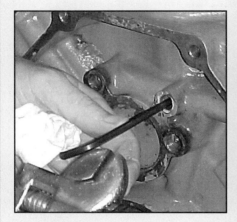

When using separate oil gallery restrictors as in this Ford block, thread in restrictors and tighten, then install the plug.

Seal galleries using Teflon sealer on the plug threads. Unlike Allen-head plugs, restrictor/plugs have male hex heads, making them easier to install and remove.

When using an external oil pump on a Chevy block machined for internal pumps, don't neglect to plug the internal oil gallery (arrow).

Teflon-based pipe dope is handy for sealing oil gallery plugs.

Oil galleries such as in this NASCAR Dodge block are sealed with O-ringed plugs. Install new O-rings and secure with retaining rings.

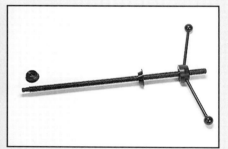

Bearing puller with mandrel at left. Needle bearings must be installed with such a tool. Photo courtesy Goodson.

block. Apply Teflon sealer to the threads and run the plugs in tight.

Oil Gallery Plugs & Restrictors

Oil restrictors and plugs vary widely. They range from separate restrictors with thread-in plugs, thread-in restrictor/plug combinations or plugs with O-rings secured with retaining rings. For blocks using separate restrictors, run them in until they bottom, then install the plugs. Seal plugs with liquid Teflon or Teflon tape.

Caution: To prevent Teflon sealer from getting into oil galleries, don't apply sealer to the first two threads. For restrictor/plug combinations, install an O-ring on the end of the restrictor, apply a sealer to the threads and lubricate the O-ring. Install restrictor/plugs. For an O-ring sealed plug, install a new O-ring. Lubricate the O-ring, then install it with threaded hole to the outside. Push the plug in the hole past the retaining ring groove and install the retaining ring.

INSTALL CAM BEARINGS

How you install cam bearings depends on the bearing type. Sleeve bearings can be driven or pulled in, but needle bearings must be pulled in to prevent damage. With a bearing driver or puller, match the mandrel to the bearing. It must fit the bearing ID, the shoulder against the edge of the bearing and clear the bearing housing in the block. Make sure there is slight clearance to the bearing ID to prevent the bearing from trapping

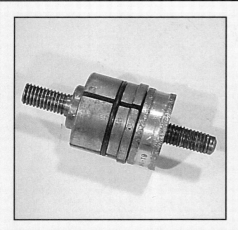

When using expansion mandrel, expand mandrel to fit bearing, then back off mandrel a full turn before installing the bearing.

Bearing with solid drive mandrel fitted to drive bar. Draw witness line on back of bearing at oil hole to help align it with oil hole in block.

Remove burr at edge of bearing with pocketknife or bearing scraper.

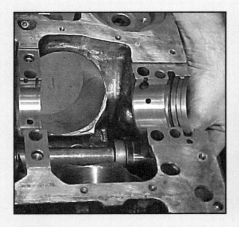

Align bearing to bore, paying particular attention to oil hole alignment.

Using the cone to center the bar, drive or pull the bearing into place.

Check oil hole alignment.

the mandrel after it is driven in. To prevent the same when using an expansion mandrel, expand the mandrel to fit the bearing ID, then back it off a full turn.

Before installing sleeve bearings, check their edges. If you feel a burr, remove it with a pocketknife or bearing scraper. This will make cam installation easier. Hold knife or scraper at 45° to the bearing and run it once around the bearing ID to remove a hair-like shaving. Also, to make aligning the bearing oil

hole with the hole in the block easier, draw a witness line across the back of the bearing shell in line with the oil hole.

With bearing fitted to the correct mandrel, install front or rear bearing from the opposite end of the block. Use centering cone on the bar to center it in the bearing bore, align the bearing with the oil hole, then drive or pull it into the housing. Once the bearing is in to the correct depth, remove the mandrel and check oil hole

alignment. This is easy to do with an inspection mirror and good flashlight. Continue installing the bearings. After you get the center bearing installed, switch ends and install remaining bearings.

INSTALL MAIN BEARINGS & SEAL

Check that you have the correct main bearings and recheck crankshaft journal diameter. Checking and rechecking is tedious, but parts can get mixed up in an engine shop. Besides, no one has

When you are away for more than a moment, cover your engine to ensure it stays clean.

Recheck main bearing journals. Make sure you have the right bearing inserts, too.

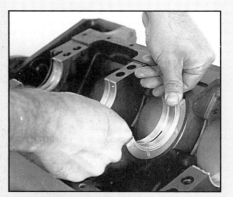

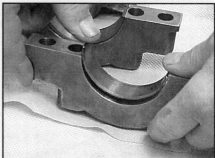

After wiping bearing bores, parting lines and bearing inserts clean, install inserts in block and caps.

Stagger split-lip seal ends 1/4 to 1/2 in. above/below the parting line. Lubricate the bearing and seal.

Signal's split full-circle seal for Chevy blocks install in place of split lip seal. Install seal on crank before installing in the block.

ever been faulted for being careful during any engine-building stage.

Providing all checks out, wipe the main bearing bores and cap parting lines clean with a solvent soaked shop towel. Give bearing inserts the same treatment. Install bearings in the caps and block. How you install the rear main seal depends on whether it's a split- or full-lip seal. If it's a split-lip seal, install half in the block and the other half in the cap. Stagger ends 1/4 to 1/2 in. so they don't align with the cap parting line.

Install full-circle seal later.

A variation for Chevrolet crankshafts using split lip seals is Signal's double-lip seal with one split. When using this seal, coat lips with 30w oil and put it on the crankshaft before you install the crankshaft. Secure the seal with two O-rings. The thicker lip installs toward the crankcase to seal oil and the thinner lip installs away in the other direction to seal out air from entering an evacuated crankcase.

INSTALL THE CRANKSHAFT

Lubricate bearings and seal. Hold the crankshaft securely over the block, then lower it straight down onto the bearings.

Noting cap position and direction, fit each to the block. Tap cap into register with a soft mallet. Seal rear cap with RTV silicone sealer. Run a thin bead of sealer from the rear main seal or seal adapter on each side to the cap register. Apply a small dab of grease to the ends of a split-lip seal. For a

Lubricate bearings and seal, then set crankshaft squarely into block and onto bearings.

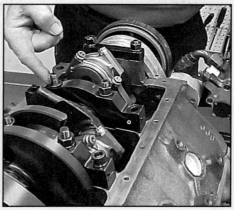

After fitting caps to block in correct location and direction. lubricate threads and bottoms of bolt heads or nuts and install with hard washers.

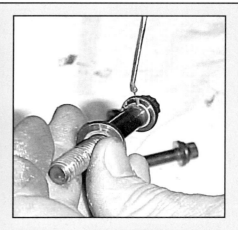

Flattened welding rod works well for apply lube to bolts.

Torque main-cap bolts/nuts in three equal steps. Torque outboard bolt after inner bolts. If used, torque cross bolts last.

deep-skirt block, lubricate and install side seals after the cap is fully seated.

Lubricate the underside of the bolt heads or nuts and stud or bolt threads. If you don't have high-pressure assembly lube, mix some moly paste with motor oil in a small container to a near pourable consistency. Install the washers and nuts or bolts. Before tightening them, pry the crankshaft back and forth in the block to align thrust-bearing inserts. Snug the main cap with the thrust bearings while holding the crankshaft forward, then triple check the crankshaft endplay. A 0.003–0.005-in. range is good with 0.007 in. as the high end. Providing float is good,

torque bolts/nuts to a specified value in three equal stages. For example, if final specified torque is 90 ft-lb, snug them, then torque to 30 ft-lb, 60 ft-lb and finish up with 90 ft-lb. Check final torque and give the wrench a "second click."

Outer main cap bolts typically have less torque, say 75 ft-lb versus 65 ft-lb, so reset your wrench and torque them. If your block has cross-bolted mains and spacers are used, install them last. Slide in each bolt while holding correct thickness spacer in place. Install all bolts and spacers, then torque bolts in two stages and in sequence. This is typically done in a zigzag pattern from the front to back of the block.

So if cross-bolt torque is 40 ft-lb, torque them 20 ft-lb first and finish with 40 ft-lb.

INSTALL CAMSHAFT

Lubricate the lobes of a flat-tappet cam with lubricant supplied by cam manufacturer. Smear it over the full surface of each lobe. Apply assembly lubricant to the bearing journals and lobes of a roller cam. Refer to Chapter 7 for installing the camshaft and timing set. Fit a long bolt or handle to the cam nose, then carefully guide it into the block. Avoid bumping the lobes into the bearings. Rotate the cam so dowel or key aligns with crankshaft positioned at TDC.

Install timing set, be it chain, belt

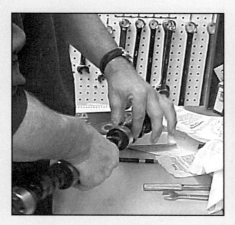

Lubricate cam lobes and bearing journals.

Using long bolt or handle for control, avoid contact with bearings as you guide cam into block.

Install thrust bearing and, if used, thrust plate, then sprocket.

Universal cam-handle kit. Photo courtesy Powerhouse Products.

Rotate crankshaft to line up cam sprocket with cam.

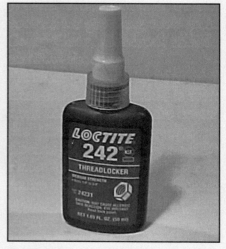

Blue Loctite is sufficient for securing most engine fasteners.

or gear type. When using belt drive, plate with gasket and sealer installs first. Lubricate and install Torrington thrust bearing on cam nose then thrust plate, if used, followed by cam sprocket or gear. If thrust plate is used, position over the nose of the cam and secure with bolts. Install any spacer or oil slinger on the crankshaft. Check that the cam rotates freely by turning it by hand with the sprocket or gear loosely installed to the cam nose.

Install the timing set. Drape the chain or belt over the cam sprocket, then set the crankshaft sprocket in the belt or chain so the timing marks are aligned. I suggest you start with the cam advanced at 4°. Have the cam sprocket bolts and hardware close at hand and ready to install. With the crank sprocket hanging in the chain or belt, slide it over the crank nose. Rotate the crank sprocket back and forth as you push back on it until it engages the key. When the crank sprocket is

engaged, slide timing set back until cam sprocket contacts cam nose. If the cam and crank are aligned, the cam sprocket should engage the dowel. If it doesn't—chances are it won't—rotate the crank slightly one way or the other while pushing back on the cam sprocket until it engages the dowel. Secure the cam sprocket. Apply a drop of blue Loctite to the sprocket bolt/s, then install the bolt/s and washer/s, if used, and thrust button or fuel pump eccentric to the sprocket. If a

If a thrust plate is used to control the camshaft float, do a preliminary endplay check before installing the cam. Loosely assemble the thrust plate, sprocket and thrust-bearing assembly, if used, then check clearance with a feeler gauge.

Set up the dial indicator square to back of the cam to read float.

Apply sealer to the outer edge of the seal, back up the front cover close to the seal bore to prevent damage or distortion and use the driver that seats firmly against the steel OD to drive it in place.

Apply a thin line of sealer to the block, install the gasket and apply the sealer to the gasket.

Fit cover to dowels (arrows) or center cover to crankshaft with damper.

lock plate is used, bend tabs over the bolt heads to the lock bolts.

Check Camshaft Endplay

Set up the dial indicator so plunger is square to the back of the cam. Push forward on the cam, zero the dial indicator, then push back on the cam while viewing the indicator dial. The endplay should be 0–0.004 in. Adjust the float with shims. If a thrust button is used, install front cover before making check. Apply sealer to both sides of the gasket, then install the front cover. Center front cover to the crankshaft with damper or alignment dowels, then secure with bolts. Install the water pump. Use pump to pry against front cover to move camshaft back in block.

After checking and adjusting float, finish camshaft installation by installing the cam plug. This will be easier done later when the engine is off the stand, so don't forget it. This large, short-flange plug can be a bugger to get started straight. Remove it and try again if it starts crooked. Apply sealer to flange, then drive in plug with large punch and hammer. Complete plug installation by applying epoxy to flange.

Install Crankshaft Damper—To ease damper installation and removal, apply anti-seize compound to the crank nose. Lubricate damper nose, then start it onto crankshaft while aligning damper with key. Push and rotate damper it until it engages key, then

Apply thin coat of anti-seize compound to nose of crankshaft and oil to damper seal surface. After it engages with the key, pull the damper onto the crankshaft with a damper installer. Do not drive on the damper.

With number #1 piston at TDC, adjust timing pointer to read TDC.

Adjustable pointer is locked in position with bead of RTV silicone.

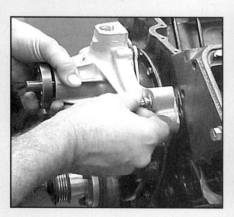

Install water pump with gasket/s and sealer.

Push the cam forward in the block, zero indicator, then pry against front cover to force the cam back in block. Read endplay.

The front cover is fitted with the camshaft endplay adjuster. Make adjustment with the center screw and lock with a jam nut.

install damper tool. While holding the threaded center section, rotate nut to pull on damper. Once it bottoms, install the damper bolt with the washer and torque to spec. Hold crankshaft from turning at the flywheel flange with two bolts installed or use hammer handle between pan rail and counter-weight.

If needed, set cylinder #1 at TDC using the procedure detailed, pages 150–152. Adjust timing pointer to indicate TDC. Lock pointer in position. To ensure pointer doesn't move, apply a bead of RTV silicone to the edge of the pointer and front cover or pointer body.

INSTALL RODS & PISTONS
Assemble Rods to Pistons

Organize connecting rods and pistons with pins and retainers. Use spiro locks and Truarc retainers with non-chamfered pins. Wire locks must be used with chamfered pins. Install a lock/s in one end of piston-pin bore. Retainer grooves may be machined for double-wound spiro locks or two TruArc retaining rings.

Install wire lock by fitting one end of lock into groove opposite pick lock groove, then push lock into groove using a small screwdriver. Be very careful as this will require some force. Have some Band-Aids handy. One slip can mean a nasty injury. Once in the groove, slide the pin into pin bore and seat lock in the groove by

Complete cam installation by installing cam plug after engine is off stand. As shown, oil gallery plugs must also be installed.

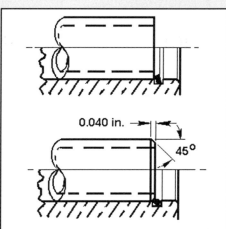

Chamfered piston pin (bottom) must be used with wire-lock pin retainers. Squared off pin is for spiro locks and Truarc retainers.

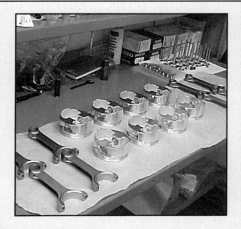

Rods and pistons organized with those for right bank at back and left bank at front of bench. Use a system to help ensure you assemble rods and pistons so they will be correctly oriented.

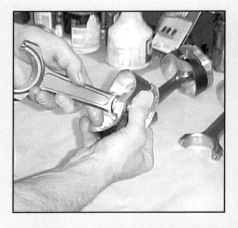

Lubricate pin and pin bore, then slide pin through pin bore and small end of rod.

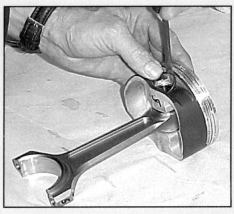

It's easy to slip and injure a finger or hand when installing wire locks, so be careful.

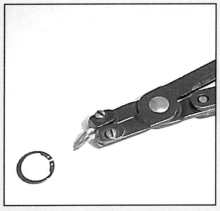

Use retaining ring pliers with bent tips to install TruArc retaining rings.

striking the end of the pin with a brass drift. Support the piston on a soft pad so you don't damage it. Install a spiro lock by pulling it apart only enough to wind into the groove. When seated, the lock should be half way into the groove. Using retaining-ring pliers, install Truarc retainers with the convex side against pin so retainer ID contacts pin and OD bears against ring groove. As a check, the rounded edge of the retainer will be against the pin end and sharp

edge will be out against the ring groove.

After you've installed lock/s in one end of the piston-pin bore, coat pin and pin bore with assembly lube and start pin in bore. Orient rods to pistons—numbers match—so large rod chamfer will be toward crank-journal radius and valve reliefs will match the valves. Slide pin through small end of rod and piston until it's against lock. Install the other lock/s in the same manner. Check to see that they are

fully seated in grooves, particularly wire locks. Double-check that both wire locks are seated by striking end of pin as before.

Install Rings & Bearings— Ready rod-and-piston assemblies for installation into block. Using a vise with soft jaws, set the piston on top of the vise and *lightly* clamp the rod. With rings matched to pistons and bores, start by installing the oil rings. Install the oil ring expander and position ends over one end of the piston pin.

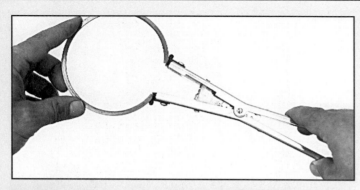

Use ring expander for installing thicker compression rings, especially the second ring.

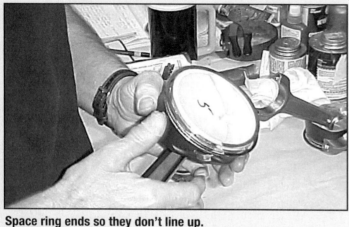

Space ring ends so they don't line up.

COMPRESSION RING

OIL-RING RAIL

1-1/4"

FRONT

OIL-RING EXPANDER

1-1/4"

PIN BORE

1-1/4"

OIL-RING RAIL

1-1/4"

COMPRESSION RING

One way of spacing ring ends. Just make sure ring ends don't align.

Make sure expander ends aren't overlapping, then install top rail followed by bottom rail. Overlap expander ends so rail ends are positioned to each side of expander ends by about one inch. Double-check that expander ends aren't overlapping. It's OK to spiral on oil ring rails and the thin top compression rings. Otherwise, use a ring expander to fit compression rings over the piston and into the grooves. After the oil ring, install the second compression ring and top ring. Check that the top side of the compression ring is up, then expand the ring, lower it over the piston and release it into the groove. As you expand the ring, support it with one hand while you

expand it with the other. Install all rings in the same manner.

Install Piston-and-Rod Assembly

Make sure the cylinders are perfectly clean by wiping them down with brake cleaner and a paper towel or lint-free cloth. Rotate the block to level the deck surface of one cylinder bank and lock the engine stand. Rotate the crankshaft so the front throw is at BDC. Coat the cylinder with 30w oil or, for a fast ring break-in, use Total Seal's Quick Seat. This dry film lubricant will seat the rings while running in the engine prior to dyno testing it.

To use Quick Seat, clean each

cylinder as described, then coat it with a light penetrating oil such as WD-40 or CRC. Wipe cylinders dry, then apply the powder-like Quick Seat with a finger to the bore surfaces. Clean cylinders will change to a greenish tint color. The cylinders are now ready for the piston-and-rod assemblies, so don't add anything more to the bore walls. If they are not clean, the powder will assume a black or silver tone. In this case, clean the problem cylinder again and reapply Quick Seat. Proceed if all is OK.

Just as you did when installing main bearing inserts, wipe rod-bearing inserts, bearing bores and cap parting lines clean. Fit bearing inserts into rods and caps, then

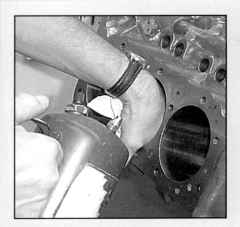

Clean cylinder with brake cleaner and paper towel or lint-free cloth.

Apply Total Seal's dry film lubricant Quick Seat to cylinder walls for fast ring seating.

Clean bearing inserts and bearing bores, then install inserts.

Adjustable tapered ring compressor covers a small range of bore sizes.

With ring compressor solidly against deck, tap piston into cylinder.

After all rods and pistons are installed, tighten nuts or bolts to specification. Stretch is the most accurate way of tightening bolts.

smear motor oil on them, the piston skirts and rings. Don't oil the rings if you're using Quick Seat.

Fit ring compressor to piston. If you're using a clamp-type ring compressor, compress the rings. As for an adjustable tapered compressor, adjust it to match the bore size. Smear 30W oil on the skirts, and then push the piston into the compressor so the oil ring starts to compress. Support the assembly in a vertical position so the rod hangs straight down, then

lower it into the cylinder. Make sure the compressor is seated squarely against the deck by tapping against its edge, then tap the piston into the cylinder. The butt end of a hammer works well for this job. Stop if a ring pops out from under the compressor and hangs up on the deck. If this happens, start over. When compressor relaxes as the top ring enters the cylinder, push piston down the bore while guiding the rod over the crank throw with your

other hand until the rod is hard against it.

Lubricate threads and undersides of nuts or bolts. Oil the bearing and install the cap on the rod. Check that it is oriented correctly by referencing numbers and chamfers on it and the rod. Snug nuts or bolts, then back them off to release the tension. Position the crankshaft so you can fit the gauge to the bolts, then zero the gauge. Tighten each bolt until the stretch is to specification. It will be about 0.007

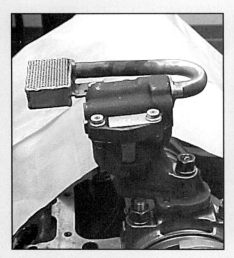

Install oil pump with the driveshaft and pickup.

Mount belt driven pump, making sure ports are oriented correctly.

Sprint car setup, cam driven oil pump and crank driven water pump are mounted to two-piece front cover. Photo courtesy Barnes Systems, Inc.

Windage tray mounted to heads of main cap bolts. Note safety-wired mounting bolts.

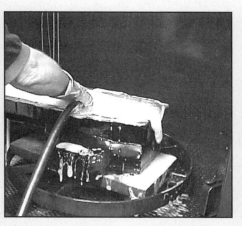

Make absolutely certain the oil pan is clean by giving it a good scrubbing.

Allan applies a thin coat of Devcon 149000 Rubber Adhesive to the pan rail.

in. give or take 0.001 in. Rotate the crank at least once to check that it turns freely. Reposition the crankshaft for installing the next rod-and-piston assembly.

If rod bolts are new and you are using torque rather than stretch to tighten them, loosen each bolt several times, then retighten them to a specified torque. Doing this will reduce the effect of friction at the threads to give a more accurate bolt stretch.

INSTALL PUMP & OIL PAN
Install Pump

If you have a wet-sump engine equipped with an internal pump, install it and the pickup. For a driveshaft that installs with the pump from the bottom as with a small-block Ford or Chevy, fit it to pump and install them as an assembly. Make sure the Tinnerman collar is on a Ford driveshaft. Install new sleeve on a Chevy driveshaft. Use a gasket without sealer. Instead, wipe some

grease on the gasket to hold it in place. Set pump with driveshaft and gasket in position, and then secure pump to block with bolt/s or nut/s and lockwashers. If your engine will use an external pump, install it. Using the appropriate brackets and fasteners, mount pump to block or engage it to the nose and bolt it with gasket to the front cover.

Install Oil Pan

If you haven't done so already,

He carefully lays the gaskets in place.

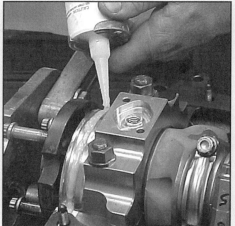

Apply sealer in groove, then install the end seal. Apply extra dab of sealer to the gasket-and-seal ends. Do the same at the other end.

Studs make pan gasket placement a bit easier. Double-nut the stud to tighten it.

Apply a thin line of sealer the full-length of the pan gasket.

Position oil pan on the engine. Studs make this operation easier.

wash the oil pan. Tank it, soak it, scrub it, brush it, blow it out, and dry it. Make absolutely certain the pan and any scrapers, screens or baffles in the pan are very clean. If they are removable, remove and clean these components separately, then reinstall them. If the windage tray mounts to the main cap bolts or studs, install it. Or if it sandwiches between the oil pan and block, install it with the oil pan.

Unless you have a deep skirt block, you'll need two gaskets and two end seals to install the pan. Start by placing the gaskets on the pan rail to determine which is right or left and up or down. Although weatherstrip adhesive, affectionately referred to as "gorilla snot," will do the job, rubber cement will hold the gaskets in place while you fit the end seals to the main caps and gaskets. It will also be easier to clean the gasket surface when the engine is refreshed. Lay gaskets in place, then apply RTV silicone to the grooves in the rear main cap and front cover. Push the seal into the groove and fit each end to gasket. Do this at both ends. Apply extra sealer over each gasket-and-end seal junction. Run a thin line of sealer the full length of the gasket.

Set oil pan straight down on pan rails. If you're using bolts, loosely install those at the four corners to secure the pan in place. These bolts or nuts are usually larger due to the extra force needed to draw the pan down against the end seals. Install all nuts or bolts with lockwashers. Install scavenging lines from the pan to the external pump.

Install Rear Main Seal

If a full-circle rear main seal is used, install it to complete bottom-end sealing. Because of access, this job will have to be done after the engine is off the stand. Find a large-diameter driver that seats firmly against the

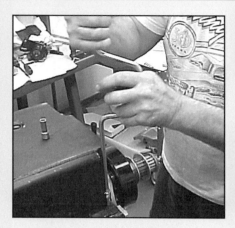

Install nuts or bolts and tighten. Using a speed handle, tighten several times as the gasket relaxes.

Due to pan distortion and gap, this pan required more silicone at the end seals.

To ensure the rear main seal stays in place, six evenly spaced Torx-drive pan-head screws were installed with flat washers so they overlap seal.

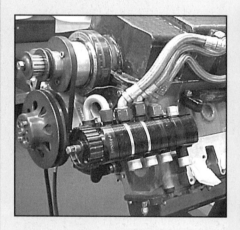

Before flipping the engine over, connect the scavenge lines to the pump and pan.

Make sure heads are clean. Head is sprayed with solvent in preparation for a good scrubbing and rinsing.

Valve and spring organizer helps to ensure valves and springs are installed in the correct position.

seal OD. Oil the seal lip and apply sealer to OD. Fit over crank flange with lip pointing forward, then drive it into place until the seal is flush with the rear face.

ASSEMBLE & INSTALL CYLINDER HEADS

Set the cylinder heads on a bench along with the valves, springs, spring retainers, locks, seals and, if used, spring locators or cups. You will need some lubricant and maybe an assortment of shims.

Organize the valves with the cylinder head in which they will be installed. An organizer like the one shown above works well.

Install Valves & Seals

Position the heads on the bench with the exhaust side up and combustion chamber toward you. Install each valve on its seat. Lubricate the stems and slide valves into place. With shop towels placed so they will be under the heads, roll them over so spring

sides are up. Watch that the valves don't slide out of the guides.

If spring locators or cups are used, fit them over the valve guides and onto the spring seats. Lubricate the valve stems. You may opt to delete the exhaust valve stem seals. Another approach is to remove the "pucker" spring from the top of each exhaust stem seal. If the engine is for drag racing, you won't need them at all. Carefully fit each seal over the valve stem tip and groove, and then push down

Have assembly lube nearby for installing valves and seals.

Lubricate valve stems and install valves on seats.

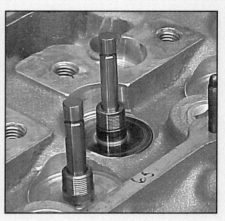

If spring locators are used, as shown on this aluminum head, install them.

Lubricate the valve stem, then carefully fit the seal over the valve stem and push down against the top of the guide.

Using a tool that shoulders against the seal OD, tap the seal down until it bottoms against the top of the guide.

on top of the guide. Using an installation tool that shoulders against the seal OD, tap the seal lightly, down against the top of the guide.

Check & Install Valve Springs

Check spring installed height at the valve and compare results to the specified spring height. Use a valve spring height gauge or telescoping gauge and outside micrometers for measuring spring seat-to-retainer distance. Set gauge to 0.250-in. or less than specified installed height, then position the gauge on the valve spring seat. Push the valve up into the guide, and then install the spring retainer with locks. Adjust gauge until it touches bottom of retainer, and then tap very lightly against valve stem tip to seat locks. Readjust gauge and read height. Record this figure.

To measure seat-to-retainer height, or installed spring height, with a telescoping gauge, seat locks first by pulling up on retainer and tapping valve stem tip. Check that the valve is on the seat, then expand the gauge between the spring seat and retainer. Check gauge with calipers or outside mics and record the results. Measure heights with all of the valves. The lowest reading will be installed spring height. Use shims to reduce height to same amount so they are within +/-0.020 in. If you are using dual or triple springs, be careful to measure from the correct spring retainer step.

Seals installed on guides. Note that tension spring has been removed from exhaust seal.

With spring retainer and valve spring gauge in place, seat locks by tapping on valve stem tip.

Read installed spring height directly from the gauge.

For convenience, Bob records results on head for later reference. Shims will be used if needed to equalize with the lowest measured installed height.

Use telescoping gauge to check spring seat-to-retainer distance. Measure gauge with outside micrometers or calipers to get installed spring height.

Check Valve Spring Pressure— Check spring pressures at specified installed height and open height. Check also for coil bind at open height. As discussed earlier, there should be a minimum of 0.015-in. clearance between the coils for both inner and outer springs so there will be at least 0.060-in. travel before coil bind is reached. Check both springs. It is possible that the inner spring will be the limiting factor.

The two major specifications to work with are seat pressure, or spring force at installed height, and open pressure, or spring force with valve at full lift. As an example, the specification for a spring may be 195 lb @ 1.975 in. seat pressure and 540 lb @ 1.275 in. open pressure. A tolerance of +/-10%. means these springs are OK between 175 and 215 pounds on the seat and between 486 and 594 pounds when open. For racing purposes I prefer a tighter tolerance range, say +/-5%. Using this

tolerance, checking ranges for these springs would be 185–205 lb and 513–567 lb, respectively.

Reference specifications given for your valve springs to check pressures at both heights. If shimming is required to bring a spring up to spec, check clearance between the coils at open height. Use a 0.015-in. feeler gauge. Also check that the springs will compress 0.060-in. more than the open height. Organize springs with shims as you proceed through the

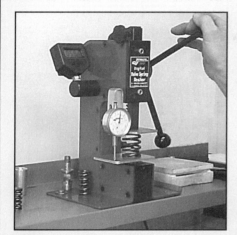

Check all springs at installed and open heights. Organize them with shims needed to correct seat pressure.

Compress spring and install locks.

Slipped over stud, hollow dowel is driven into place with punch. Work around edge of dowel to drive it in straight.

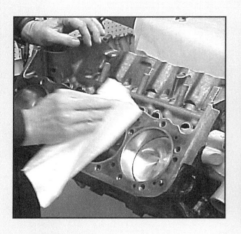

Wipe decks clean.

First check to make sure it's in the correct direction, then install head gasket. Some have a forward and rear position for routing coolant to the cylinder heads. Push gasket over dowel and against deck surface.

checking process.

Note: For breaking in a flat-tappet cam, temporarily install light valve springs or low-ratio rocker arms. Run in engine for at least 30 minutes, and then replace springs or rockers arms with the correct ones.

Position heads on intake side, then place the shim/s, if used, then the spring and spring retainer over the valve stem. Compress the spring enough to allow room for installing locks. While holding locks in place, release spring compressor. Give valve stem tip a light tap to ensure the locks are seated. Move to the next spring and install it. Once all valve springs are installed, install the heads on the engine.

Rocker Arm Stands

If your heads are equipped with separate rocker arm stands, you may or may not be able to install them on the bench. If they bridge the head-bolt holes, you'll have to install heads on the engine, then install the rocker stands. Otherwise, how you do it is your option.

Install Heads

If you removed the cylinder head dowels from the deck, reinstall them now. Drive each in until it bottoms. Likewise for the studs. Install them if you're using them in place of bolts. Apply sealer to threads that go into the water jacket. If they are blind holes, make sure they are dry. Wipe deck surfaces clean with a

183

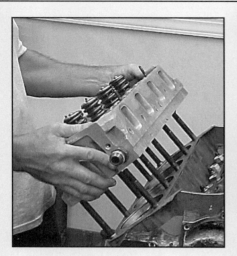

Install heads. When using bolts, loosely install at least two before installing the other head.

Bolts that go into holes exposed to the water jacket are coated with sealer. If bolts go into blind holes, use thread lubricant. Lubricate undersides of heads.

Apply thread lubricant to threads and bottom of nuts or bolts, then install flat washers.

Allan Powell torques head bolts. After final torquing, go back over them as a final check.

Use torque angle meter to ensure torque-to-yield bolts are tightened accurately.

For installing a separate rocker arm stand, position it on the mounting bosses with shims, if needed.

shop towel soaked with solvent such as lacquer thinner or brake cleaner. After the deck dries, install the head gaskets, fitting each to the dowels. Check that they are oriented correctly. If there is a front, they will be marked accordingly.

If you are using bolts apply lubricant or, if bolt holes go into the water jacket, sealer to the threads. Have a couple of head bolts close at hand, then lower cylinder head onto block deck so it engages the dowels. Loosely install

two bolts to keep head from accidentally falling off. Thread in the remainder of the bolts or nuts and washers.

Run bolts or nuts down, then torque them in sequence in stages as specified by the manufacturer. Torque may vary depending on the location and length of bolt or stud. After you've finished, go around one more time to ensure you didn't miss torquing one.

If using torque-to-yield bolts you need an angle meter. Torque bolt

to a low value, and then rotate bolt through the specified angle. This will put the bolt at its yield point to provide an accurate and consistent clamping load. Don't retighten bolts once tightened in this manner. Also, don't reuse torque-to-yield bolts.

VALVETRAIN

If separate rocker arm stands are used, position them on the rocker-arm-stand bosses with shims, provided they are needed. Apply a drop of

Apply Loctite to rocker-stand bolts…

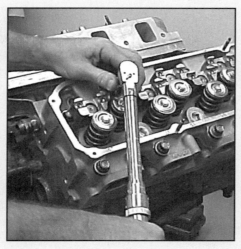

…and torque bolts to spec.

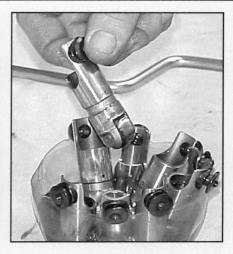

Soak roller lifters in assembly lube.

Install roller lifters so they align with cam lobes.

When using a dog-bone guide plate, the spacer goes over each stud first.

Plate goes on next. Install over studs and flats on lifters; apply Loctite, then secure with washer and nut. Torque nut to spec.

Loctite to the bolt threads, then install and torque bolts as specified.

Install Lifters

Lifters and pushrods go in before the rocker arms. If you are reusing roller lifters, it is best to install then in the same bores. As for flat tappets, they must be installed on the same lobes, providing the same cam is used in the same engine. Otherwise, don't even think about reusing flat tappets.

Soak roller lifters in assembly lubricant before installing them. Coat feet of flat tappets with lubricant supplied by the cam manufacture or a moly lube paste. Smear assembly lube on OD of each lifter and slide it into the bore. Align roller lifters with the cam lobes and, if tie bars are used, position the alignment spools toward the lifter valley. If possible, lift one lifter of each pair and install the bar or install them as a pair with the bar. For those guided by plates attached to the valley, fit plates to flats on the sides of lifters and secure them using the appropriate hardware. Apply red Loctite on fasteners, install and torque them to specification.

Install Pushrods & Rocker Arms

Check the ends of the pushrods. If one end is necked down as shown on the following page, install it in the rocker arm. Check for long and short pushrods, too. Those for intake and exhaust may

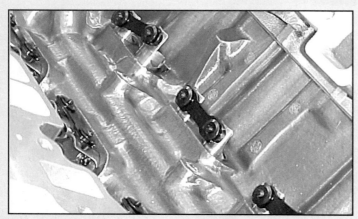

Install guide bar by lifting one lifter, then fit bar over alignment spools.

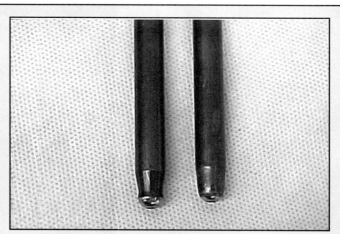

Necked-down tip shown at left is rocker-arm end of pushrod.

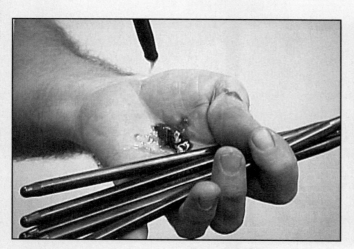

Apply high-pressure lube to tips, then install pushrods.

These shaft-mounted rocker arms install in pairs. Fit pushrods to each, and then loosely install bolt at each end.

take different lengths.

Coat ends with high-pressure lube, then slide pushrods into place, centering them in the lifters and, if used, the guide plate slots. Oil the pivots and tips, then set rocker arms into position, placing each over stud or rocker arm stand while fitting the pushrod to the rocker arm. Loosely install nut or bolts. Look for lifters lowest in their bores. Using clearance provided on cam card for cold lash, adjust each of these rocker arms.

For shaft-mounted rocker arms, tighten the jamb nut while you hold the adjusting screw. Use the nut for adjusting stud-mounted rocker arms. In this case, hold the nut while you tighten the set screw to the lock nut. Note any lash change and readjust the rocker arm. This will allow you to get a feel for any lash change so you can set the initial lash accordingly. Indicate with a felt marker the rocker arms you adjusted, then rotate crankshaft 180° to move

other lifters low in their bores. Rotate crank another 180°—120° if it's a six—and adjust lash at next set of valves. Go though this process until you've adjusted all rocker arms. Repeat to make sure you've lashed all valves.

When using a stud girdle to support stud-mounted rocker arms, recheck valve lash. As the stud girdle is clamped to adjusting nuts, a slight deflection may occur. This results in slight valve lash changes. So with a feeler gauge in hand and

While holding the pushrod in the rocker arm fit the rocker arm to the stud.

With lifter on base circle of cam—low in bore—check and adjust lash.

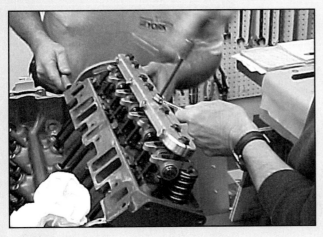

Picture illustrates typical thrash that usually occurs when completing engine for morning dyno test so engine can be installed in car next day for a weekend race. Allan adjusts valves while Bob installs accessories.

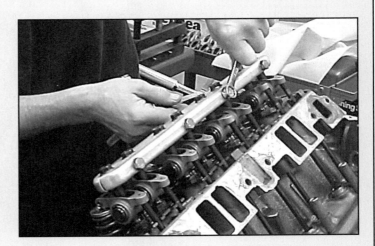

Check and readjust valve lash after stud girdle is installed. Allan has feeler gauge in one hand to check lash as he tightens girdle bolt.

the lifter low in the bore, loosen girdle bolts at each rocker arm just enough that you can turn the adjusting nut. Recheck lash and make an adjustment if necessary. Retighten nut, setscrew and girdle bolt then recheck lash. Continue process until you've achieved the correct lash at all valves.

INSTALL INTAKE MANIFOLD

Before you go any further, seal the engine to prevent nasty things from getting into it. Many an engine has been damaged by an errant fastener finding its way into the crankcase or combustion chamber. To prevent this from happening, tape over or plug the exhaust ports and other openings such as those for the distributor.

Valley Tray

For a raised-runner manifold, install separate valley tray. Seal it at the ends and along the bottom edges of the heads with a bead of silicone. The aluminum tray shown is secured at the ends with three #4 pan-head screws. The breaks in the tray along the side at each head provides enough rigidity in the tray to ensure a good seal without the need for additional fasteners.

Check the fit of the manifold gaskets by positioning each on the cylinder head. Use witness marks or dowel holes in the gaskets and heads. Manifold gaskets don't normally require sealer except at the water passages, however a thin application of rubber cement on

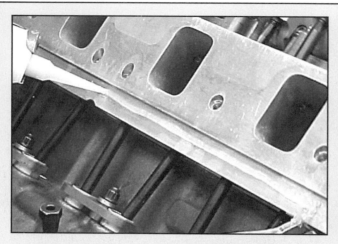

Seal valley tray with continuous bead of silicone along bottom edges of heads and across ends of block.

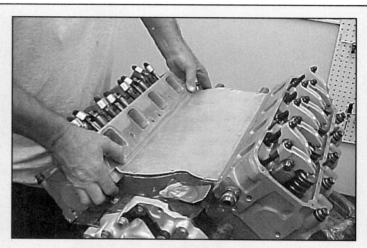

Lay tray over lifter valley and snap into position at heads.

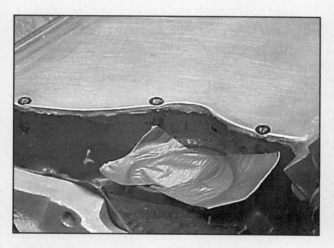

Ends of tray are secured with pan-head screws. Duct tape over distributor hole keeps out bad stuff.

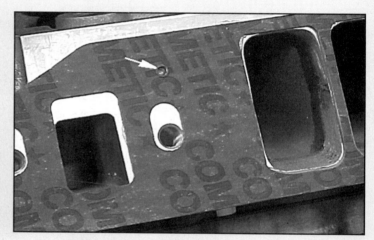

Align gaskets to the head using witness marks or dowel holes (arrow).

the head, particularly around each intake runner, ensures the gaskets will stay in place. This is particularly critical along the narrow section at the bottom of the runners. Run a small bead of silicone or non-hardening sealer around each water passage opening and bolt hole that enters the water jacket, then position gaskets on the heads. As you did when installing the head, apply sealer around water-passage openings and bolt holes. Rather than using end

gaskets, run a heavy bead of RTV silicone across each end of the block between the heads. Apply extra sealer at the four corners.

Here's where two sets of hands are better than one. Set manifold square into position on engine. Referencing the witness marks, adjust position of the manifold by sliding it back or forth until the marks line up to your satisfaction. Using a small flashlight or inspection light to illuminate the dark recesses, peer into the runners to double-check runner alignment.

When you're satisfied that the manifold and heads line up, install manifold bolts with flat washers and snug them in sequence. For those that thread into holes entering the water jacket, apply thread sealer to the threads first. Finish manifold installation by torquing bolts in stages and sequence.

INSTALL VALVE COVERS

Button up the top end by installing the valve covers. Use a thick gasket such as Cometic's

Allan uses rubber cement on the head to hold the gasket in position. Run bead of RTV silicone around each water passage opening and bolt hole that runs into the water jacket.

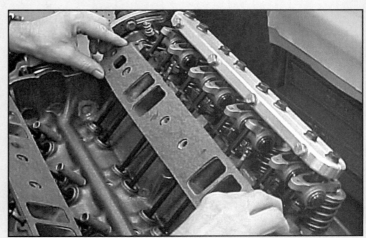

Lay gaskets in position using marks or dowel holes.

Apply silicone sealer on gasket around water passages and bolt holes, too.

Run heavy bead of silicone across block in place of gasket end seals.

0.188-in. thick KF gasket. Don't use sealer. The valve covers will have to come off more than once to check valve lash and possibly change valve springs or rocker arms. Studs are particularly helpful because of the thick gaskets and flanges of the typical race-type valve cover. They also hold the gaskets in place while you R&R the valve covers.

Lubricate valve springs to minimize friction at startup, then install valve covers with gaskets.

Tighten valve cover nuts/bolts a little at a time to prevent damage to the flange. Because a thicker gasket tends compresses more, check fastener tightness several times. For valve covers equipped with spring oilers, connect lines between them. If breathers are used, install them.

INSTALL FUEL PUMP, ACCESSORY DRIVE, FLYWHEEL & IGNITION SYSTEM

There are too many combin-ations to cover final engine dress in detail, particularly accessory drives, but there are some basics. To begin, assemble as much of the engine as you can now with the exception of some induction system compo-nents such as a carburetor, super-charger, or turbocharger. It's best to install these after the engine is on the dyno or in the engine compart-ment. I cover high spots using photographs and captions.

Note: Now that the engine is off the stand, install the cam plug.

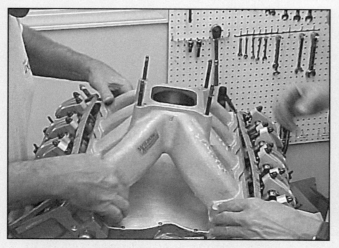

Lower manifold straight down on engine so it aligns with witness marks.

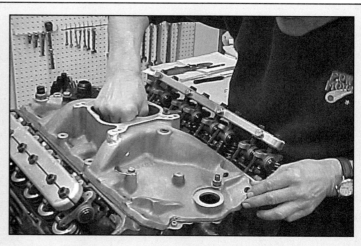

Shift manifold to achieve best port and runner alignment.

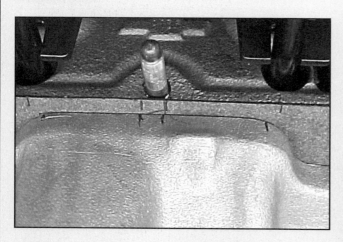

Sometimes you must balance differences, particularly when rules say you can't open up manifold runners to match cylinder-head ports or vice versa.

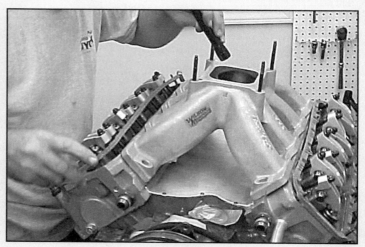

Bob uses a flashlight to check manifold runner alignment with ports in heads.

Check also that the oil gallery plugs are installed.

DYNO ENGINE

Be extremely careful at this point. Many a new engine has been damaged from improper install-ation such as incorrect coolant or lubrication plumbing.

Secure manifold with bolts fitted with flat washers. Seal bolts that install into holes entering water jacket.

Use spray-on gel to lubricate valve springs.

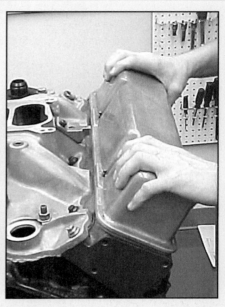

Lay gaskets in place, then install valve covers.

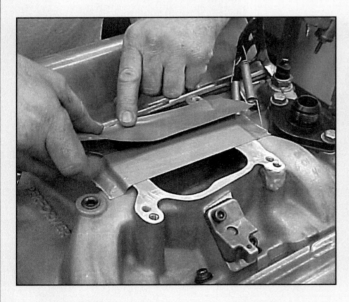

Seal the manifold. Duct tape or a lift plate works.

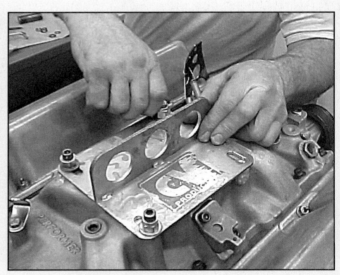

Example of basic accessory drive is CV Products power steering pump and alternator arrangement for a Dodge. Bracketry for a dry sump pump is provided, lower right.

Accessory drive begins with hub mounted to crankshaft or damper.

Installing a power steering pump bracket on Busch Ford.

Late-model Chevrolet accessory drive. Slot for tensioning power steering pump belt is at rear of pump. V-belt pulley mounted to the front of the water pump drives the alternator.

Check pulley alignment with a precision straightedge. It is critical that pulleys align to ensure belts run true and stay in place. Use shims, spacers or whatever is needed to achieve alignment.

Install the mechanical fuel pump. A small-block Chevy requires a pushrod and plate, then the pump. Lubricate wear surfaces.

Set cylinder #1 in firing position, say 10° BTDC. With finger in plug hole, turn crankshaft in normal direction until you feel pressure and you know piston is coming up to the firing position.

Lower distributor into position. Hold distributor body while you work rotor side-to-side to engage it with drive gear. Compensate for distributor shaft rotation as it engages drive gear.

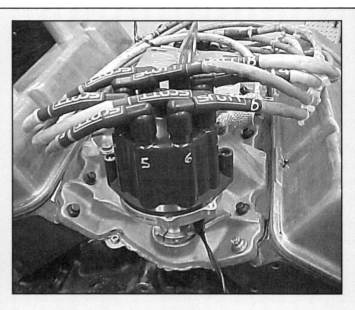

Secure distributor in firing position. Indicate cylinder numbers on sparkplug leads and distributor cap. Install sparkplugs and connect leads.

Remove engine from stand and install flywheel. Use Loctite on bolts and torque to spec. Use locking sealer on bolts that thread into holes running through flywheel flange and into crankcase.

With a cherry picker and lift plate on the intake manifold or other attaching device to support the engine, set the engine into position.

No gaskets here. Use high-temperature RTV silicone sealer on exhaust manifold flanges. Note thermocouple taps on primary header pipes. EGT (exhaust gas temperature) data is critical for tuning an engine.

Thermocouple leads installed in headers.

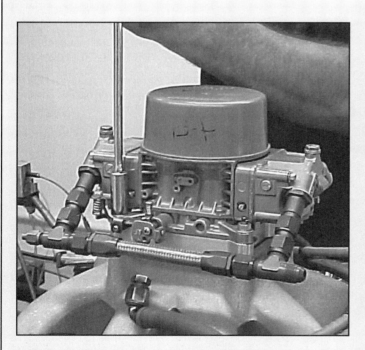

Install carburetor or other induction equipment.

Connect coolant and lubrication plumbing, making sure lines are routed correctly and connections are secured. Once connected, add oil. Dyno system will supply coolant.

Use 1/2-in. drill motor to prime lubrication system by turning the dry sump pump. If oil pressure is not indicated, disconnect pressure line at engine to help until system is filled. For a wet sump engine with internal oil pump, remove the distributor and turn the pump with drill motor and shaft.

Assortment of carburetor jets. Use EGT and O_2 sensor to jet carburetor to obtain correct air/fuel mixture.

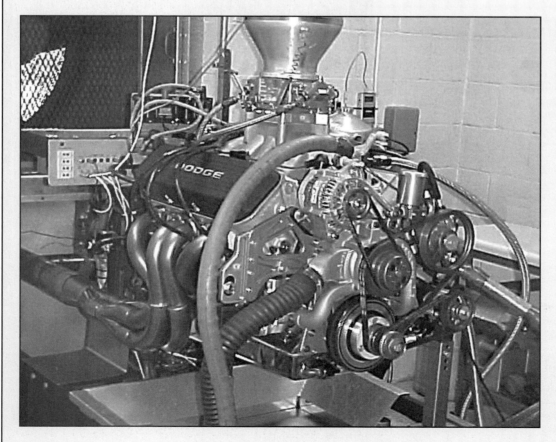

Double-check that all systems are connected, then spin the engine with the ignition off. Check for leaks and oil and fuel pressure. Have timing light ready to check timing.

Once all systems are OK, run in engine at moderate load and rpm while monitoring all systems. Check for leaks and set timing. Run engine for about 20 minutes to break in flat tappets.

After running in flat-tappet cam, replace light springs or low-ratio rocker arms with race setup. And if you used hotter plugs for the run-in, change to cold plugs. Allan Powell lashes valves rocker in preparation for some serious "pulls." Next stop, the race car.

METRIC CUSTOMARY UNIT EQUIVALENTS

Multiply:	by:	to get:	Multiply by:	to get:
LINEAR				
inches	x 25.4	= millimeters (mm)	x 0.03937	= inches
feet	x 0.3048	= meters (m)	x 3.281	= feet
yards	x 0.9144	= meters (m)	x 1.0936	= yards
AREA				
inches2	x 645.16	= millimeters^2(mm)	x 0.00155	= inches^2
feet2	x 0.0929	= meters^2(m)	x 10.764	= feet^2
VOLUME				
quarts	x 0.94635	= liters (I)	x 1.0567	= quarts
gallons	x 3.7854	= liters (I)	x 0.2642	= gallons
feet^3	x 28.317	= liters (I)	x 0.03531	= feet^3
feet^3	x 0.02832	= meters^3(m^3)	x 35.315	= feet^3
fluid oz	x 29.57	= milliliters (ml)	x 0.03381	= fluid oz
MASS				
ounces (av)	x 28.35	= grams (g)	x 0.03527	= ounces (av)
pounds (av)	x0.4536	= kilograms (kg)	x 2.2046	= pounds (av)
FORCE				
ounces-f(av)	x 0.278	= newtons (N)	x3.597	= ounces-f(av)
pounds-f(av)	x4.448	= newtons (N)	x 0.2248	= pounds-f(av)

TEMPERATURE

Degrees Celsius (C) = 0.556 (F – 32)   Degree Fahrenheit (F) = (1.8C) + 32

ENERGY OR WORK (Watt-second = joule= newton-meter)				
foot-pounds	x 1.3558	= joules (J)	x 0.7376	= foot-pounds
Btu	x 1055	= joules (J)	x 0.000948	= Btu
PRESSURE OR STRESS				
pounds/sq in.	x 6.895	= kilopascals (kPa)	x 0.145	= pounds/sq in
TORQUE				
pound-inches	x 0.11298	= newton-meters (N-m)	x 8.851	= pound-inches
pound-feet	x 1.3558	= newton-meters (N-m)	x 0.7376	= pound-feet
pound-inches	x 0.0115	= kilogram-meters (Kg-M)	x 87	= pound-feet
pound-feet	x 0.138	= kilogram-meters (Kg-M)	x 7.25	= pound-feet
POWER				
horsepower	x 0.74570	= kilowatts (kW)	x 1.34102	= horsepower

COMMON METRIC PREFIXES

mega (M) = 1,000,000 or10^6 centi(c) = 0.01 or 10-2

kilo (k) = 1,000 or 10^3 milli (m) = 0.001 or 10-3

hecto (h) = 100 or 10^2 micro (u) = (u)0.000,001 or 10-6

NOTES

GENERAL MOTORS
Big-Block Chevy Engine Buildups: 1-55788-484-6/HP1484
Big-Block Chevy Performance: 1-55788-216-9/HP1216
Camaro Performance: 1-55788-057-3/HP1057
Camaro Owner's Handbook ('67–'81): 1-55788-301-7/HP1301
Camaro Restoration Handbook ('67–'81): 0-89586-375-8/HP1375
Chevelle/El Camino Handbook: 1-55788-428-5/HP1428
Chevy S-10/GMC S-15 Handbook: 1-55788-353-X/HP1353
Chevy Trucks: 1-55788-340-8/HP1340
How to Hot Rod Big-Block Chevys: 0-912656-04-2/HP104
How to Hot Rod Small-Block Chevys: 0-912656-06-9/HP106
How to Rebuild Small-Block Chevy LT-1/LT-4: 1-55788-393-9/HP1393
John Lingenfelter: Modify Small-Block Chevy: 1-55788-238-X/HP1238
LS1/LS6 Small-Block Chevy Performance: 1-55788-407-2/HP1407
Powerglide Transmission Handbook:1-55788-355-6/HP1355
Rebuild Big-Block Chevy Engines: 0-89586-175-5/HP1175
Rebuild Gen V/Gen VI Big-Block Chevy: 1-55788-357-2/HP1357
Rebuild Small-Block Chevy Engines: 1-55788-029-8/HP1029
Small-Block Chevy Engine Buildups: 1-55788-400-5/HP1400
Small-Block Chevy Performance: 1-55788-253-3/HP1253
Turbo Hydramatic 350 Handbook: 0-89586-051-1/HP1051

FORD
Ford Windsor Small-Block Performance: 1-55788-323-8/HP1323
Mustang 5.0 Projects: 1-55788-275-4/HP1275
Mustang Performance (Engines): 1-55788-193-6/HP1193
Mustang Performance 2 (Chassis): 1-55788-202-9/HP1202
Mustang Performance Engine Tuning: 1-55788-387-4/HP1387
Mustang Restoration Handbook ('64–'70): 0-89586-402-9/HP1402
Rebuild Big-Block Ford Engines: 0-89586-070-8/HP1070
Rebuild Ford V-8 Engines: 0-89586-036-8/HP1036
Rebuild Small-Block Ford Engines: 0-912656-89-1/HP189

MOPAR
Big-Block Mopar Performance: 1-55788-302-5/HP1302
How to Hot Rod Small-Block Mopar Engine Revised: 1-55788-405-6/HP1405
How to Maintain & Repair Your Jeep: 1-55788-371-8/HP1371
How to Modify Your Jeep Chassis/Suspension for
  Offroad: 1-55788-424/HP1424
How to Modify Your Mopar Magnum V8: 1-55788-473-0/HP1473
How to Rebuild Your Mopar Magnum V8: 1-55788-431-5/HP1431
Rebuild Big-Block Mopar Engines: 1-55788-190-1/HP1190
Rebuild Small-Block Mopar Engines: 0-89586-128-3/HP1128
Torqueflite A-727 Transmission Handbook: 1-55788-399-8/HP1399

IMPORTS
Baja Bugs & Buggies: 0-89586-186-0/HP1186
Honda/Acura Engine Performance: 1-55788-384-X/HP1384
Honda/Acura Performance: 1-55788-384-X/HP1384
How to Hot Rod VW Engines: 0-912656-03-4/HP103
Porsche 911 Performance: 1-55788-489-7/HP489
Rebuild Air-Cooled VW Engines: 0-89586-225-5/HP1225
The VW Beetle: A History of The World's Most Popular Car:
  1-55788-421-8/HP1421
The Volkswagen Super Beetle Handbook: 1-55788-483-8/HP1483

HANDBOOKS
Automotive Detailing: 1-55788-288-6/HP1288
Auto Electrical Handbook: 0-89586-238-7/HP1238
Auto Math Handbook: 1-55788-020-4/HP1020
Automotive Paint Handbook: 1-55788-291-6/HP1291
Auto Upholstery & Interiors: 1-55788-265-7/HP1265
Car Builder's Handbook: 1-55788-278-9/HP1278
Classic Car Restorer's Handbook: 1-55788-194-4/HP1194
Engine Builder's Handbook: 1-55788-245-2/HP1245
Fiberglass & Other Composite Materials Rev.: 1-55788-498-6/HP1498
The Lowrider's Handbook: 1-55788-383-1/HP1383
Metal Fabricator's Handbook: 0-89586-870-9/HP1870
1001 High Performance Tech Tips: 1-55788-199-5/HP1199
1001 MORE High Performance Tech Tips: 1-55788-429-3/HP1429
Paint & Body Handbook: 1-55788-082-4/HP1082
Performance Ignition Systems: 1-55788-306-8/HP1306
Pro Paint & Body: 1-55788-394-7/HP1394
Sheet Metal Handbook: 0-89586-757-5/HP1757
Welder's Handbook: 1-55788-264-9/HP1264

INDUCTION
Holley 4150: 0-89586-047-3/HP1047
Holley Carbs, Manifolds & F.I.: 1-55788-052-2/HP1052
Rochester Carburetors: 0-89586-301-4/HP1301
Tuning Accel/DFI 6.0 Programmable F.I.: 1-55788-413-7/HP1413
Turbochargers: 0-89586-135-6/HP1135
Street Turbocharging: 1-55788-488-9/HP1488
Weber Carburetors: 0-89586-377-4/HP1377

RACING & CHASSIS
Bracket Racing: 1-55788-266-5/HP1266
Chassis Engineering: 1-55788-055-7/HP1055
4Wheel & Off-Road's Chassis & Suspension: 1-55788-406-4/HP1406
How to Make Your Car Handle: 0-912656-46-8/HP146
How to Get Started in Stock Car Racing: 1-55788-468-4/HP1468
Stock Car Setup Secrets: 1-55788-401-3/HP1401

MOTORCYCLES
American V-Twin Engine Tech: 1-55788-455-2/HP1455

STREET RODS
How to Build a 1932 Ford Street Rod: 1557884781/HP1478
How to Build a 1933–'34 Ford Street Rod:1-55788-479-X/HP1479
How to Build a 1935–'40 Ford Street Rod: 1-55788-493-5/HP1493
Street Rodder magazine's Chassis & Suspension Handbook
  1-55788-346-7/HP1346
Street Rodder's Handbook, Rev.: 1-55788-409-9/HP1409

ORDER YOUR COPY TODAY!
All books can be purchased at your favorite retail or online bookstore such as amazon.com and barnesandnoble.com (use ISBN number), or auto parts store (use HP part number). You can also order direct from HPBooks by calling toll-free at 800-788-6262, ext. 1 or at www.penguin.com.